# Arctic Twilight

## Kevin McMahon

James Lorimer & Company, Publishers
Toronto, 1988

**Canadian Cataloguing in Publication Data**
McMahon, Kevin
Arctic Twilight

ISBN 1-55028-092-9 (bound)  ISBN 1-55028-091-0 (pbk.)
1. Arctic regions. 2 Arctic Archipelago (N.W.T.)
FC3963.M35 1988     971.9     C88-094506-0

F1090.5.M35 1988

James Lorimer & Company, Publishers
Egerton Ryerson Memorial Building
35 Britain Street
Toronto, Ontario M5A 1R7

Printed and bound in Canada

5 4 3 2 1  88 89 90 91 92 93

*For Angela*

*This is how one pictures the angel of history. His face is turned toward the past. Where we perceive a chain of events, he sees one single catastrophe which keeps piling wreckage upon wreckage and hurls it in front of his feet. The angel would like to stay, awaken the dead, and make whole what has been smashed. But a storm is blowing from Paradise; it has got caught in his wings with such violence that the angel can no longer close them. This storm irresistably propels him into the future to which his back is turned, while the pile of debris before him grows skyward. This storm is what we call progress.*

Walter Benjamin

# Contents

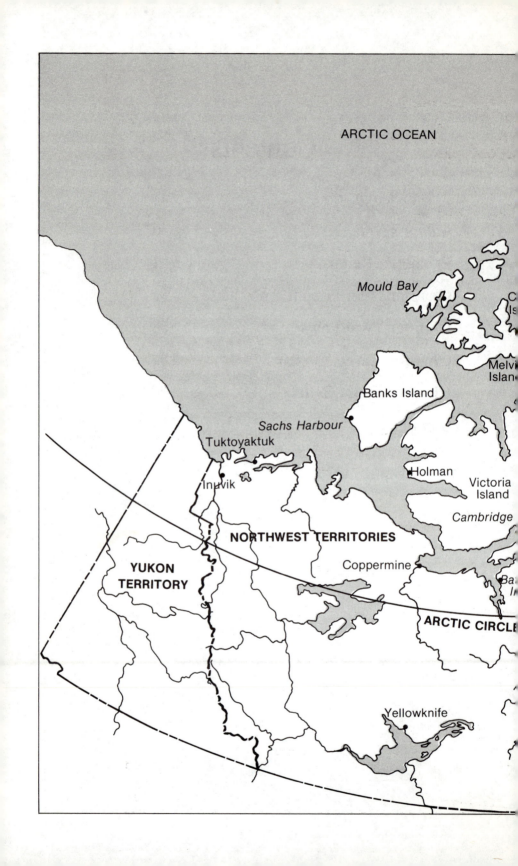

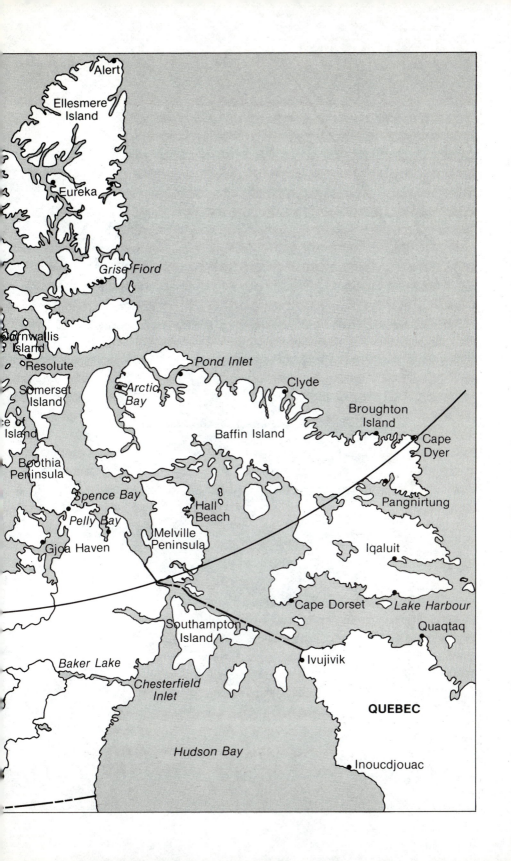

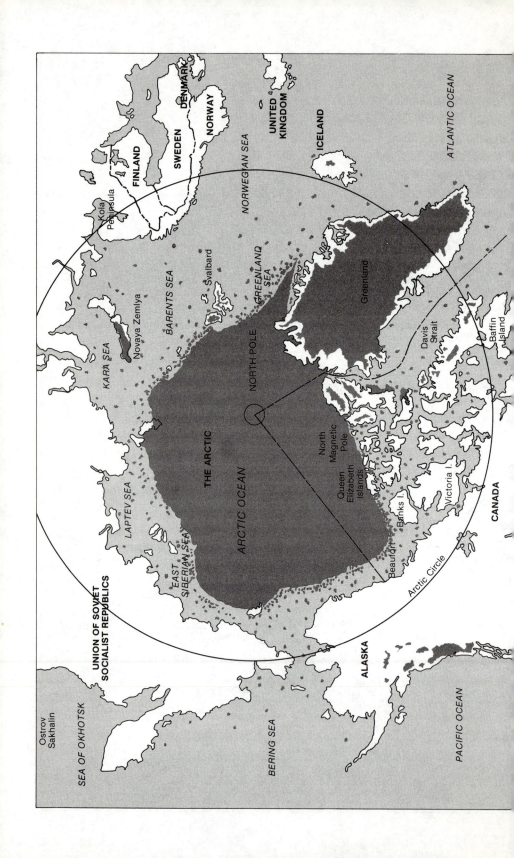

# Acknowledgments

I have a great many debts to the people who, in their various ways, helped to buoy me during this work.

First, I wish to thank the people in the towns and villages of the Northwest Territories through which I travelled in the autumn of 1987. The open disposition of northerners was well known to me before I journeyed to the Arctic and, everywhere I went, I found their reputation for generosity as deserved as it is understated. People opened their homes to me, some for extended periods, and spent hours and days patiently recounting their experiences, thoughts and feelings. Their stories are the foundation of this book and my hope for it is that the many who will recognize their words and ideas here find them true to the spirit in which they were communicated. To all of them I offer my humble and heartfelt gratitude.

The Canada Council, the Canadian Institute for International Peace and Security and the Ontario Arts Council all provided generous support without which this work would have been impossible. I thank particularly Nancy Gordon and David Cox of CIIPS for their continuing interest and support and Lorraine Filyer and the editorial collective of *This Magazine* for theirs.

Many of the ideas here developed during several years of writing for the *Standard* in St. Catharines. I owe thanks to many colleagues there who supported me in this, especially to Murray Thomson, my editor there, who constantly encouraged me to explore areas of thought and writing that are not commonly considered within the range of newspaper work.

My specific involvement and interest in the Arctic grew from working on *The Northern Front*, a radio series which was produced for the Canadian Broadcasting Corporation's *Ideas* programme. I am indebted to my collaborators on that project, Ursula Franklin and Peter Chapman, for their continuing advice and assistance.

Vit Wagner, Doug Herod, Carrie Beres, Ed Innocenzi and my brother, Michael, also kindly lent me their time and thoughts and, in different ways, provided much needed direction at crucial points.

Several people worked closely with me in the preparation of the manuscript. Heather Robertson and Curtis Fahey were unfailingly helpful and patient editors. I was first drawn to this subject by Max Allen and to him I owe many thanks for his vital contribution to the writing and for the passionate commitment he inspires. I am also deeply grateful to my friend John Ferri for his exuberant support and for the crystal intelligence he brought to our many discussions of the ideas here. Rita McMahon, my sister, was a tireless, enthusiastic and ever cheerful researcher without whom I would surely have floundered. Whatever fine points this work may have can be attributed to their collective effort.

I feel inadequate to convey my appreciation to my parents whose sensibility, faith and constant support have maintained me through the tempestuous times during which this book was written. Their compassionate vision, profound respect for others and the sheer joy with which they embrace life have instilled in me great strength and hope, for which I daily give thanks.

This work, like everything else in my life, has been immeasurably brightened by the intellect and spirit of Angela Stukator, with whom I have walked many miles and from whom I have learned more than my words can say. To her, with love and admiration, I dedicate this book.

# Author's Note

Throughout I have used *Inuit* to describe the people of the Arctic whom anthropologists label Eskimoan, from the linguistic family to which they belong. I have avoided the older term, Eskimo, which comes from the French Esquimaux and means people who eat raw flesh. Many people in the Arctic now consider this a perjorative term. Properly, *Inuit* refers to the people of the eastern Arctic while those in other areas, such as the Mackenzie Delta — the Inuvialuit — prefer other terms. Often I have used *Inuit* when referring to these other peoples also, for simplicity. Likewise, many of the events and situations in this book have been experienced by other peoples of the north, specifically the Athapaskans of the sub- Arctic. I have confined myself, however, to dealing only with the Canadian Arctic and its people. Readers will notice a discrepency throughout the text in the usage of names, with Inuit often referred to by their first names and southerners by their last. In this I have adopted the convention used by the people themselves in their particular context and wish no other meaning to be attached to this differentiation. As will become clear, Inuit are often quoted speaking of themselves in the third person — indicating that their words have been filtered through a translator. Inuktitut words used in the text are from the dialect of the eastern Arctic. Military acronyms have generally been written in lower case, as a more accurate reflection of the way they are used.

# Reigns

The end of the first stage of Thomas Anguttitauruq's life came to him when he was about five; he is unsure now of the year though he remembers perfectly the shape, which was that of a tin of processed meat. It was a can of *Klik*, a heavily salted and compressed paste of pork which tasted nothing like what Thomas knew as meat. But what fascinated him was the tin itself. He would take it from the caribou skin sack which kept it safe and turn it over in his small hands as if it were a cube of crystalized magic.

"It was so beautiful, the picture on it was so beautiful, the colour on it was beautiful; a thing which I never seen before. I was always wondering how they wrote those label on it and the picture on it. I was always wondering how they did it. And it was very precious to me. I wouldn't let other children touch it."

Thomas lived then with his parents on the shore of Garry Lake, northwest of Hudson's Bay, in the Arctic. Their camp was a snug and solitary speck on the vast and hard white desert of the tundra. The colours of that world are the earthen browns of the tundra, rusty orange and mossy greens of lichen, oxygenated reds of blood, the glittering whites of snow and ice, the purples and deep blues of the endless northern sky. Its textures are the coarse pile of muskox fur, the porous grain of whale bone, the wind-polished surface of rock. Into this world, the tin box painted in shiny, lacquered Fifties reds and yellows, bearing a portrait of a Wonder Bread sandwich, straight from the cupboard of *Ozzie and Harriet*, came as if from another planet.

"All that time, I don't know nothing about white culture at all. Living out in the land, not knowing, never seeing. I saw a little house at the mission that was around Garry Lake but they don't have electricity. I didn't notice that electricity existed. Same with light bulbs. Then I heard of other things but I thought they were some of the fairy tales. Like my grandmother and grandfather tells me Inuit fairy tales almost every night. And some things you hear about. They told us that they have great big boats, just like a house. I thought that was all fairy tale. They say there was flying machines. And I thought that was also a fairy tale. I don't believe them because I never seen them."

We met in Gjoa Haven, on the south coast of King William Island, in the Hudson's Bay, mens' wear section. He had heard I was looking for an interpreter. At the time, he was taking a government-sponsored accounting course for his job as an executive service officer, a sort of go-between for the village and various levels of government. It was hard, the course, but okay. *Numbers*, he said and I knew how he felt. Among his many attributes was his photocopier memory; he would listen to an elder speak for ten minutes straight and then repeat the story or argument in intricate detail, always resisting, as near as I could tell, the temptation to edit.

When he spoke about his own life, Thomas identified three stages altogether, each marked by a clear division beyond which there were whole constellations of previously unimaginable things. When he was about ten, still running around in caribou-skin clothes, these unimaginable things included the priest's eyeglasses, birthdays, cotton, paint, phonographs and rubber boots. At twenty they included the concept of hippies and such gadgetry as telex machines. Years after he experienced a telex machine he still thought it was haunted.

I, on the other hand, was born, only a few years after Thomas, into a cosmology in which all of these things were common as dishwater; as were huge white convertibles, television sets and nuclear weapons. As we have grown up, Thomas has had all but the convertible, and much more, gradually piled upon his world. Leaving his "pure Inuit" stage and entering the "age of the white man" — when he met up with teachers, traders and bureaucrats — his old world was completely painted over. In the third stage of his life — the "Space Age", when he worked in a military installation — his old world was, for all intents and purposes, blasted into oblivion. It still existed, of course, but Thomas didn't recognize it anymore. When I met him, Thomas was forty years old. Sitting in his kitchen late one night, he said, "You know, it's as if a white man had lived for 1,000 years."

My business in the Arctic was to talk to people about sovereignty. This is a vexing question, sovereignty. The original concept, of course, was quite simple: the demand of kings, supposing their rights heaven-sent, to do whatever the hell they pleased. Most nation states uphold the pretense that this right has now dropped down to their people and we think of sovereignty questions in terms of the squabbles and intrusions nations visit upon each other. For lawyers and warriors, sovereignty is a matter of the integrity of borders variously to be ensured with proclamations or guns. For economists, control of financial direction; for artists, the collective vision of a people.

Few citizens breathe easily about their sovereignty anymore. There are those that feel acutely insecure physically, like Israelis, and never stop manoeuvring and mobilizing to protect their sovereignty. And those that feel insecure in every other way, like Canadians, who never shut up about the question, or very precisely define what is being asked.

I was raised in Niagara Falls, a town whose economy has been entirely built upon turning one of the world's great natural wonders into a massive bit of flood-lit plastic kitsch for the amusement of Americans, who have blasted and blackened its twin on their side of their border. The people of the town are as American as you can be, short of having a Social Security number and pledging allegiance to a currency featuring Cycloptic pyramids. They drink in American bars, gasp at the fires on American local television news, think American thoughts and speak with American accents. For eight months of every year, they rub their hands in worry and anticipation over the success of the coming tourist season. When the summer heat inevitably cooks up the overweight and underdressed hordes, a uniform grouse about sovereignty — of a sort — is raised by the local populace over the cacophonous chingling of cash registers. The Americans, they shout to each other, think they own the joint. Which, in many ways, they do.

During the two years I lived in Britain the country was constantly tearing at itself over a variation of this. The British were concerned about the decline of national sovereignty under the weight of American attitudes that were influencing increasing numbers of people to drag themselves up in the world by acting not quite British.

The righteous, emotional, uppity side of Canadian's typical ambivalence about national sovereignty often sputters up in public fretting over the Arctic. Roughly one-fifth of the country has an Arctic character, though Canadians generally think of the rock islands jutting towards the North Pole when they think Arctic. "Think" puts a bit too fine a point on it, though, since almost nobody knows anything whatsoever about this toque of territory jauntily slapped on the country's head. Not that there are not books, reports, manuals, proceedings, studies, meditations and memoirs galore. Yet the place itself remains a region of epic, half-remembered myths and the people who live there are obscure. Urban Canadians, particularly those of my generation, imagine some cold and peculiar place that can bizarrely double as the setting for both those stoic wilderness Hardy Boys of *Lost in the Barrens* and the mass media engineering hype about the rises and falls of a Dome Petroleum.

Yet the Americans need only sail a ship, every couple of decades or so, through one of the several routes between the islands known broadly as the Northwest Passage for everyone to get on their high horse. While the Canadian government is currently planning to enter into an all-embracing economic union with the United States — to create one gargantuan Honeymoon City — the public has been convinced the country needs a fleet of nuclear submarines to keep them from dropping by uninvited in *our* Arctic. Our sovereignty, we say, is threatened.

All around the top of the world, people feel this. The frozen land where the United States and the Soviet Union meet is fully wired with opposing weapons systems, each guardians of sovereignty, which are being made new, and improved. The aboriginal people, atop whom these systems and their different sorts of baggage have landed, are struggling to regain something of the already diminished sovereignty they had when Thomas was a child. In the Canadian Arctic, the national government is flailing away in between, trying to maintain what it considers its sovereignty. The means each is using to advance its claims — and therefore the logical conclusions they are moving towards — are as different as a respectful request and a nuclear bomb. But each think itself up to the same thing: survival.

Like many journalists, I had written about weaponry for years and about the Arctic too. Yet I had never stepped foot north of the 60th parallel. And my only personal encounter with a nuclear weapon had been once on a country lane in England during a cruise missile convoy protest. I fretted also about Canadian sovereignty in the Arctic, also for vague reasons of national pride. The specific legal and strategic questions can be easily grasped. Canada wants to control the waterways, America refuses to be controlled. The region is being overrun by guns. Everybody has their beady eyes on its oil and minerals and dreams of shipping and pipelines to move them south. The Inuit still have what we are pleased to call "land claims" outstanding. Yes, but …. There was much I did not understand.

I went north with some trepidation. The Inuit were said to be inscrutable; friendly but false. They don't like to be questioned, people wrote, they find it intrusive and rude. I assumed they would be bitter. I found these things to be only partly true, or, more accurately, both true. Some of the stories the people told were bitter. But none were reluctant to tell them. Much of the time I used a tape recorder and one of the first men I spoke with, an elder, took the microphone gently from my hand and began recalling the story of his life as if he had been waiting years for this moment. Everywhere people gave me a seat and a cup of tea and talked until I was tired of listening. Time was of no consequence and obfuscation was only ever at their own expense.

Often my conversations, particularly with the old people, were about what life used to be like. I suspected sometimes that this was a pointless area of inquiry. What mattered was what it was like now. For twenty years Inuit organizations have been trying to ditch the stereotype that they live in *iglus*. My feeling, though, despite all that has been written, was that southerners still had no idea how recently they had. And it made all the difference in the way you thought about them; and about how fast and deep the changes have been. Elders always wanted to talk about this. It was the only way, they felt, to make me understand.

The focus of the sovereignty question, I had thought, might be found in the many communities across the Canadian Arctic where all three parties concerned — the United States, Canada, the Inuit — met, which primarily meant communities where there are military installations. As I travelled in the autumn's gathering dark, and listened, the questions began to seem about more and more fundamental things and the journey became one of following tangled reigns that trail all over the Arctic and lead elsewhere. Trying to learn who, exactly, reigned over whom.

What was to be learned about sovereignty, Canadian and otherwise, was to come as much from hearing Thomas describe the meaning of having my home town, complete with flashing lights and giant Ferris wheels, grafted atop his camp as in listening to a young soldier, also about my own age, describe that day's rehearsal of a nuclear war. One way or another, both have been done, nominally, for Canadian sovereignty — which is to say, in our names — over the past thirty years in a place that is part of the country and, yet, so very far away. As I listened, I came to think that we are, the people of my generation, such little princes and princesses.

Creation stories are the most important ones to the Inuit and many would have leavened Thomas Anguttitauruq's nightly ration of fairy tales. All things originate in the Arctic for the Inuit — even the white man — and there is a tale to explain whatever can be known.

There was a girl who refused to get married. Eventually her father, exasperated, said if she didn't smarten up she was going to end up marrying a dog. Sure enough, words being magic, a dog showed up that night and had her. When the puppies were born, she was exiled with them to an island. One day, when her father came around with food, she got him back for his fateful words, having her children tear him to shreds. Then she made little kayaks for them from his boots and sent them out into the world telling some to turn themselves into Indians — "you be savage, kill whatever comes around" — and some into whites — "work hard and invent all kinds of things." Over the course of Thomas's life, the white dogs returned with a vengeance and as he grew their gadgets got handier and more complex; their bites, though, got nastier and deeper.

Gjoa Haven, where Thomas lives now, was named by Roald Amundsen, who was the first man to navigate the Northwest Passage, in 1903, sailing in the Gjoa, and who took refuge in the harbour for two winters. Its Inuktitut name is Uqsuqtuuq, which means "a place of a lot of blubber." Thomas's family came to it gradually, moving northward.

"At that time we were living in an iglu in the winter time; like, the only things we buy from the store were flour and tea and the grown-up people buy coffee and ammunition, sometimes they buy kerosene for the stove and lantern; and sled boards and runners. Everything else we get from the land and from the animals; food and clothing came from the animals that my father and grandfather got."

Over great tracts of tundra they moved slowly, in the wake of the animals. The whites they knew consisted of fur traders, the priest — they travelled to the mission at Easter and Christmas for feasting and games of skill for prizes of oatmeal and jam — and the odd Mountie. They had only the barest conception of government. About 1955, Thomas's brother, hunting in the north, along the coast of the mainland, stumbled upon a military installation being constructed and found work.

Soon after, the rest of the family began to move north to meet him. By then Thomas was raring to go to school — whatever exactly that meant. He had known this since the day a Mountie showed up in the family camp with an interpreter and begun asking the most marvelously bizarre questions. Like: What day was everyone in the family born? Thomas had been reading magazines published in Inuktitut syllabics from the time he was three and a half but he had never heard questions anything like this before. "We never were aware of the days that we were born and all that, or what year." His interest was hopelessly piqued. Afterward, he badgered his father relentlessly to send him to school. There he reckoned he could learn English so that he could understand everything like the Mountie's interpreter.

When they made Gjoa Haven, he was left with the priest to be packed off to school. He began to spin. First it was losing his fur clothes. Cotton and wool were unbearably itchy and rough, they stunk and were so light he felt naked. Rubber boots crippled him. Wonderous, though, it all was. The priest gave him a jacket and that night he sat up examining every stitch, every fold. He was proud as a peacock in that jacket. So it went. One amazement after another descended into his world from the air, uncommon and delightful as a fairy tale.

School, operated by nuns, was more on the uncommon side. "Another strange experience. The nuns were always wearing cloaks. When I saw them coming to meet the plane I couldn't see their arms. I heard before that nuns were all holy and they sacrifice and all. I thought maybe they cut off their arms to do some sacrifice." As it turned out, of course, they had arms the better to swat him with when he stepped out of line, which was often. Growing up in the borderless expanse that is the Inuit world and culture, he could not imagine how many lines there were in the white world. Lines to stand in, lines to keep you out or in, lines to emphasize what language to use, to tell you how to work and how you should play. Thomas had been told that nuns, by nature, were gentle and he soon felt he had been misinformed. They would, for example, tolerate none of the children's screechy Inuit songs, which they suspected to be little mouthings of black magic. "I started thinking that Inuit ways were all wrong."

After school he found work back at the military installation — a Distant Early Warning (DEW) radar site — which at first seemed a relative picnic. "I find out for the first time that even in white culture you are quite free. Except: the time you got to work and the time you go to supper." He shovelled, cleaned, swept, moved and washed things under the eye of supervisors who always seemed willing to explain. At first it suited him fine but the time came when he started wondering why he was doing all the work and they were doing all the explaining. He envied them, started to feel stupid and, eventually, quit. Back home in Gjoa Haven he spent his days hunting with his cousins. So much time had passed since he was on the land that he had forgotten almost everything. He had turned in to one lousy hunter. He moved back to the DEW Line.

He said, "That's where I felt more comfortable. I didn't have to go out hunting."

By then he had a family and eventually his children wanted to go to school. Back in Gjoa Haven he tried to learn as much as he could about hunting. Once more it did not go well but he was determined to succeed.

The first time he went out on the land by himself he purposely did not bring a tent. He would build an *iglu* for the night — sure he could do it, he'd seen it done hundreds of times. He cut out the blocks of snow and set them one atop another with great care in the spiralling arrangement well known to him. They collapsed. He tried again, the *iglu* collapsed again. Again. And again. That night he slept outside. The next day he travelled further still, tempted to stop while there was still light but pushing himself until the soft blue dome of the Arctic afternoon imploded into darkness. He slept outside that night, shovelled out an abandoned *iglu* the next and finally, on the fourth day, built one big enough to sit up in.

So it went. He could catch seals but always ripped their pelts to bits trying to skin them. Same with fox. Inevitably he tore their heads off. He would stitch the furs back together and try to sell them. But the fur traders aren't that easy to fool. They have been at this for 400 years.

"It makes me totally confused. I thought I was not going to make a good hunter and at the same time I was not going to be a good worker unless I went back to the DEW Line. That's the only place where I could earn a living to feed my family."

Thomas was powerless in his own land. He had, in a manner of speaking, lost his sovereignty. He is not unique, Thomas. Neither in his dogged determination to survive with self-respect nor in his confusion over what that now means.

Trudging around the village with Thomas, I heard many similar stories, as I did in other places. Gjoa Haven is larger than most, a collection of 700 people at the tip of a tongue of a bay on the southwest corner of the island, 2,500 kilometres or so straight north of Winnipeg. Its centre is the new administration building and it is tacked down on three corners by the large modular school, the Bay and the power station. At the head of the bay, a sloping hill is dotted with storage shacks, furs tacked to their sides and horns to their rooves, surrounded by small boats, bits of fishing gear, dogs. In Gjoa Haven pretty well all the adults have lived, as it were, for 1,000 years.

Historians chronically speak of the military opening up the Arctic, as if it had been a kind of locked and mysterious room before some clever army engineers happened by with the keys. Really, the military swept over the Arctic — first during World War II and more so during the Cold War — like an iron cloud, carpet bombing the place with boxes. Their job was the assertion of sovereignty. Every place a box landed became a beachhead for industrialized society. The boxes soon became the foundation for the Canadian government, which the military had given cause to worry about its sovereignty. Boxes were added, and more of our society — with its various virtues and vices, machines and organizations, ideals, morals, values and goals — were shipped north. What adult Inuit recall when they look back, not always in anger, is decade after decade when the skies rained boxes. The skies rain boxes still.

I asked a man once what his father was doing before he started working at a military base in the 1950s. He said, "Never beginning. People hunting. Starting from there, all the way through; never beginning." Times, and time, changed, like *that*.

In few places in today's world is it possible to see the kind of polarities that exist in the Arctic. The apotheosis of our technological culture has been dropped on top of one that still maintains the most ancient intuitions of humankind. Listening to the people, I came to feel they had a profound grasp of what sovereignty really means, right now, though the word rarely crossed anyone's lips. Inuit are not dramatic about what they have seen. They can describe the most extraordinary things in achingly placid tones. *And then the world changed*, they say, as if it were the wind. But they have seen a great deal. And they know it.

Travelling is always a form of mapmaking, idiosyncratic, personal and imprecise; always an attempt to find one's own way through a land and yet inevitably influenced by those who have come this way before and by the directions the natives provide. In a country where you don't have the language, as I didn't in the Arctic, native directions can seem confusing and contradictory; you see the land through the gauze of your own culture and can never be sure how it looks to the inhabitants. But travel too is always interior, we go looking for the commonality of the thing. What I was trying to understand in the couple of months that I travelled across the Arctic islands was my own culture in a single moment in a specific place. Yet, in this I found myself, as never before, moving on planes that constantly shifted through time and space. I find it useful to think of the image that I have tried to construct of these, in the following chapters, as a series of overlays on a single map.

"From the Stone Age to the Space Age," somebody said, "with no age in between." True, yes. But there was more than the simple and total obliteration, the flash followed by long darkness that that implied. Here too, the ancient culture lived, imperilled, but tenaciously, still; men could cross the harshest territory on the planet, travel hour after hour, over mile upon mile of a flat and frigid, windswept, concrete land and return, in silence, with food for their families; glancing, just in passing, at a nuclear weapons installation as they entered the village. Beneath the projected and precise, electronic landscape, within which lighted squares moved along predetermined lines, inscrutable figures wandered too, in circular patterns, guided intuitively by the muted but steady breathing of the land under their feet. Where these images merged the polar ice became a mirror and in it was reflected, in all of its twilight possibilities, the face of the future.

# Chapter One

# Friends

Flying north: the lines beneath begin to separate and diverge. The hyperkinetic, densely etched graph of the city recedes quickly. The band of industrial boxes and the arterial cabling bordering it gives way to neat crescent-shaped blocks of red roofs and blue pools. Soon the suburban geometry is ragged also, the blue pools scatter and dissolve into the perfect quilting of golden and chocolate cross-hatched squares.

Thereafter, for hours, there is only that incredible carpet of trees. Trees with a hairline part for a railroad; trees shaved to a bald patch of stumps or blasted away by the dark crater of a town; trees opened by yellow grasses or with gray-white mountain peaks poking through them; trees splashed with lakes. You fly a long way in Canada, before you run out of trees. Eventually it happens, they shrink into the land and darken; they fan out and fade away until they are stunted and then shrubs and then gone.

The land is smooth now, just a vaguely undulating white hardness, with random streaks of grey. This is the polar desert, a marble table top of unknowable size, wide open in every direction. Down there the soil is shallow as paper and the ground is permanently frozen. Trees are as high as the length of your thumb and a tire tread can divert a river. The precipitation is equal to that of the Sahara and it almost always comes as snow; on average, the temperature is minus twenty-five Celcius. Winter, which lasts from September to May, can bring winds, also, of 100 miles per hour or more.

Even flying right above the ground, in most parts of the Arctic, most times of the year, you could travel for days without spotting the slightest twitch of life below. Only about two dozen of the world's species of mammals can survive in the Arctic. Proportionately, the same is true for birds, fish and insects. The dense, rich blanket of life that covers the planet in the temperate zone thins as you travel north until here it is the merest patina over which, occasionally, washes a streaming, beating migrating herd. Anthropologist Marshall Sahlins called hunting peoples "the original affluent society." It is impossible, at first, to see that this could ever have applied to the Inuit. From the air, their land is a great blank canvas, as lifeless and undifferentiated as the surface of the moon.

Deep blue shadows reveal steep sea cliffs as the plane sweeps out off the northern Canadian coast and a different sense takes hold. Most of the sea is covered with a skin of opaque, grey-white ice riven with long, stretch-mark-like tears; it looks like rubbery wax paper. On the lip of the horizon, the sun is riding the shallowest arc imaginable, as it will all autumn. This perpetually slanted illumination creates an unfathomable ocean of violets, pinks, hard blues and grays, off-whites and soft blacks. The sea, the ice and the sky meld into one. Low puffy stacks of cumulus clouds become indistinguishable from the coastal mountains; you cannot tell the long stratus clouds from the ice or the water from the air. A sense of depth is lost entirely. You appear to be moving within a limitless continuum of mingling and transforming states; within a realm of pure light.

Twilight is the state of being in the Arctic, where the Light and the Dark are seasons. Space, time and energy have meanings here that are completely different from those you absorb in the delineated, evenly modulated temperate zone. Before you have even landed, you feel you have entered another dimension.

Hall Beach came into view suddenly. It always happened that way here. There are no roads in the Arctic, no arteries to herald another core. Every village is a compressed and solitary core unto itself. There are forty of them all told, tiny dots sprinkled along thousands of craggy miles of the Northern coastline and around the Arctic islands, the sum total of their population less than that of Stratford, Ontario.

"Every one of them is an artificial community," a town official said in Iqaluit. Iqaluit is the first stop after Montreal and unofficial capital of the eastern Arctic, the town grew up from the seed of an American bomber base; all the largest and most important villages were begun by the military. There had always been a thin spread of people along the coast but never so concentrated. Inuit gave these places names that meant "a beautiful cove" or "mountains" or "never a day passes." On maps they were called Clyde River and Cape Dorset and Resolute Bay, after explorers, towns in Europe and boats.

*Sanirajak*, they called Hall Beach. Flat land. The coast, along the northwest corner of the Melville Peninsula, is a hopelessly level plain of gravel and silence. It runs so unflinchingly into the Foxe Basin that Inuit hunters can barely distinguish between the tundra and sea ice here in winter. People elsewhere had spoken of its flatness with a wary tone, which I now understood. The village below amounted to a few homes loosely tacked to the shore. It was easy to imagine one good blast of Arctic wind sweeping the whole thing into the sea. Not so the Distant Early Warning radar station. It sat a little back from the water and looked like a huge iron golf ball in a trap of jagged metal. It wasn't going anywhere.

The plane came down at the radar station, a complex of long tin and wood buildings — trains, they were called — on stubby stilts, surrounded by receiving dishes and crowned with the elevated orb of the radar dome, about the size of a municipal water tank. It looked old, yet temporary. It had obviously come in sections, been unloaded and bolted down. Elsewhere it might have been mistaken for light industry but for the radome and other protrusions that gave it away as an electronic fort. Some of these looked like grotesquely large, industrial strength, TV receivers. Others I couldn't fix at all: 120-feet-high, concaved obelisks the colour of charred iron. Drive-in movie screens from Hell.

There is one road from the DEW Line site and it runs into the village, a mile or so away. Four hundred people live here. All are Inuit but for the usual southern contingent of teachers, nurses, managers and police. The village was arranged in three strips of prefabricated houses broken by two churches, a community centre under construction — the air was filled day and night with the sound of hammers — a Bay and a Co-op, a school and a brand new nursing station. Two long propellers at the top of high poles, an experiment in electricity production, spun ceaselessly.

The dark season was approaching when I arrived in the village. The sky was always purple. The bay was starting to crowd with small ice floes, hard dollops of whipped cream that bobbed in the water and made constant swishing sounds. People said, "Won't be able to put out boats soon." Behind the houses the pond ice was still soft enough for kids to spend every day skating. Their cries made the several dog teams tethered to the ground nearby strain and squeal.

Just a few days before, the annual white whale hunt had ended. Fresh whale guts were strewn up and down the shore, creamy white heads and bits of flipper lying amid much older debris: pieces of antler, a rib cage, bits of fur, vertebrae, and hunks of twisted metal, old chairs, oil drums. Decay is exceedingly slow in the Arctic. For ages and ages, memories lie right on the surface.

On the edge of the DEW Line, for example, there are Thule houses still standing. For hundreds of years, this was the heartland of the Thule from whom contemporary Inuit are directly descended. Climate and migration patterns traditionally made the peninsula one of the richest hunting grounds in the North — teeming with caribou, seal, walrus, whale and fox — a kind of Arctic breadbasket.

Thule houses were semi-subterranean, their rooves of turf and skin supported by the jawbones of Bowhead whales. The tidy line of four houses at Hall Beach, dug into the side of a low hill, had collapsed rooves, but were otherwise intact. They were a thousand years old. The greying whale-bone support beams had spilled out through the doorways and been scattered, like strewn baby building blocks. In the background, the dome of the radar station rose over the hill, a full, metal moon. A sinister obelisk stood nearby on the shore. It was obsolete now and a dozen ancient black ravens wheeled about its pinnacle, screeching.

There was continuity here. The Thule had brought to this part of the Arctic the same kind of sovereignty problems that, after a millennium, had occasioned the hardware now smothering their sturdy homes. According to legend and archaeology, they had won this land by war.

Before the Thule came, the legends say, the Arctic was inhabited by the Tunit, who were "large and gentle" but also "terrifying." They were caribou hunters who had no dogs, no kayaks, no bows and arrows. What they had, and what frightened the Thule, was powerful magic. Archaeologists call the Tunit "the Dorset" and say they lived from 500 BC to 1000 AD, having developed out of an older culture still. Among the things that distinctively mark Dorset ruins is their extraordinary art: tiny amulets and carvings, the size of a fingernail, made with stone tools and yet wrought so deftly that they have the appearance of life, of soul, with the slightest of detail. They exude, everyone notes, a feeling of magic and a knowledge of darkness. Polar bears fly, guiding the shaman to the netherworld. Gatherings of tiny faces contort into Munch-like howls. Humans and animals, carved of precious drift wood, have curious slits at their throats, pierced with ochre.

Around 900 AD the Arctic climate began warming, opening up waterways. For the next 300 years, the Thule washed across the Arctic from the area of the Bering Sea. They were great maritime hunters and ingenious technologists who invented many of the devices Inuit still use: bolas for bird hunting, snow goggles, tridents, whale boats, balleen mattresses, dog sleds. They lived a wealthy and fairly sedentary life, often in large villages, living high off the walrus and whale. Because they spread across the Arctic so thoroughly and quickly there is a common cultural and linguistic thread from Greenland to Alaska.

They lived, the legends say, peaceably with the Tunit for some time, but then fights broke out. The Thule, who were more numerous, drove the Tunit from the land. Neither were innocents. The Greenland Inuit told a representative story, set on this shore: A very long time ago, the Tunit visited a Thule camp when the men were away and raped all the women. The Thule men, on learning of this, went seeking revenge and found the Tunit in their stone houses, bows and arrows hanging uselessly outside. Alerted, the Tunit rushed for their arms. Too late. "The Eskimos wounded them with their harpoons," the storytellers said, "they took pleasure in killing the powerful but unarmed men by piercing their skulls." This sort of thing could only go on for so long.

The Dorset, writes Canadian archaeologist Robert McGhee, had been developing a way of life perfectly suited to their environment for almost 3,000 years. The archaeological record that traces them until the arrival of the Thule stops at that moment. They just vanished. "We can only guess at the causes of the disappearance," McGhee writes. He assumes, however, the legends are correct. The Inuit are well known to have long and exacting memories.

The Thule flourished until another climatic change. The Little Ice Age, which began around 1200 AD, forced them to disperse and develop the more nomadic and flexible Inuit culture. A few hundred years later Europeans would begin to arrive and other adaptations would be required. But the cultural heritage of the people would not be hit with massive forces — on the order of an ice age — until the modern military came. Thirty years ago there was neither radar station, nor prefabricated village, nor almost any of the current residents along this shore. A few families lived here in homes not unlike those of the Thule. I was in Hall

Beach looking for what few of those people remained. Such recent images, I thought, would still be fresh frozen on the surface of their minds.

On the way to Simeonie Kaernerk's house I passed two kids throwing a football back and forth, end over end. They matched, these two: beaming cherubs in ski jackets, with fine shiny black hair and eyes that made me smile. Their toy wooden sledges, *qamutiiks*, onto which they had both strapped plastic models of souped-up cars, were parked nearby. The kids here were unabashed as puppies. After a day in the village they all knew my name and yelped it whenever I walked by. And they were always everywhere. At midnight I would hear them, running around in the twenty below, laughing.

One said, "Catch."

"I didn't know you guys played football up here."

"We don't play. We just practice."

Inuit houses are buttressed typically by piles of things awaiting their moment: wood, rope and wire, skidoos in various states of repair, furs and other parts of animals and, always, a big wooden box up against one wall, for meat. Simeonie Kaernerk's house was particularly well endowed with such a collection and I suspected his box might be near to full; its flip top lid was sagging beneath a stack of frozen furs and a couple of fresh caribou heads.

Simeonie had been born some sixty years earlier near Hall Beach and had always lived here. He had a grizzled face with the faintest line of black mustache the width of his upper lip, huge ears, brown leather skin and quizzical eyes behind plastic, double-bridged aviator's glasses. It was the arms, however, that struck me. They swelled from his shoulders and tapered to rough hands; the kind of arms one needs to hoist a walrus into a boat. Simeonie hunted whenever the weather was fine. When it wasn't, he sat in, beneath a wall-sized tapestry depicting polar bears, listening to the broken warble of a two-way radio — intelligence from the outpost camps — and staring out the window.

It was grey the first day I visited. Simeonie and Abigail, his wife, were sitting in and the house was alive with children. Children playing around and children exploring. We talked for hours and the ruckus of the kids rose and fell. Nobody ever shushed them. Seven kids belonged to this house including Johanasie, the baby, who was adopted. Abigail, who was also sixty, had the eyes of a child and the dexterity of a cat. She sat on the couch, legs folded beneath her and the baby on her lap.

Simeonie was talking and Abigail was absently toying with the baby's penis as she listened. She would squeeze it and then look at his face, to see what kind of reaction she got. Later, when her cigarette ash sagged heavily toward the floor, one of the children appeared and cupped his hands beneath it, took it away and came back with an ashtray. If we were a couple of thousand miles to the south, I could not help but think, there would be an official busybody around to demand this child be taken away. I had some chocolate that I gave to the daughter of Napatchie McRae, who was translating. The child wandered away with it and soon returned to drag her wet brown hands down the length of her mother's white duffel parka. Nobody panicked but me.

Generally, an Inuit child has to be playing fast and loose with a knife or walking on too-thin ice to be reprimanded. The Inuit see their children as full human beings from birth, capable of decision and reason, as opposed to bits of unshaped clay waiting to be sculpted by the good ideas of society. They are expected to learn at their own pace through observation and experience with the intervention of adults restricted mostly to encouraging traditional games that teach them responsibility as individuals and within the collective. This was what had made life so miserable for Thomas Anguttitauruq among the nuns, who had ten rules for every occasion. Anthropologist Jean Briggs has described a quality the Inuit call *isuma*, a kind of intelligence that includes knowledge of one's responsibilities towards

society, which Inuit believe can only grow in its own time.
People, they say, can only be nurtured.

"Even though they live in a comfortable house they don't seem
to be as happy," Abigail said. She was talking about the children.
When she looked at herself at their age, and looked at them, they
just weren't. Children are the barometer in any society and every
discussion with the Inuit revolved, one way or another, around
their welfare. "It was happier days," Simeonie said like an echo,
"especially for families. There was nothing to disturb them."
Everyone said that. Never: it was an easier time. No one said
that.

To listen to Inuit describe their life then, to read the libraries
of anthropological reports, is to realize that, even in the Fifties,
we might as well have been living on different planets. This is a
banality, of course, but is too easily overlooked. Everybody
knows aboriginal people have a different relationship with their
environment but none of the terms that trip easily out — a close-
ness, a bond — quite suffice. Intuitive processes operate that our
science can't understand and our language can't explain. Details
can be listed endlessly, but only a leap of imagination, a leap
*within*, can provide an inkling of a hunter's perception of being,
a perception European culture submerged long ago. Life is life.
Biological pathways, obviously, never vary. But consciousness
makes all the difference.

Simeonie's family, and several others, lived in an area not far
from what is now the village. In summer their homes were earthen huts lined with moss; in winter *iglu*. "If there was heating
oil available they were really warm," he said.

It's impossible to generalize about traditional patterns of life
among the Inuit. Across the Arctic, the cultural threads are common but the individual weaves — clothing patterns, dialects,
hunting techniques — are highly particular amongst scores of
tiny groups. Most people spent much of the year on the move,
pausing for months or days, following the lifestreams flowing

sporadically through the land. In winter, your dogs, if you had enough of them, would pull you across the rolling plains and the mirror-flat sea ice. In summer they would walk alongside through the fields, dragging the details of the household.

The knowledge of when to move or in what direction or what kind of weather you would soon meet was a matter of constant interpretation of a thousand signs. Smelling the air, listening to the wind, watching the stars, touching the earth and other perceptions not easily described. Perceptions, Edmund Carpenter wrote, that came through the bowels. Signs, like work and food, were shared among collectives which varied in size depending on the time of the year — large groups, for example, hunted seal along the coast in winter while families tended to scatter inland for caribou and fish during summer. "When an Eskimo went out to hunt seal," the French anthropologist Jean Malaurie wrote, "he did not say 'I am going to try to catch a seal' but 'to have my share of seal.'" This was the simple definition of the collective. It was also a common consciousness. A man literally could not know what he thought outside of the group. It took the senses of many to sort out the thoughts of the earth.

The hardest thing to learn, Simeonie said, was to predict the weather. This he had begun to grasp at the age of ten. Now he could say, without question or boast, that he was much better than the weather office, which made loads of mistakes. This is the most important of a hunter's skills because even slight changes in the weather at the wrong moment can be fatal. The sea ice that you were travelling on could be solid as rock one minute, then the wind would swing around, conspiring with the unfelt current beneath, and a bridge several miles wide would become, in an instant, a drifting, shrinking island, bound for the open sea. Just this sort of thing had once happened to Simeonie and nearly been the death of him. For a week he floated, anguishing. Not out of fear of dying, so much, but of his family's helpless worry.

That sort of thing happened all the time. Storms pinned people down at home and prevented hunting. Migrating animals, for inexplicable reasons, did not arrive at the time or place expected, as they always had. Polar bears appeared, silently, from nowhere.

It is impossible to exaggerate the respect the Inuit have for the power of the land or for its continual gift of life. The essence was too strong to be diminished by speaking of it in a heated bungalow with a TV incessantly yapping in a corner. "The walrus," they would say, speaking not of a species but of a spirit. Or: "The river needs fish." Not the people; the river. A hunter was successful because an animal gave itself up, as a gift, and its spirit was ritually placated so that it might come again. At the end of a hunt, they would slice off something nice, like a head, and leave it behind as their gift to the other animals. Survival demanded a respectful attitude.

For the women, neither the work nor the anxiety was any less. Abigail explained how to make a pair of skin boots, *kamiqs*: the process began with cleaning the skin — one way if for summer, another for winter — and drying and stretching it; followed by scraping and tanning and chewing it, to make it soft. She would wrap her hands around someone's feet to measure them, and then cut the pattern and sew the pieces together with a stitch precise and tight enough to be waterproof. Usually the boots had two layers made this way and there were, also, socks, pants, shirts and coats to make. And other things to do. But it was a good life.

Who comes?
Is it the hound of death approaching?
Away!
Or I will harness you to my team.

So goes the Inuit poem.

"They were happier times," Abigail said. Everything is getting different now. Making *kamiqs* is not so enjoyable as it used to be.

Napatchie said, "She can't stop herself from putting the skin in her mouth. It's difficult for her. It's painful. And she just can't get it right using her false teeth."

The European arrival in modern times started with a kind of slow and sporadic shelling at the very edges of the Arctic. This began at the end of the sixteenth century, with the arrivals of Davis and Frobisher, and lasted for 200 years; lobbing towards the Inuit now a handful of nails, now venereal disease. At the turn of the eighteenth century, gradually increasingly waves of whalers, missionaries and explorers began arriving. Inuit quickly developed a savvy to deal with them. "The Esquimaux," British explorer John Franklin wrote, "immediately evinced their desire to barter, and displayed no small cunning in making their bargains, taking care not to exhibit too many articles at first."

The Inuit offered caps and boots, sculptures and whale bone to the strangers — *qadlunaaq* they would come to call them, people with bushy eyebrows — in exchange for knives and nails, tin kettles and needles. Saws were valued highly. Early white hunters and traders took whatever the Inuit would give and learned a fair bit from the indigenous population about how to survive a place that amazed, enchanted and terrified them. The explorers, as a rule, thought the indigenous people too crude to offer much but souvenirs.

The Inuit thought the whites peculiar, ill-tempered and potentially dangerous. Initially, they called them *arnasiutiit*, woman kidnappers, and took note of the fact that people who touched them often died not long afterward. But they were useful also; a breeze on the edges of the land flecked with metal and wood. When, as often happened, expeditions failed, when the European ships were crushed by the merciless sea ice, when sailors starved or froze, their graves became treasure troves for the people. Word spread quickly of a failed expedition and Inuit travelled a long way to pillage the remains.

People in coastal camps near seasonally ice-free seas knew Europeans and Americans first and it wasn't, really, until the twentieth century that the European influence became pervasive. In 1900, people living on the west coast of Hudson's Bay had forty years of regular work with whaling ships behind them. The Inuit who met Amundsen about the same time on King William

Island had never seen white men before. When Amundsen had his men laden his ship's deck with food and knives as gifts, the Inuit were too frightened to accept. In 1924, after travelling across the Arctic by dog-sled visiting Inuit villages, the Danish explorer Knud Rasmussen felt he had seen a people "unaffected by white culture." Though he knew what was coming: "Before long the white man will have conquered everything — the land, the people, their thoughts, their visions and their belief."

During these years, the traditional pyramid of white power in the Arctic — missionaries, Hudson's Bay Company and Mounties — was built ever stronger and higher until the group imagined itself a veritable Holy Trinity. And Inuit life had acquired a definite tincture. Waves of imported pestilence swept through camps. One historic group, the Sadlermiut of Southhampton Island, was wiped out altogether and almost everybody else was weakened. In the Thirties and Forties, many camps saw more people die than were born.

Christ was worshipped everywhere and the authority of the shaman was being undermined by white missionaries. Yet traditional belief in the need to appease Inuit gods and the spirits of the animals was tenacious. And there were appealing things about Christianity. "The miracles in the Bible, for example; for the Inuit — no problem," Fr. Robert LeChat said. Fr. LeChat had worked in the Arctic much of his life. He lived now in Hall Beach, in a rectory that smelled like cookies and warm blankets. "For the Inuit there was no difference between the spiritual world and the world of men." The story of how the white dog was created, for example, took place many years after Adam and Eve who, they said, were born in the Arctic.

By the 1940s virtually all Inuit hunters were also trappers, in the employ of the Hudson's Bay Company, trading fur for bullets and sugar. The traders called all the shots and often enough conducted business in a way that extended beyond the merchant's petty meanness into brutality. In one infamous case a stock of food some starving Inuit had clumsily attempted to pilfer was destroyed as a lesson to the community; better a loss and some more hunger than theft and full bellies.

The ethnologist Diamond Jenness has written that even by now people were slaves to the new economic order of the frontier. True, probably. Yet, Inuit, from their perspective in the present, never said this. In the first place, they didn't need much from the south. One man gave me his shopping list for 1940: two rifles, thirty-five bullets, 100 pounds of sugar, five boxes of coffee, two boxes of tea and some duffel. All tolled, $100, or about ten pelts.

Most important: the rhythm of Inuit life was a bass line steadied by the beating of the heart, but the melodies and harmonies were ever altering to maintain synchronicity with the land. They were, that is, improvisational geniuses. Initially, white men were fairly easy to knock off given the range of adaptations that were always necessary.

Their machines, for example, were helpful and mastered in a trice, be they rifles or whale boats. From the whalers of the 1800s, Inuit learned to pilot large ships in no time. Everyone who visits the Arctic is struck by the seemingly innate mechanical ability that allows Inuit to fix boat engines with shards of bone or tear apart a broken skidoo in a storm and make it get them home. Rather reluctantly, most southerners will admit that Inuit almost always understand machines better than their owners. Malaurie wrote of having the shutter speed of his camera repaired by a man who had never held a camera, but gauged it to within one-twenty-fifth of a second by recalling the sound it made when fired.

And it was always the case with Inuit that they had no way of knowing how much damage the whites were going to do until it was too late; until smallpox, measles, diphtheria and tuberculosis had diminished huge numbers of people to nothingness. Until their open sexuality had been corrupted with jealousy and disease. Until there were no bowhead whales left.

Many anthropologists and Inuit politicians have argued that there is a sick-making consistency in the attitude and the damage

Europeans have brought to the Arctic for 400 years. The differences between those who came for the first 360 years and those in the past forty have been matters of scale. But scale matters. Of the times before World War II the people I met still said: Never beginning.

Simon Keanik was the oldest. Probably he was eighty. Who could be sure? There was not the slightest creak about him. He lived in Gjoa Haven and he allowed himself, with a minimum of effort and a few jokes, to be cajoled into talking without payment. He had, as a younger man, guided explorers, scientists and the like from one end of the land to the other. "I always had to build *iglu* for them without being lazy or without getting greedy for a payment." The things he got from the whites, he said, made his life easier. And, he reckoned, vice versa. They couldn't have travelled in the North without the help of the Inuit. They were learning things from each other in those days. They were friends.

Simon said, "They passed a lot of good things to us and we passed a few good things to them. You know, in the beginning we were helping out each other so well in order to survive."


In the Fifties, a metal wind blew into the Arctic. It seemed, to most people, like nothing at first: a plume of dust in the distance. The silver glint of a small plane above a camp, where no one was sick and no traders expected. A score of white tents inexplicably inflating on the horizon. A rumour passed through the steam of tea from one hunter to another at the end of a day — 100 miles away, he had heard, there was money to be had. In distant places, unknown and seemingly of no consequence to the Inuit, this wind had been gathering for years.

Pearl Harbour to begin with. Once the Japanese had the Americans good and enraged, they added fear to insult by capturing two of the Aleutian Islands off Alaska. The United States, with Canada's permission, strode up the northwest coast like a cleated colossus, dropping air bases, roads and an oil pipeline as it went. After the Japanese were routed, the airports were used to supply planes to the Soviet Union. Another series of bases was built on the east coast to do the same for Britain. Previously, substantial building in the Arctic had seemed too formidable. The place was a vise — the ground impenetrable and the environment crushing. The installations barely clawed at the edges of the Arctic but they proved — in the usual tradition of war — what could been done with a little will and a lot of money.

Inuit living close to the subarctic, realm of the Indians, had always known battle. And, of course, people had fought amongst themselves. But contemporary Inuit knew nothing of what could properly be called war. Simon Keanik had a story for every occasion on any subject one chose, but war left him stumped. "Ever since he's growing up and the white people started coming in he heard that white people have wars," said Thomas Anguttitauruq, who was interpreting. He couldn't tell a story about it, though. "It's too confusing."

In *An Arctic Man*, Ernie Lyall, an old Hudson's Bay Company hand, wrote that southerners had a hell of a time justifying the war to the Inuit. The Mounties had just about gotten them convinced that Inuit methods of keeping order — extreme tolerance, followed by exile and, as a last resort, execution — were no longer on. There had already been jailings for what the Inuit community considered necessary killings. They saw, Lyall wrote, a double standard. "How is that the white man can kill hundreds of people every day and get away with it?"

The sheer girth of World War II operations astonished those few Inuit who witnessed them. The Aivilik, living on Southampton Island where an airfield was built, later said it made them rethink their notion of the cosmos. Having seen the same whalers, missionaries and police come and go year after year, they had concluded that there were fewer whites in the world than Inuit. They were shocked to find out how wrong they had been.

Moses Atagoyuk was a child then, living near an installation on Baffin Island. What did he remember? "Lot of interesting. I was with a friend I grown up with. He's living in Broughton now.

Mostly we were learning to play cowboy shooting. Saw movie every night. Mostly a cowboy movie."

Moses is now a CBC announcer in Iqaluit. We talked in a padded sound booth, where our words plopped straight to the floor. A harried and ham-fisted engineer in the adjacent control room pushed the wrong button and a snippet from the noon news broke in. "... latest convoy of American warships ..." was all we heard.

Moses, who didn't speak much English, said, "During World War II, the Americans, I saw machine guns and everything."

"They kept weapons here?"

"Yeah. After World War II: no more war! They threw in the water. All kinds of guns. Bullets. Everything."

"Just threw them away?"

"Yeah. No more Germany. No more war. That's it. Good life."

But so much stronger was the wind now blowing off the flattened plain at Hiroshima.

In Ottawa, right after the war, Prime Minister MacKenzie King saw a circumpolar map — showing that the fastest route between the United States and the Soviet Union was over the Arctic — for the first time. He thought it a devilishly clever view of the world and he instantly understood what it meant for Canada. It only strengthened his resolve to dampen the Canadian military's great and growing enthusiasm for cooperating with the Americans on Arctic military ventures of all sorts. King was adamant about international cooperation and profoundly distrusted military men. Thus the Canadian military first came to gaze upon their American counterparts as would a small boy awed by the neighbourhood toughians who got to wear leather jackets and whose breath smelt of plutonium.

The diplomats and ministers of Louis St. Laurent's government took a different view. By the early 1950s, American demands for Arctic weather, navigation, radar, fighter and bomber bases were endless and strident. St. Laurent's men, who had invented the concept of Canada the Peacemaker, yearned for the United Nations to work. Their passion, however, turned quickly enough to despair. They were also nervous about the emerging American dominance of Canada, but this was offset by the chill they felt as Stalin turned into a homicidal maniac. And having lived under Britain's mouldy and suffocating skirts, America, at the time, looked so sexy. Manhattan and Marilyn Monroe; a bright future in the making. Dixie Cups had just been invented and everyone thought them a brilliant thing to do with a tree.

St. Laurent's men, wrote diplomat John Holmes, who was one of them, came to believe in "the common sense of common defence and common profit against a common enemy." No more Mr. Nice Country. Deals were made.

The grandest deal, in 1954, was for a line of radar to give the Americans warning of a nuclear bomber attack, distant and early. The Canadian government had long resisted this. Ministers felt it was unnecessary and would cost a fortune. Reports to the American government, however, kept arguing that their problem was something deeper: "Basic Canadian attitudes natural to their political and economic climate." Apparently, they did not understand the threat.

Analysts such as David Cox, of the Canadian Institute for International Peace and Security, and American historian David Alan Rosenberg have since established that the American military were not, as everyone supposed, worried about their cities being sneaked up on. Rather, their war plans envisioned, when push came to shove, blasting the Soviet Union to Kingdom Come. These plans assumed that a few bombers would undoubtedly escape the initial attack and they wanted the radar to guide fighter jets in an air battle over the Arctic. Newspapers called the project the Arctic Maginot Line after a useless fortification built by France before World War II that did nothing but depress the French until the Germans' tanks rolled in. As so often happens with newspapers, it was a bit of accidental prophecy. The long depressing stalemate of the Cold War was beginning.

While the Canadian government dithered, the American Air Force set out to solve certain technical difficulties that the Arctic posed for radar. It hired the best scientists it could find and gave them their own laboratory at the Massachusetts Institute of Technology (MIT). They called it the Manhattan Project of air defence. We might, from our perspective, consider it the Star Wars of the 1950s. Months of theoretical doodling at MIT produced two prototype stations, one on an island in Alaska and one in a cornfield in Illinois. When these turned out to be successful, the scientists produced a report saying it was imperative the radar line be built immediately. Or else.

The plan called for forty-two DEW Line stations to be built in Canada, a necklace of domes and support installations embedded in the tundra every fifty miles from the Alaskan border to Davis Inlet. Some, like Hall Beach, would be industrial villages — dozens of buildings over several square miles — others just a handful of huts. Soon after the scientists' report was released, the Soviets exploded a hydrogen bomb. And that was that. The wind had gained the force of public terror. Never a gentle Victorian breeze of broken timber and discarded nails, by the time it reached the Arctic, it was a gale of shrapnel.

Building sections, steel towers, oil drums, electronic equipment, paint, wood, wire, plastic and food barged up the Mackenzie River. An ocean-going fleet approached with more from the east as did another from the west, 300 ships all tolled. Two hundred transport planes arrived. Convoys of steel-treaded tractors appeared on the tundra. Bulldozers were parachuted from flying boxcars, frogmen dynamited open harbours, thousands of soldiers piled ashore in amphibious landing craft. Between 1954 and 1957, 1.25 million tons of heavy machinery and 75 million gallons of petroleum blew into the Arctic. In a flash, the Inuit were overwhelmed.

An old man said, "In those days, the Russians didn't realize there were some people living up here. Same with the Americans, they didn't realize. Same with even the government of Canada, they didn't even recognize that there were some Inuit living up here, even though it's their own country. Seems that way."

"It is a mountainous, treacherous country, snow and ice covered, and barren," a military pamphlet said. "In the placement of stations the actual terrain was a secondary consideration. They had to be where they had to be, even if it meant building them on mountain sides, ledges or peaks." A faint attempt was made not to land square on top of the Inuit, but there's no pleasing everyone. In their planning, for example, engineers initially plotted the line straight through Igloolik where archaeologists trace a 4,000 year-long chain of uninterrupted habitation. After a confused pause, it was rerouted about sixty-five kilometres south, to a remote beach named after the American explorer, Charles Hall.

Simeonie Kaernerk's elders were not amused. "They felt like it was disturbing their hunting grounds for fox. They weren't too happy. He didn't see what disturbance it would cause."

Elijah Qammaniq lived down the road from Simeonie. He recalled his father saying just the opposite as the cargo planes began to arrive on the tundra. His father, Elijah said, was dying at the time. He told his kids: "If you are asked to work there or anywhere, just take the job. Because life is not always that easy." He didn't want to hear this, Elijah. Like Simeonie, he preferred hunting. But then his father died. And then his father's dogs died. Elijah took a job. He was just back from work the day we talked. His watch was still set to DEW Line time, which is uniform from one end to the other.

Matthew Ehaloak, who was twenty at the time, stumbled into the construction on the way back from trapping, as he might have a blizzard. Driving towards home, he could see, in the distance, a small city of low, white Arctic army tents with fingers of smoke above them in the spot where only his camp used to be. When he got there he found white men swarming all the over the place and strange Inuit too. A lot had happened while he was away. People were pouring in from distant places. Personally, Matthew wanted nothing to do with this. His elders, however, insisted.

Same thing happened to George Porter. He was just back from the land, tying up his dogs, when his father, a white trader, came to meet him. "He said: 'Son, I want you go to work.' I ask him where. He said they are building the DEW Line and they are picking up Eskimos to work on the DEW Line. That's how I got started." George was now the head of maintenance for the village of Gjoa Haven. When he told this story, he crinkled his brow right down to his mustache, indicating his upset at the time, and said, "But *I* am an Eskiiiimo!" His father didn't care. He could see the way things were going.

Camps high on the Arctic islands and low on the mainland heard of the commotion. A kind of exodus began, with people travelling for weeks and months by dogsled to reach the line.

There were those, too, who were just plucked up, like Dorothy. Take Alan Ayak. In 1955, he is a twenty-five-year-old hunter at Bathurst Inlet, an isolated coastal village which, even now, few whites have ever seen. All his family lives there. One day he is sitting at home and a plane appears, descending. A couple of men get out and ask if he wants work. He says yes and vanishes. Before the day is out he is 200 miles away and has left the world of the hunter forever. He spends the rest of his life working on the DEW Line. The first time he gets a vacation, it's a two-week break. Too little time to make it, by sled, back to Bathurst Inlet. He starts taking his vacations in Winnipeg.

Old Simon said, "He was pleased when this was being built because the younger people were getting a job and earning some money. At the same time, not knowing how to speak English, not knowing exactly what's going on, it makes you feel a little wary."

People started piling up around the construction sites. About 250 of an estimated 800 Inuit adult men across the Arctic came to the line for work. There had never before been such a gathering of Inuit. Nor of whites: the Inuit worked beside 4,000 men brought from the south. They hauled water and materials, picked ice, filled oil tanks and emptied shit tanks, cleaned the camps and unloaded airplanes. Then, as now, construction workers shipped to the Arctic wanted to get the job done with and get home. The work week was six and half days long.

In places too remote and rugged to be barged, smashed or blasted into, Inuit would be dropped in with shovels, to dig airstrip foundations. Then a slightly bigger plane than the one that brought them would come with a bulldozer. Then a bigger one. And so on. George Porter rode with a Caterpillar train across the tundra, guiding it along the trail of little red flags dropped by a lead plane. Later, to his chagrin, they had him peeling potatoes in the kitchen of a camp. This was no job, he thought, for a hunter. Eventually he worked his way up to being sent to carpentry school in Calgary. Just then the government came into the Arctic, hiring every Inuk who had learned English. George's career was set.


Officially, the Inuit were not to be troubled by the military. The agreement signed by the U.S. and Canada said, "The Eskimos of Canada are in a primitive state of social development. It is important that these people be not subjected unduly to disruption of their hunting economy." A manual published by the ITT subsidiary that got the contract to run the line said, "The Eskimo is politically and in every other way a first-rate citizen." A book on the subject said, "Canada will never allow her Eskimos to become serfs or slaves."

The Canadian government sent Jack Ferguson to tour the DEW Line in the spring of 1956, ostensibly to find out if all the pledges were being kept. He always suspected his real job was to spy on the Americans. The radar sites were U.S. Air Force bases now and nobody but nobody in Ottawa knew what was going on up there. Sovereignty, however, wasn't Ferguson's problem. He was a young sociologist, just out of school, and keen as could be to learn about the Inuit. What he saw travelling the line, as his report made clear, appalled him.

In the boom camps encircling the radar sites the banging and trundle of construction reverberated through every Inuit tent and shack and was, Ferguson felt, disintegrating the foundations of social organization. There was no time to go out hunting and what game there was nearby had disappeared. People started relying on food and clothing shipped to the sites from trading posts. When, as sometimes happened, the shipments didn't get through, men could eat in the military mess halls but women and children went hungry and were forced to beg at the back door. One of the DEW Line cooks gave Ferguson a letter he had received from a woman:

"To sir cook: would you please let us have a piece of meat to cook even thou its small. We got nothing to eat. My children will be starving while there Dad working and getting good meat every day while we get hungry having nothing to eat."

Money, however, fluttered down like snow and stacked up around them in great drifts. Fur prices had been falling and only the very best hunters and trappers were making much. Traditionally they would have led the community, their influence granted by virtue of acknowledged wisdom and experience. That order, Ferguson reported, was now being turned on its head. Great hunters still had great status, but it was already becoming more romantic than real. Younger men, less experienced at trapping, could earn six times as much money on the DEW Line as they could on the land. They were learning how to drive big trucks and intending to stay put. Practically speaking, they no longer gave a hoot for the sagacity of the great hunters who were beginning to look underprivileged by comparison.

Anthropologist Hugh Brody has written that the nineteenth century stereotype of the Inuit — permanently grinning at horrific circumstance — was used by the British as a useful model to hold up to the factory workers back home. As Darwin's theories were useful as a warning to them. What Ferguson saw was the process in reverse. The factory was coming to the Arctic to wipe the grin off Inuit faces.

The Western doodads filling the employees' packing crate shacks — furniture, radios, cameras, shaving cream, Coca Cola —were crowding other, fundamental, things out. Communities were being lost: men no longer hunted together; old dances and songs, already frowned on by the missionaries, had become the property of the old, replaced for everyone else by American movies at the Air Force base. "The Eskimos," Ferguson wrote, "file into the room and stolidly watch the movie (unless there is a gunfight, when they murmur) and then quietly file out again." And families were breaking down: The work week left men too exhausted to play with their children or talk to their wives. Women, robbed of their own work, had been reduced from partners to babysitters. Kids were learning nothing. Elsewhere, some people who heard of the boom sweeping the land even stopped trapping in anticipation of the wind of wealth blowing their way.

Sometimes, Simeonie said, people from his camp would go over to the construction site, just to watch the dome rise. These domes, as it happened, were the first significant break in the career of the technoprophet and inventor Buckminster Fuller. The design grew out of Fuller's ecological ideas. It is based on a mathematical formula that produces maximum area and strength from minimal materials. Fuller thought that his architecture could reform the extravagance of consumer society through efficient design. He propounded the idea of self-contained Arctic colonies and believed "the entire population of the Earth could live compactly on a properly designed Haiti." These ideas made him famous during those crazy Sixties. His American pavilion, also a geodesic dome, was the toast of Expo '67 in Montreal. Before the CN Tower came along, the geodesic dome at Ontario Place was the symbol of Toronto.

Military organizations are not renowned for adherence to ecological principles. Forever, everybody who lived in the North had had to split each match to make four. And wood had always been golden. Now, as Fuller's white domes bloomed across the Arctic, they became symbols of waste on an unimaginable scale.

The military arrived with enough gear to stay forever and, predictably, brought considerably more than was required. Buildings were erected and never used, warehouses full of supplies abandoned, mountains of food let spoil, tons of construction materials thrown out. A fully rigged hospital was abandoned. In one community, a detachment walked away from a liquor and oil stock that, it was said, took the Inuit almost twenty years to exhaust. Five years after the DEW Line was finished, half the sites were deemed obsolete and shut down.

Inuit had never seen such bounty. No shipwreck, this. It was manna from B52s. Whole villages were built from discarded wood and metal. Simon and some of the other men from Gjoa Haven travelled out to an abandoned site and disassembled several of the buildings, carefully straightening each old nail as they went. They piled the materials onto sleds, hauled them back to town and resurrected the buildings as a co-op store and a church.

Contradictions were becoming apparent. Greenland Inuit found themselves sudden beneficiaries of the supply run-off from an $800 million American bomber base at Thule. On the other hand, they were forced to move away from their ancestral camp, which happened to be on the spot the bombadiers wanted. They were promised some riches for this, which they never were able to collect. "Now we are richer than the Danski. We don't have to work anymore," they told Jean Malaurie of all the surplus food that was coming their way. "That's just a manner of speaking. You can't eat half of what's in these cans; it's too salty."

Every age brought its own diseases to the Inuit, who always, as it were, had an immune deficiency. The whalers brought syphilis. The fur traders smallpox. The military brought bulemia, illness of the twentieth century. In the modern world, they said, we gorge and purge.

The military also gave the Inuit their first demonstration of the extraordinary power industrial society could muster and showed them that it could do whatever it pleased. In Iqaluit, when the bomber base was being built, the American commander got sick and tired of having to walk a couple of miles up the coast to the Inuit village where the Bay store was located. So he had his men toss a road through the coastal hills and build a bridge over a river, a task they cleaned up in four days.

Jack Ferguson was one of the first people to spell out clearly the social costs of industrialization in the Arctic. Imagining someone might care, he filed a blistering report back to Ottawa. He said: look, the frontier society was bad enough, but the place was being turned into an industrial wasteland now. The people were being converted into sedentary peasants. Communities were splitting between an economic elite and a traditional underclass. The people who keep their jobs at the end of this were going to be immeasurably more secure than the many who would inevitably be let go. The social structure was being skewered. Unemployment was being invented. Little good, he thought, could come of this. The Inuit were at a crossroads where all the sign posts had meaningless words written on them.

The responsible bureaucrat in Ottawa, upon receiving these criticisms, wrote a memo in response that was largely a critique of the grammar in Ferguson's report, with an airy dismissal of his point tacked on the end.

There were others — administrators and scientists mostly — who felt queasy about what was happening in the North. A bureaucrat wrote, "Once the break from the traditional ways has been made there can be no turning back .... How will they regard all these plans we are making on their behalf?" Doubtless this also crossed the minds of many of the southern men working on the tundra; men who, like all those that had come before them, were shocked by the apparent desolation of the place; men who, despite the usual blend of romanticism and racism, believed they respected the Inuit. Certainly they felt, in their own humble ways, heroic when they were able to fly people out to hospitals or slip table scraps under the back door.

The military was not so sentimental. At an international meeting on Arctic developments in 1952, an American Navy report had laid out its thinking on these matters with the subtlety of a bazooka: "The Eskimo is a potential source of manpower that will be invaluable to our future military efforts in that region and which, if utilized to the full extent, will result in a material saving to our government." It went on: "The Eskimo compared favourably with the semi-primitive people of such Latin American countries as Mexico, Peru, Brazil and Argentina."

They were never going to be reliable, however, until they were fully assimilated into the white race. "It is generally recognized that any Eskimo enjoys the privilege of civilization but it will take some time before they can be taught to assume the responsibility of civilization." To teach them this, the military had built a town in Alaska that had five stores, two coffee shops, two movie theatres and a beauty shop.

Yes, a Canadian official politely inquired, but did the Navy feel any provision need be made vis-a-vis the native economy against the possibility of operations being relocated? Nope. "The U.S. Navy did not consider that in any way their concern."

For a society whose people will pay for any amount of bombs as long as they don't have to look at them, the Arctic turned out to be a kind of perfect military playground. Just beyond the horizon was an enemy they hated to bits but couldn't afford to fight. Godforsaken as the place was, though, the men were separated from the boys just by being there. Practicing turned out to be almost as good as the real thing. And there was nobody around to natter at them, complaining that the cannons were too loud.

They played war games, flew their fighters, and their bombers, practiced their anti-submarine techniques, tested their fallout suits and fired their flame throwers. They mapped the land and they charted the sea. They held exercises and troop movements that they gave names like Operation Muskox, Operation Sweetbriar and, my favorite, Operation Nanook. They studied Arctic biology, geology, zoology, oceanography, hydrology and astronomy. This bustle of activity was coordinated by the Canadian Defence Research Board. "Any increase of knowledge of the north," its chairman, Omond Solandt, offered at one meeting, "was a worth-while contribution to defence." The Arctic Institute of North America, the leading research organization of the time, was almost entirely financed by the American military.

With hindsight, it is easy to criticize, to be left breathless by the notions prevailing at the time — "The field of environmental protection covers the protection of the serviceman and his equipment against the adverse physical effects of his environment" — but I search in vain for a scrap, a line, a marginal note indicating the remotest sense of respect, as opposed to responsibility, for the people or the land.

It is the special joy of military bureaucrats to live within an amoral universe, the ethical details of which are always subjugated to ideology, that thing to which they bow down. And, at a fast clip, who knows how many ants one crushes? In 1952 a joint exercise called Sun Dog Three was held in arctic Quebec at what is now called Kuujuac. The premise was that Soviets had taken over an airfield as a bomber refueling base. The enemy soldiers marshalled the Inuit for their various bad deeds. In the critique at the end of the exercise, the good soldiers were dressed down for having made "no use" of the local population. They were told to smarten up. Then everyone packed up the game and went home. Two months later, it emerged that the bad guy soldiers had apparently given the Inuit measles, against which they still had weak immunities. Nine hundred people were eventually stricken. Seventy of them died.


At noon on Thanksgiving Sunday, Hall Beach was still quiet. Nobody moving but me and a small brown pup, strolling together along the purple shore. Nothing better to do. I was waiting for Jonah Anguilianuk to wake up. The pup was just killing time. The night before had been Octoberfest at the DEW Line — free beer for everybody. All the bureaucrats in the village and the men who work at the site had been invited. "They say," said a young southerner who had just arrived, "it's the best party they do all year." Good enough, I said to the pup, to lay Jonah mighty low.

He kept telling me to come back in an hour, every hour on the hour until five. The pup and I covered a lot of ground that afternoon.

A long, slow dispersal began when the military's Cold War building binge subsided and the lay-offs came. The few hundred Inuit employed in 1957 dropped to 100 in 1960 and just kept dropping to something in the neighbourhood of seventeen. A nickel and copper mine built at Rankin Inlet at the same time had operated just long enough to attract people from across the territories, bloating it to one of the biggest communities in the Arctic. After seven years the land had been stripped and the company pulled out. The Canadian government arrived, on the runways built by the military, to begin concentrating people into settlements. The sites chosen for their strategic value became the major government centres, which meant the major economic ones also, since government is now the main economy of the Arctic. Migrations began from one community to another, people searching for work.

Jonah was grumbling when he finally raised. Sure, yeah, it was a good enough party. "Would have been better if I could have taken my wife." Sorry, bub. No Eskimo wives allowed. Jonah had worked for the military for twenty years, since he was sixteen, thus accumulating several plaques. In five year increments, Felec Services, the ITT subsidiary that runs the radar line, issues each man an official company plaque, thanking them for defending North America. Jonah's plaques shared the wall with a shrine of Polaroids, stickers and knick-knacks. There was also a laminated wood poster of the Bee Gees smiling into a breeze and a tin golden eagle with wings spread wide and a clock mounted in its belly.

Jonah said, "I wanted the job because I always wanted to have fun with money, like the rest of the kids." This he had done. His home was well appointed, the furniture expensive and new, the stereo stacked the tell-tale three components high, the camera equipment professional. Outside were a new truck, a new trike and a new snowmobile. All the men who worked for the military had homes similarly laden. VCRs, beer label mirrors, you name it. They were middle-class homes. Homes like mine. The men worked a lot of hours and they were proud of what they had made. Sitting with David Kanatsiak, a janitor on the line, his daughter, translating, said, "He really likes his job because he's making good money." She added, sharply and spontaneously, "I know you are making less money than he do. He really likes it."

There was a defensiveness in the way the men spoke of what they had. Everywhere people wanted jobs now, but everyone, including — in fact, particularly — the southerners, valued hunting above working. For obvious reasons. But nobody could afford to hunt anymore without a fair bit of money. Bullets, they said, are expensive.

It was like the company T-shirt they all wore, which bore a cutesy cartoon fox. "Fox Main, N.W.T." it said, using the code name of the radar station as if it were a municipality. The name came from the Foxe Basin but the picture was associated with the fields of hopping white Arctic fox that Simeonie had known as a child. The week I was in the village everybody was talking about a fox that had recently been spotted out near the station. Napatchie and her husband were driving the kids out every few days to have a look. The young guys that worked at the weather station on the site had been feeding it chocolate cake, but the fox, knowing no better, insisted on caching it beneath the gravel of the station driveway, where it was mushed by trucks. Variations on the T-shirt were available. At the Bay they sold one that had a smiling polar bear wearing headphones and watching a radar screen. Baseball caps, being uniform-like, were more serious: they featured a crest with the Maple Leaf and the Stars and Stripes meshed beneath a satellite dish firing lightning bolts.

The problem for Jonah was time. "Working," he said, "is my life. When I was young I started working. It's my life now." Thirty years on, things have not changed much. Men shipped up from the south still want to make their money and get the hell *out*. Southerners working in the North have a kind of binary notion of planetary geography in which the world is composed of two places: the Arctic and Out. Everybody works six days a week. Inuit at the radar stations are the outsiders — shovelling, driving, unloading, fixing, emptying — and the whites insiders — scanning, plotting, thinking. None of the Inuit complain about the work — easier than hunting, they say — but they never let up about time.

Jonah said, "When you grow up on the DEW Line you want to stay there. But you can't get time off and you don't learn about hunting. If you work in the government you can always get time off and learn hunting. I want my son to work in the government or something."

The first time I visited there was a caribou head sitting on the kitchen floor, skinned with med school care from muzzle to eyeballs and staring at the ceiling. Jonah's son, one of five children, had been learning to hunt from his uncles. Jonah only got to go hunting on his summer vacation. Sundays all he felt like doing was sleeping. The worst of it, though, was the several months a year when the men were sent to remote radar sites. "I have to go all by myself, no wife and kids."

Redundantly, and stupidly, I said, "Do you miss them?" Redundantly, and obviously, he said, "I always miss them. Same as everybody."

Playing pool in the bunker and yukking it up with the lads was no substitute. Same as everybody.

Old Simon Keanik's wife in Gjoa Haven heard that I had met a man she knew in another village. How was the family? she asked. I shrugged. "I thought you white men were so smart," she said. "You don't ask the most important questions." She was hoarse with laughter.

Noah Adglak lived across the road from Jonah, in a house facing the sea. He had the opposite problem. All the time in the world to hunt but no money. The men in the village who didn't have a job with the military or the government just had uncollectable debts. Some owed housing payments for five years back. Napatchie McRae's husband, Al, who was from Scotland, was the housing manager. "Wot," he said, "are ye goan tae do?"

Noah was forty-four and deputy mayor of Hall Beach. For the longest time he had resisted taking this post because he wanted to find a job. No plaques here. Only: magazine pictures of a polar bear hunting and of a seal skins hung to dry, a Hudson's Bay calender and the ubiquitous print of The Last Supper. Noah took his unemployment very personally. It had depressed him, he said. He had had "emotional problems."

He had been badgered into taking the deputy mayor post by the other villagers until he finally accepted. "He hasn't been told why he was elected," Napatchie said, "but he thinks it's because he was trying to help whenever he could."

Noah said his father taught him this. One day, when he was a kid, his father inexplicably scooped him up and took him on a sled journey. For two days they rode in crystal silence, nothing said and nothing to hear but the slisking of the runners over the snow and the barking heartbeats of the dogs. Noah had no clue where they were going. They ended up in a camp. The family who lived there had adopted a child when its mother died but had begun to abuse it. Two days journey away, Noah's father kept hearing about this abused child. He had come to help them learn to look after it. Giving up on this after a few days, he took the child away.

"That's how Adglak started thinking this is what he should do. To help out people. His father didn't have to tell him that."

We spoke for a long time about this and that; the changes he had seen, the various problems the villagers had, the responsibilities of the council and, as always , about the children. Like so many people I met, he replied to each idiosyncratic question with an unhesitant, long, detailed answer, in a soft and even voice, as if he had just been thinking about the very issue I happened to raise.

At one point, presumptuously, I said — blurted — that he seemed to me a very wise man. "I would be wiser," he said, straight out, "if I didn't have emotional problems."

The way he spoke of this was less than a complaint and more than the autonomic self-deprecation, the feeling that your skin no longer fits properly, that is usual with the unemployed. Clearly, the situation was impossible. Unemployment came to the Inuit like a disease and people of Noah's age often seemed just plain confused by it. You couldn't really blame anybody. Not even yourself. He had all kinds of arguments with the government but the unemployment problem was not one of them. That he had no job, that this had made him sad and then sick was an intangible, plaguey kind of problem. A storm that you couldn't wait out, and a hunger you couldn't fill. A shrinking ice island moving toward the open sea.

Walking back from Noah's house, across the village, Napatchie said, "Imagine Noah's father going all that way just to get that kid. Imagine that."

I was still trying to imagine it the next afternoon when I came upon a fresh walrus carcass on the beach. Mid-afternoon, it was by the clock, but I noted long blue shadow lines were already falling from the points of a set of caribou antlers, tacked to the roof of an equipment shed. Like lines of movement in a cartoon; still wandering. Every day now the band of ice floes along the shore was broader and denser. They had stopped bobbing and swishing, and had become a mute crowd of petrified curlicues. Simeonie had caught the walrus and laid it out on the beach. It was a thick, rectangular pad of bright red pourous concrete. A pudgy seal pup lay at one end, the grinning head of a Beluga whale at the other. I was meant to help myself.

School was just out. The Laughers were everywhere. Here a pair were wedging their boat into the floes, there a pair were driving their dogsled off cliffs. "Hey, Kevin!" "Hello." "Hallo!" "Kevin!" "Hey, Kevin!" "Kevin!" "Hey!" They compulsively talked to strangers.

Down the road from the radar station had come a school bus painted bullet-proof green with "United States Air Force" stenciled in small white letters on its sides. Its windows framed identical green men, like in one of those pressed tin toy cars that come from Taiwan. At the front, a man was spieling. Honchos touring the Arctic installations, they called themselves Operation Arctic Star. They were on R and R hour, trolling for images of Eskimos. The bus halted in front of the co-op and a green bunch went inside. I knew they would be buying up the blobbish whales some of the unemployed men carved from the ugly local grey stone. The store manager had told me she always kept a good supply on hand for them. A few minutes later they returned to their windows and the bus made a slow turn at the far end of town and trolled back up the road. The Laughers were momentarily silent. Beyond the village, a Canadian Airlines jet was dropping onto the plain, trailing a streak of dust and stone chips the length of the airstrip to the base of the dome. I wished it would fly Operation Arctic Star elsewhere.

"He goes out hunting not just for himself," Napatchie said when I asked about the walrus. "He wants to make food available for other families who don't have anyone to hunt for them. The best way of living is to share food. That's one way of showing people that they don't just do hunting for themselves and their family."

This was an unending subject with Inuit elders. When you asked them about the most spectacular changes they had seen in the past forty years, expecting to hear how handy they thought flush toilets or how magical television, they would say: "The lack of sharing." As a means of survival it was superfluous and people were starting to see it as a cumbersome, anachronistic habit, no more necessary than having old people walk away from camp so that their children might survive.

Simeonie said, "There were younger Inuit working at the DEW Line. That's where it all got started. When they wanted some meat the people wanted to give them some meat and they didn't want payment. But they insisted on paying them. That's when people started thinking they got to expect payment." Abigail said, "Borrowing wasn't even considered then."

Nothing had been more basic to Inuit society and no loss was felt more deeply. In every community the meat of the land — "country food" they called it — was still the staple and still shared among family and friends. Families shared incomes but no one quite knew what to do about money on a larger scale. The disparities in the villages were so clear and yet, after all, everyone was getting fed. Men who mainly hunted were the poorest, yet it was they who were the most revolted of all at the idea of selling meat to their own people. This was the flip side of unemployment and a problem slipperier still. It made them feel like traitors against themselves.

*"Wage Earners,"* Elisapee Davidee spat out, with the sort of righteous disgust with which a dirt-poor peasant might say *princesses.* "You go to a Wage Earner's house and all they want to talk about is The Cost Of Living." The thing was: she was a TV producer in Iqaluit. It was a small operation, granted; in a small town. But TV producers are TV producers. Yet she spoke of Wage Earnerness as if it were one or another of the heinous human attributes that no one owns up to, like hypocrisy or racism. They all did that.

One of my roommates in the hotel in Hall Beach was an electrician named Ivan Uvilluk who spoke very slowly and clearly in a voice that came from somewhere very deep. He was thirty-eight. He said, "I don't like the idea of buying. I don't like to buy from another Inuk. Either he gives me some meat or he doesn't. Same with me. If he wants some meat I give it. If he wants to pay I don't give it."

We were talking in a spare room of the hotel, late in the evening, avoiding the squalling television in the lounge. The room's heating had packed up. We puffed little clouds of steam at each other, but it was tolerable. Ivan was saying, "We didn't have money before, so we don't share it; but a lot of people share ..." when the choleric manager of the hotel returned, spied us talking in the room and became hysterical. Do you have permission to use that room?! That room is only for rentals! Who said you can use it?! You can't just go *using* it like that! This was what the people were up against.

They were also up against themselves. Jean Brings has written that Inuit always understood the difficulty of sharing and acknowledged it publicly in jokes and stories, reinforcing sharing by making everyone aware of their own ambivalence. These dynamics, however, began to break down as people were given reasons for not sharing, which ranged from the southern insistence on the virtues of capitalism to government largesse. Now Noah said, "There's another help that is available." Yet this knowledge did not keep Inuit from castigating themselves for being too tight-fisted.

Of course, southerners yammered about Inuit being too loose with money. I spent an afternoon once with a former Bay manager, now a teacher, who gleefully tore strips off every other white he had ever met in the Arctic. His voice was paced by Benzedrine: "They just don't understand the Inooits, eh? They think they're so great. Soo great. Here for a year. Make a bundle. Split. What do they know? What do they know? They don't care about these people. These people can do anything just as good as you or me. Oh, sure. You can't have them running the Bay, eh? They want to share everything all the time. If some relative comes along and he's hungry, your Inooit ain't going to say no. Na, can't have them do that. Otherwise, anything."

What Inuit feared from this ethic was not that anyone would go hungry. They feared the fading of the collective responsibility that lies at the heart of all of their traditions and beliefs. As always, they looked to the children to measure the advance.

One day I went to Atanaarjuat School to talk to a class of ten-year-olds. The teacher was introducing me — I was smiling — when Abigail barged into the classroom, with Johanasie a bundle on her back. Without a word to the teacher she began giving the children a talking-to about sharing and niceness in general. There had been a nasty outbreak of thumb-tacking and she was there to tell them that this was cruel.

For ten minutes she spoke without stopping, her frame straight as a rod, her parka tight at her throat, the baby a silent peering lump. Her voice would rise two notes toward percussive anger and then slip down four into a loving song of encouragement. She spoke of teasing and helping, of taking and of giving. She talked until all of the children were rapt. Until even the tall one with *Quiet Riot* stencilled on the back of his jacket and a hot pink chiffon sash around his head, Ramboish, stopped smirking. She talked until her voice had gone right around the room and massaged every head. It was more, I felt, an improvised poem than a lecture. When they were all smiling, she turned, abruptly, and left.

"She went to tell the kids not to fight each other," Napatchie said, "She told the younger kids to obey the older ones. And the older ones to be nice."

Two flag poles set in red and white oil drums anchored with cinder blocks were all that marked the entrance to the radar site. One was not supposed to go beyond here without special permission, though nobody and nothing enforced this. Instead, every building was festooned with signs that said, "Warning: Authorized Personnel Only" and prominently featured a skull and cross bones. Administrative voodoo, I assumed, was cheaper than chain-link fencing.

I was reminded of Alvin Hamilton. He was minister of Northern Affairs in John Diefenbaker's brand new government when he passed this way in 1957. Radar was hot technology then and the USAF was refusing to allow even Canadian cabinet ministers to approach the site without a prior security check. Worse, they weren't even flying the Canadian flag. Hamilton was plum outraged.

"I just landed on those places without permission and told them to put up a Canadian flag higher than the American flag. And if they didn't have a Canadian flag to pull down their flag. That this was sovereign soil of Canada and every pebble was

worth ten times more to me than the whole American people —
200 million people."

That fixed their wagons. Hamilton pulled the stunt mostly as
balm for the sting the government was still feeling from having
been hoodwinked by its own military advisors into signing the
North American Air Defence Agreement with the U.S., putting
the defence of the continent under American control. Only days
in office, Diefenbaker had been convinced by the military that
the deal was all but signed by the previous government. It's just
a formality, they said. This was an outright lie. The previous
government had been stalling because it didn't trust the
American promise to consult Canada during a crisis. It wanted
guarantees.

As it happened, these would eventually be obtained and turn
out to be plain worthless anyway. When the Cuban Missile Crisis
came along Diefenbaker's cabinet conscientiously spent two
days debating the merits of putting Canadian forces on nuclear
alert. Meanwhile, Canadian ships went to sea and pilots readied
for flight, their commanders having instinctively followed the
American lead.

Alvin Hamilton was still sitting member in the riding of Qu'-
Appelle-Moose Mountain, Saskatchewan. I had interviewed him
in Ottawa, in his centre block office at the end of a work day. He
was tired. He took off his shoes, laid down on his couch and rat-
tled into my tape recorder for an hour, as if he were paying me
for this. When he got to the part where he tells the Americans to
pull down their flag, his head lifted slightly and he lowered his
voice to a tone of gravelly, prairie rage. It was the tone *Maclean's*
magazine had in 1956 calling Canada "the world's most northern banana republic" for its military subservience. But in those
days it was not possible to mistake *Maclean's* for *Time* on the
newsstands either. It was yesterday's nationalism. Hamilton was
just an old man now, charging around on a mythical horse whose
name he had forgotten. He laid there beneath a photo of himself
posing with the Mulroneys.

A few months earlier, Brian Mulroney had signed an agreement with Ronald Reagan to rebuild all the Arctic military sites at a cost of $1.5 billion, most of it paid by the United States. There would be a new radar chain, new bases for jet fighters and various other attendant hardware.

The work had been considered by NORAD in 1979 and by a House of Commons committee in 1981, both of which saw something that had been known since the 1950s: bombers could fly around the DEW Line, if they cared to, by way of the sea. No one worried much about this for twenty-five years because nuclear missiles had made bombers pretty well obsolete. Neither committee thought the work worth doing. When Reagan came into office everything changed. In 1982 a plan called Strategic Defence Architecture 2000 was written, which aims to develop air defence "that would actually last through a nuclear strike." The Strategic Defense Initiative — a.k.a. Star Wars — just made it more perversely legitimate. "It doesn't make any sense to build a house with a roof over our heads," the military said, "while we forget to put walls around the sides."

Canada sells $1 billion worth of military hardware to the Americans annually, notably including the guidance system for the cruise missile, which the Arctic weaponry is meant to guard against. It was hardly in the position to say no. In any case, Mulroney had just come into office. He wanted closer ties with the Americans. And his military advisors told him the deal was all but signed by the previous government. It's just a formality, they said.

Passing between those flags, happily waving at each other on the tundra, riding in a truck painted bullet-proof green with "United States Air Force" stencilled on the sides, I thought: it was like one long TV rerun. Only, as you watched, the laugh track got increasingly insane. *I Love Lucy* as Dorian Gray.

The supervisor of the DEW Line site was giving me a tour in his pick-up. "Lately," Bernie Doiron said, "we have put a big emphasis on having the village and the community here mingle more." His example was this: when Fr. LeChat needed a part for the church, Doiron had it flown up from Winnipeg and delivered the very next day. Which is more than anyone else could do.

The station sprawled over four square miles of the coast. There were twenty-four buildings altogether — warehouses, workshops, garages, offices, powerhouses, airplane hangars, barracks, radar rooms — all on stilts and clad with tin. Doiron motioned to a warehouse: "Everything comes on the sea lift once a year, tractors, napkins, everything." It was, of course, completely self-sufficient; it could store five million gallons of fuel, had its own dual power system and its own fresh water lake, which also supplied the village, although the Inuit preferred to drink melted ice.

Thick clusters of cable, marked by little flags, trailed all over the site winding around dense piles of refuse to the various dishes. The site was weighed down and mapped out by junk: a collection of old machines here, a couple of hundred oil drums there, a stack of broken transformers yonder near a heap of concrete blocks. The refuse was strewn so far and wide it seemed like a territorial thing, like a monstrous cat urinating metal in the corners of the backyard. The garbage, strangely, made the tundra look more desolate than usual. The bits of twisted metal and rusting oil drums produced the irrational feeling that the land had been laid waste, rather than found this way.

On the way back in I noticed there were Christmas lights strung around the base of the radome. "We do it just like down south," Doiron said, "put them up and then never take them down."

Pete McKinney, a West Virginian with a big mustache and a hell of a handshake, supervised the entire radar line from an office at Hall Beach. He also pressed the community service bit. "The native population and the stations have a very good relationship. I believe," he drawled, "it's one that will continue and grow in the future as they become more aware of what we do and we become more and more aware of their capabilities. The two seem to mesh well together."

Okay: "How are you more aware of their capabilities?"

"Northern labour is available. It is there. And the native has become aware that his skills are such that he can do and can compete in an open environment where those skills are required."

He went on for a while longer. At the end, he asked for my tape, so he could make a copy of it. He said he had never heard his voice on a tape recording before. Later I asked if I could take his photograph. He had to check that one out with the H.Q. in Colorado. H.Q. replied in the negative. "It could be misrepresented," they had said.

The stuff about the village had to do with the competition for the contract to run the North Warning System. Construction was already proceeding at a furious pace; all that summer the site had been swarming with engineers and electricians. In both supervisors' offices there were already plaques hanging, praising their cooperation. Four consortiums were now bidding on the operational contract and Felec, which had had it for thirty years, was sweating. For one thing, it didn't exactly have a sterling record of employing northerners. Of the eighty people working on the site, eight were Inuit. As it turned out, both men were wasting their breath. The company lost the contract.

Men might work a lifetime on the DEW Line, taking vacations a few times a year to visit their families. Doiron thought of himself as a Montrealer, his wife and daughter were there, but he had been working here for more than five years. "It's a way of life and you get used to it," he said. "It depends on your personal goals." He was telling me about the internationalism of the place. One Christmas Eve they had got to talking and found they had people from Quebec, New Mexico, France, you name it. They spoke seven languages amongst them.

I had heard this sort of thing before. Villages of the exiled that flattered themselves as being tiny UNs. Once in Spain I had come upon a peasant village which an American draft dodger named Ric had managed, in the days when Franco made it easy, to purchase lock, stock, people and the mountain they all sat on. He was converting it into a vacation spot for wealthy Britons. Every year the peasants were more overwhelmed by men and women who, among other things, dropped their drawers the minute they arrived. Ric's lieutenants were from Scotland and Germany and New York and known only by their first names: "Bill; just call me Bill." "We're an international family," Ric said. "We all live together and we all communicate."

At one time there had been Eskimo Houses around all the radar sites for the families of Inuit workers. As the government settlements grew up and families moved closer to schools, some of these fell into disrepute. After some serious trouble that ran to murder, they were dismantled. Now wherever a village sat beside a military installation there was a degree of seething, unspoken jealousy among the young Inuit men. The southerners had money, status and prestige to dangle. "Those old guys," said a young one who had worked for the military, "think they're so lucky being able to get all these young girls." When venereal disease turned up in these villages, the list of contacts always ended at the base.

But the atmosphere in these places is not what might be imagined. They are neither wild nor woolly but infused with the fastidious and brittle sterility that is born of the multitude of rote suppressions required of men who spend a lifetime alone. For centuries, this has been the most difficult of things for Inuit to fathom: why whites try to get along in life without women.

Doiron was saying, "We have quite a few people who have been here twenty-five, thirty years." There was an exercise room, pool tables, a bar, a reading room, a curling rink and lots of television. "We get ten channels." We were passing through the bar. Several older men were slouched at stools vacantly gazing at the evening news from Detroit. Fires were raging.

The atmosphere at the weather station, just beyond the radar site, was something else again. It was a kind of miniature version, operated by guys in their twenties: a few small buildings crouched beneath a baby radome, used for tracking the helium-filled weather balloons that were released, with great excitement, every evening. "We make a mistake," Andrew Clark said, in a voice filled with delicious danger, "And The Whole Thing Could Blow Up! Kaboom!! The service has lost three sheds this year."

Inside their main building, the walls were covered with maps; elaborately segmented, highly numerical sorts of maps. Against these on every wall stood heavy metal boxes with thick glass windows behind which needles were scratching and bobbins jumping. Measuring the world outside. The room was shot through with a *U2* anthem simulblasting from the TV and stereo. On a rooftop in Los Angeles, Bono was making a spectacle of himself. In a corner, a multi-layered schematic of a space ship, in dazzling reds, blues and yellows, was revolving slowly on a computer screen. Air-guitars were being played. Brownies were on offer.

For some reason, Andrew Clark said, the weather guys and the radar guys don't get along. He couldn't figure it out. "They think we're dummies," he said. "We are treated almost like the Inuit. The Inuit are treated like they don't exist." He was part Cree — "I've lived on reservations, but that's not the point" — and sensitive to racist subtleties. He was listing a catalogue of these when a knock came at the door. An old woman, a couple of teenagers and various children stood in the black night. "We use the phone?" the teenage boy said.

"Happens every night," Andrew said. The little family was now jostling and jabbering into two lines amid the scratching and clicking of the machines. The station is connected into the DEW Line's phone system. When the fathers are off at remote camps, hundreds of miles away, the only way families can afford to reach out and touch them is by begging at the door of the weather station. Elijah Qammaniq had mentioned this. His wife was chronically ill and couldn't leave the house. It drove them crazy being unable to talk for weeks at a time. Sometimes, Andrew said, there were families waiting four and five deep in the doorway.

He said, "You would think the company could take into account their worries about their families. This is a different culture. The family is everything."

Walking back along the coast in the dark, the village looked so tiny. A couple of strings of softly glowing yellows and blues, a single used-car lot in the distance with a few televisions under bushels.

The Inuit have a word that anthropologist Hugh Brody has written about. This word, for which there is said to be nothing similar in English, has at its centre, Brody writes: "The feeling of nervous awe that comes from being at an irreversible disadvantage, a situation in which one cannot modify or control the actions of another; it can also describe unpredictability." This word is *ilira*. Inuit feel this toward southerners, bound up as it is with both a kind of respect for some form of raw power and the uneasiness it produces in those forced to endure it.

The image of the radar station held more power at night. The darkness hid all of the dented metal. Purely an image of artificial light, it became a large, bright, segmented orb, set in a cluster of red and white pinpoints. Its searchlight swept the sky. A superior electronic *iglu*. The military installation, it seemed to me, could not help but produce several kinds of feelings that would be expressed using this word. *Ilira*. By any measure of raw power you cared to think of, it hugely overwhelmed the village.

In the late Fifties, Inuit living at Tuktoyuktuk encountered a first for their society. They had an ideological dispute. Overnight, the radar site there had been completed and the jobs associated with construction had evaporated. Historically, the people of the region, on the Mackenzie Delta, had more contact with southerners than any Inuit. They were used to booms. Now that the military boom had busted, they were grappling with what to do with themselves. Factions formed. One side wanted to demand that the government provide jobs or subsidies, so that the way of life they were used to could be maintained. The other wanted the people to return to their subsistence lifestyle, for the preservation of their culture. In the end, the government arrived anyway, uninvited, and began distributing welfare. But the dispute has continued throughout Inuit society since.

Governments, dog-like things that they are, have a limited capacity for grasping the shadings of human ambivalence. The debate among the Inuit is wholly academic from their perspective. They have no question about the economic future of the Arctic. "They have seen," wrote political scientist Kenneth Rea, "the 'problem of northern development' mainly as a matter of overcoming physical obstacles to the exploitation of resources — that is, as an engineering problem." His 1976 report to the federal government argued that it ought to ask itself: "Why develop the north at all?"

This sort of question goes down like an apple loaded with razor blades. For most of this century, governments and corporations have been holding their collective breath and crossing their many sticky fingers, praying that the deposits of their dreams would be found beneath the Arctic islands and the Beaufort Sea and that there would be markets to justify extracting them. Billions of dollars have been spent drilling hundreds of wells that have, in turn, located billions of cubic metres of oil and gas. Nobody has ever wanted to know about whys.

In 1977 Justice Thomas Berger held an inquiry for the federal government into whether a pipeline should be built down the Mackenzie Valley to bring gas to the United States. He said it should not, for at least a decade. But he also addressed the bigger question. He wrote: "We must cease to regard large-scale industrial development as a panacea for the economic ills of the north." The government accepted his recommendation, but exploration continued and Berger's point was lost. Three years later, the government announced the National Energy Policy to promote the "Canadianization" of the oil industry, creating a boom in the Arctic, without so much as perfunctory consultation with natives. At the same time it went ahead with a pipeline down the Mackenzie Valley, despite Berger and native protests. When the pipeline was finished and the NEP cancelled in 1984, the whole, false, economy collapsed. So it goes.

In 1987 Gulf Canada discovered a huge oil field — disingenuously called Amauligak, an Inuvialuit word for snow bird — that it says will soon be gushing like a stuck pig's jugular. Corporations, of course, don't talk that way. "We will be in full commercial production in 1992 or 1993 in the Beaufort unless some nut gets in the way." The oil boom, analysts now say, is on again and the federal government has said that the 1990s will see the "takeoff" of the Arctic as an energy capital.

The quandary this kind of exploitation creates among Inuit politicians and commoners alike has intensified over the years but will not, by its very nature, be able to go on forever. The voices one hears in it are those of the Inuit mind wrestling with itself, trying to formulate a response to a danger to which there can only be a limited reply. A mind, as it were, headed toward the sea.

The pattern is the same right around the pole. In *The Circumpolar North*, the three authors, recognized Arctic experts all, wrote: "Development is frequently justified on the grounds that it gives the natives the choice of whether to continue their traditional life or to enter the bright new world of wage employment. It is, however, rarely a fair choice, for the cards are stacked against the traditional life, which receives little or no support compared with the massive incentives provided to industry. The choice offered to the natives becomes simply whether or not to survive."

At the end of the 1980s the growth industry in Arctic exploitation is military development. The new radar line and fighter bases are just the beginning. The Canadian government will also create a military base at Nanisivik, install submarine detecting equipment in the island channels and increase patrols and exercises of all sorts. The applause for this has come from predictable quarters. "We view this project," the territorial government said of the new radar line, "as an engine to strengthen the economy of the of the Northwest Territories. It can help build a better north."

Since it formed a decade ago, the Inuit Circumpolar Conference, which represents people from Alaska to Greenland, has been against military development. It has said, "Serious efforts must be made to avert the aerial and naval arms race that is gaining momentum in circumpolar regions." Most Inuit politicians, however, have confined themselves to complaining that local people were not going to get enough of the billions being spent.

"Inuit communities," Allan Jones said, "have been very cooperative. They are very anxious to work with us." Jones was the military's consultation man. Normally he was in the Department of Indian Affairs and Northern Development but he had been sent down the hall to organize meetings with Arctic communities where new radar installations were to be built. Everything was going according to plan. Advance men travelling through the villages were having an easy time of it. They met worries everywhere but easily glossed over them.

In every village people asked about the effect more military was going to have on the animals. Would there be jets frightening them? Would the installations disrupt their movements? Would there be fences to trap them? Would there be, they asked in Hall Beach, more tests of the cruise missile because of this? A wink and a nod was always enough to bring them back to the main source of their anxiety, about which the military could assure them: jobs. How many would there be? Would the local people, for sure, get them? How long would they last? Would they be the same old dogshit jobs they have been doing for thirty years? Or what? Some communities, where unmanned radars are to be built, tried a little unsubtle extortion. You know, they said, there might just be a little vandalism out there. Howsabout a contract to keep an eye on the place? Before the locations of fighter bases were announced, communities vied with one another for them, valiantly arguing their superior strategic significance.

In the western Arctic, an Inuit-owned company put in a bid to run the radar line. The Inuvialuit Development Corporation is a small conglomerate built out of money from a land claims settlement between the federal government and the Inuit who live in the Mackenzie River delta. It threw its lot in with Felec. The head of the Inuvialuit corporation is Roger Gruben. He said, "In our area, you don't get people bitching and complaining about passive military development. It is in our economic interest. My father was part of the construction crew that built those sites at Tuktoyuktuk. Here I am, his son, trying to be a major player." It wasn't to be. The $114 million contract was won by a company called Frontec Logistics, a subsidiary of Atco which made much of its fortune servicing the oil industry. Of the contract, a company official said, "This is a big-time move into one of the last frontier areas of the world."

Ordinary people simply did not know what to think. Peter Akkikungak was a municipal foreman in Gjoa Haven where, he guessed, ninety-five per cent of the people had no cash work other than trapping, which was sorely depressed. He said, "I think I'm one of the luckiest guys in the world, just about." But he worried about the others. He showed me some coloured crystals, a sort that could be found all over the tundra. He wondered if they were worth anything. Perhaps, he thought, someone might like to open a mine here. Except: not anywhere near the animals. "Nobody wants pollution." Personally, he would have liked to open a bakery, which he thought would be a good move since people were paying four dollars for a loaf of bread imported by the Hudson's Bay. Except: the nearest bank was 700 miles away and he knew there was not the slightest chance it was going to loan him the money to do that. Banks knew, he said, "the people are just learning to live with cash." These were the circles the people travelled in.

Part and parcel with the question of sharing, these are circles within the soul. Increasingly Inuit put hope in their own corporations, believing they will be more sensitive to the land and the people. But many also recognize there is an oxymoronic quality to the very notion of Inuit corporations. Inuit were not made of the stuff upon which capitalism has been built. "The competitive spirit," wrote Malaurie, "might only be expressed as a wish to be the best in the service of the group." Their attempts to maintain this ethic within a capitalist society continue to be fraught with internal pain — there are bitter arguments about how, even *if*, these corporations should be run — and they have always come up against external pressure. In the Fifties, for example, Inuit attempts to form cooperatives were continually frustrated by the Bay, which did not want the competition, and by the government. "Senior branch officials," an academic wrote of the time, "harboured reservations about cooperative development on ideological grounds, viewing them as socialist experiments incompatible with the Ottawa government's outlook."

The Arctic has taught the Inuit something about implacable force. They have a word for use in impossible situations, like when a storm prevents movement or animals are nowhere to be found. *Ayunmut*. It can't be helped. Think of it as a verbal shrug.

"If the military wants to build here for the national interest," Simon Awa said. "Then *ayunmut*. It has to be put there." Simon was a newsman in Iqaluit. "I think the Inuit view of the military is that if they want to have something done, then there is no way of stopping them. Because they have so much power."

I asked Noah Adglak how he felt the village and the military got along. He said, "They pretty much stay to themselves. It's okay for them to come and fish in the lakes. But it's beginning to show that they will do whatever they want to do. Last summer they were shooting at whales. But they didn't take them. They shot them and left them. It seems they will do what they want to do without consulting the hamlet."

The military swore up and down they did no such thing, that guns were not even allowed on the radar sites. What was interesting was what people believed them capable of. The enormity of the Arctic, with people moving so infrequently over it, lends itself to apocryphal stories. Asking about the military, I heard many. Tales of mysterious bomber crashes. Intimations of unlawful missile bases. Rumours of explosions. I took these to be a part of people's understanding of the thing. They had come to believe that fighting guns gave you the right to do whatever you pleased; which under their circumstances was quite reasonable.

Jobie Weetaluktuk was also a reporter. He had come from print and now worked for Inuit television in Iqaluit, two sides which I thought reflected in his constant vacillation between a stone face of grave seriousness and a busted dam of a smile. He said: "Inuit politicians have limited power and there are so many pressing problems — unemployed young people, housing over-crowded with generations of families. That's what people are worried about and want politicians to deal with. Inuit politicians honestly believe what they say about the weapons but they feel impotent. They feel we might as well get on board."

There is no shortage of evidence for them to determine that this is how the system works. The government's acceptance of Berger's recommendations, for example, crystallized corporate hatred for Pierre Trudeau and the resulting pressure soon got the decision turned around. The NEP was likewise gutted because it raised the ire of the Americans.

Everybody is answering one up the line. In Ottawa I inter-viewed, one after another, two External Affairs men. As it hap-pened, one was French and one English. I was asking about the possibility of missile bases and other such things that the American military likes to imagine being installed in the Arctic some day soon.

The Englishman said, "Our interest in air defence against the Soviet threat happens to overlap with the Americans' interest. We are not just going along." The Frenchman said, "Canadians have to realize that our airspace is so important to them we can't leave them without protection, though there is a great deal of dis-agreement." The Englishman said, "We have never said that we are against SDI, only that it is not our area of expertise." The Frenchman said, "You can only go so far, criticizing, and then you start touching things that are too close to them."

Everything, I thought later, is attitude.

As was usual in Arctic hotels, the one in Hall Beach was packed out with southern construction workers. They were from Montreal and building the new community centre. It was an election year. These hotels were almost always depressing places. The builders were amiable enough but their lives were pure work. They were at it every waking hour but for the five times a day when they ate, returning in a thunder of boot clumping and back slapping to be served a plane-load of beef by young Inuit women whose eye-line never rose above thirty degrees. The air was always filled with the fumes of diesel engines and work socks. As I laid in a bed that a thousand swarthy chaps before me had sunk into, a hammock and old Ferguson came to mind.

He was now a professor of sociology at Windsor and lived in Detroit. His report, the only one ever done on the DEW Line's impact, was kept in the rare documents section of a library in Ottawa. He called the DEW Line "the last nail in the coffin." In a way, I was thinking, it was more like the first. Things had happened so fast — with the government arriving and then the mining and oil companies — that none of the dozens of bureaucrats and anthropologists and politicians who considered the changes in the native economy and culture thought there was any point in bothering to isolate the impact of the military. You could comb dozens, probably hundreds, of articles on the strategic significance of the Arctic and never read a word about the people who lived there. Naturally. That's the way it is with military analysts. To them, everything is hardware and cartography.

The problem for the Inuit was that they couldn't separate things out; economy from culture, belief from need, individual from community, men from women, adults from children. But this was the essence of the military; this was what it was about, separating one sex and one set of traits off, sending them away in a metal phalanx to defend the other half. It was the archtypical creation of Western society, with its inherent sense of competition that set the tone for all relations between people. And it had set the future for the Inuit, literally building the foundations for the new economy of the Arctic and all the attitudes it engendered. In a single flash it brought the Inuit into, as people used to say, a man's world.

I thought of the transport planes that were dropping down on the fields of fox every hour during the summer of 1955. Inuit had puzzled over the peculiar shapes and possible uses of many unfamiliar objects being winched down to the ground. Everything would turn out, in the end, to be a wedge. And all those elders pushing their children toward it must have known that. Thirty years later, their grandchildren still had the same problem. *Ayunmut*.

I thought of the young men who had reluctantly taken jobs, who were old men now. "He took it to avoid his kids envying other kids," Napatchie had said of Simeonie. "But he wasn't that happy. He likes hunting." Elijah Qammaniq had worked in the radar station for twenty-two years. He was finally driven from the place, he said, because he could never get the smell of diesel fumes out of his head.

Later, I had two conversations with men on this topic and they are the ones that stuck with me. One was with Matthew Ehaloak, who had, as a young man, come home from hunting to find a construction site atop his family camp and whose elders had insisted that he go to work. The other was with Alan Ayak, who had flown off one day with the company recruiters into a different world. I met both in Cambridge Bay.

My conversation with Matthew was translated by Joe Koaha, a gregarious and generous guy who just never stopped smiling. The Matthew that I met, who had just left the military's employ, was a nervous and rigid person. Our interview was a circle of short bursts.

"How did you feel about working at first?"

"He was pretty happy, he wanted to stop fox trapping for a while."

"So it was okay with you?"

"Yeah. Happy."

"Did you work there until now?"

"He started in '57 and went through until three years ago."

"And you were always happy that you were working, rather than hunting?"

"Yeah."

"Was it a good place to work? Nice people?"

"Yeah. Happy. Nice people."

"So you retired."

"Yeah, retired. Partly laid off and partly retired."

"Was there not enough work there?"

"There's less work now."

"Are you happy not to have to work?"

"Yeah. Sometimes it's boring. But he's happy."

"What do you do with your time now?"

"He don't have a skidoo right now, so he's staying in his house for a while to relax."

"Do you plan to buy a skidoo?"

"No. He's not buying any more skidoos."

"No more hunting?"

"No. No more hunting. Just a big relax."

To speak to Alan Ayak, I had to skulk the perimeter of a radar station one evening, waiting for him to get off. He lived in the bunkhouse and, when I asked to speak to him during a guided tour, no one was too inclined to seek him out for me. He was, as he always is, back in his cubicle room immediately after supper, watching the television news. Dan Rather, reporting from New York. "I don't get too many visitors," he said.

Like everybody else, Alan Ayak began working as a helper in a camp; he and eight other Inuit with 300 southern construction workers. Jackhammering, cutting wood for the carpenters, cleaning. A friend came with him from Bathurst Inlet but soon after they arrived he died, drowned while fishing on his vacation.

Eventually, Alan worked his way up to driving trucks and forklifts. For all of his career there, until three years ago, he had been shifted from one camp to another. Out in the camps, at night, they watched television and played pool. "Good food, good people, good money," he said. He thought of hunting, of course, but he couldn't because guns are not allowed on the radar sites.

He said, "We got all kinds of food in the station. I go by the law. Company law."

Every four months or so, he returned to Cambridge Bay, where his family lived. Sometimes for two weeks, sometimes for six. He and his wife divorced fifteen years ago. They had had three children, but two had died.

"One had pneumonia," he said. "The other, a little girl, she got really sick. We sent her to hospital in Montreal. She died. Nobody know what happened."

"They never told you?"

"No. Just a little tiny baby. She only took breast from mother. That's all. Never take no bottles or anything."

His nerves started to go three years ago. He couldn't sleep and he got the shakes all the time. He was taken off the trucks and sent back to Cambridge Bay to be close to the nursing station. He works in the big site there as a janitor. Most days he wishes he was back outside. He saves most of his money. Last year he bought his daughter a skidoo and before that a three-wheeler and before that a pickup truck. "Money got no home," he said.

Alan had a hearing aid. He spoke loudly and from the diaphram. What did he do with himself now? He spent his time in his room. What did he do there? He watched television. They got thirty-two channels. Did he ever go into the village? Not often. He had no vehicle, didn't trust himself with one. For that reason, too, he couldn't think of hunting. Sometimes, his daughter came out and got him. He still took his vacations in Winnipeg.

Dan Rather yapped in electronic silence as Alan talked. I listened and looked around the room. Eight feet by twelve feet. Regulation size. On the desk there was a form that had just arrived — a pension notice perhaps — and a package of Rothman's. On the telephone there was a big sticker, like on all the site telephones: "Don't discuss classified information! Phone is constantly monitored. Use constitutes approval."

The walls were a pallid yellow. On one hung a painting of a red and orange forest in autumn. At the foot of his bed a watery photo of a sailboat, sea and sky. At his head the usual long service plaque. On the television set there were two plastic models. One was a polar bear with cubs, Inuit-style. "My daughter bought that for me in Edmonton. She bought it at the airport." The other model was a fighter jet. Did he ever wish, I asked, he could be again in his camp on the Arctic coast? "When I get laid up or when I get fired," he said, "I might go back home."

# Chapter Two

# Laws

The meeting was convened at ten a.m., August 10, 1953 in Langevin Block, in Ottawa, Col. F.J.G. Cunningham, director of Resources and Development for the Northern Administration and Lands Branch, presiding. He opened with an overview of the duties and responsibilities of the department towards the Eskimos and of the department's policy regarding their health and welfare. He said the administration had determined that the eastern coast of Hudson's Bay could not continue to supply the Eskimos with a reasonable standard of living. Therefore, the administration had planned an experiment. A small number of Eskimo families would be transplanted from Quebec to certain settlements in the High North.

Mr. F. Fraser, Chief of the Northern Admnistration Division, then asked Mr. J. Cantley, of Resources and Development, to explain the experiment. Mr. Cantley said that eleven Eskimo families were involved, all volunteers. They would be shipped to three locations, the particulars to be decided during the trip. It was not desirable to break up family groups if possible. Mr. Cantley said the main purpose of the experiment was to see if people could adapt themselves to living in the High North. No one was certain what type or quantity of game was to be found there.

Sgt. Lt. P.E. O'Neil, of the RCAF, hoped the Eskimos would not become dependent on the base at Resolute Bay for food and clothing if the experiment failed. Mr. L.T. Campbell, of the Meteorological Division, felt the same. Mr. Cantley assured both that these Eskimos were not looking for jobs, although no one would stand in their way if such were available. The meeting was assured that the planning of the experiment was such that the Eskimos would not be an inconvenience to the RCAF.

In any case, Mr. B.G. Sivertz, of Resources and Development, pointed out that the Canadian government was anxious to have Canadians occupying as much of the North as possible for reasons of sovereignty. It appeared, he said, that in many cases the Eskimos were the only people capable of doing this. The meeting concluded with all satisfied on the terms for the experiment. Or so the minutes said.

The *C.D. Howe* reached Resolute Bay, at the southern tip of Cornwallis Island, a few weeks later. A storm was blasting the coast but the people were anxious to make shore anyway. The journey had been difficult. The air had gotten colder as the ship sailed north, ice had banged against its sides and the people felt suffocated and nauseous. The dogs howled on deck and the children wailed for fear of the doctors who, discovering lice, insisted on shaving their heads. A baby had been born.

There were seventeen Inuit and a Mountie disembarking at Resolute. Three families were from Inoucdjouac in northern Quebec and the fourth was from Pond Inlet, enlisted to teach the others to survive the High Arctic. Unlike Arctic Quebec, the sun would not rise here for three months of the winter. The Inoucdjouac people had left behind a home which they would, ever after, feel sufficiently described when they said, "There were plants there."

They clamboured ashore onto a broad apron of stone beach running around a bay backed by sloping hills. The children scattered to cower behind boulders while the adults fought to erect wildly flapping tents, banking handfuls of gravel to pin the canvass to the concrete ground. Over their shoulders, the ship was slipping away. They had come more than 1,000 miles due north and were now closer to the North Pole than to home. This was the place government officials had said would be a land of plenty. Scanning the horizon, they saw nothing but rock. They wondered if they had not been misinformed.

Miss Hinds, the welfare teacher in Quebec, later recalled warning them it might not be easy. Reuben Ploughman, manager of the HBC store, was not surprised they believed the government's claims. He said they had an inordinate trust of the government, these particular Inuit did. They had had a long association with whites. Indeed, some people felt they had lost their ambition as a result. The welfare bill in the area was high. One of the hopes for the experiment was to make them more self-sufficient.

These were the first Inuit to live on Cornwallis Island since the Thule had been driven out by the Little Ice Age 400 years earlier. Quickly, they built up a camp, but their sense of abandonment grew. The sun had disappeared soon after they arrived. Now, morose in their lamp-lit tents or groping over the land like blind men, they longed for the light. And the food was wrong. All their lives they had been used to a steady diet of char, which tastes like salmon, and plants and musky caribou and delectable ptarmigan. Now they had to swallow walrus and seal and bear for supper every day. And making clothes was a problem — the materials different and calling for new and unfamiliar methods. And there wasn't a store for hundreds of miles.

When it proposed the experiment, the government had promised they could go home in two years if they didn't like their new home. Amid their early difficulties they clung to this promise and, two years on, when the annual government inspection arrived, they called it in. They said: Thanks, but no thanks.

We'd like to go home now. And the government said: We prefer that you stay. But, okay. You can go. You'll have to pay your own way, though. That was the end of that.

Decades later it would emerge that their request to return to Quebec, which they repeated annually for years, was more than mere homesickness. The tiny village was so remote, the people so interrelated and the enmity between the Pond and Inoucdjouac natives so strong that children had few choices for mates. The Quebec people feared for their biological continuation.

"I feel personally," wrote a young bureaucrat sent to assess the situation, "that the experiment will be an unqualified success. The people are well fed and happy and seem to be satisfied with their new environment."

A mile and thirty five years from the spot where they first landed, the people I met in Resolute were anything but. They spoke of the cold and dark of the High Arctic as if they had just stepped off the boat. They were chronically slumped with apathy and rose only to curse the government of Canada in hot blasts of bitter vehemence that hung above their kitchen tables like a fog long after the literal translations provided by their children had dissipated.

"They were just dumped off on the shore."

"At that time we just looked up to white people as the people who were leading the way."

"He is sure of it: that the government tricked them into coming here."

"The government people said they think it's a good idea to stay here. We had no choice but to go by their idea."

"The government got them stuck here but good."

"The government knew there were natural resources here. So I guess that's why the Inuit were brought up here. So this could be a part of Canada."

"She tried to accept being happy. Because she had no choice."

"Desolute Resolute, that's what ah call it," said a man named Ray. "Imagine Alcatraz in the Arctic." People from other places were full of such pleasantries about Resolute Bay. When I said I was going there they would fix me with a look of mock pity and ask, "What did you do to deserve *that*?" "Resolute," the more thoughtful said, "has had its problems." Over the years, the village had gained a deathly awful reputation. But I rightly guessed that Resolute's problems would be no different from those of any other Arctic village. Only maybe a little worse.

There were two Resolute Bays. The tourist brochures trumpeting the "Gateway to the High Arctic" were talking about a former military base that was now an industrial airport complex. "The total area of the base is 128 million square metres," said John Goodman, who managed it all. "That's more than PEI. It was larger before, it has been cut back to half the original site." Anyone passing through the High Arctic islands — scientists and weathermen fanning out, oil workers moving on, polar explorers setting forth or military jumping off — did so through the base. Dignitaries visited often. Queen Elizabeth had once been here.

The village, home now for about 160 people, sat five miles down a winding road, out of sight. "We're two separate worlds," John Goodman said. Before the base was slimmed down to the size of PEI it had included the village, for administrative purposes, and many of the bad jokes about Resolute sprang from the ground where these worlds collided. What Goodman meant was that the base was self-contained — it included the post office, the Hudson's Bay Company, the Mounties and a dozen sundry services. It could ignore the village. The opposite was not true. The villagers had always been powerfully effected by the base and, of late, were even more so. They had become preoccupied with the notion that their very presence in Desolute Resolute was its fault.

The people of Resolute Bay were convinced they had been planted in the High Arctic as Canadian flagpoles. This they had never suspected until the theory was developed a few years ago by some young Inuit living in the south. It was a reasonable assumption. The military base had been American and sat smack on Lancaster Sound, the main route of the Northwest Passage. Little evidence had ever emerged to single out Resolute as a specific Canadian sovereignty beachhead but this barely diminished the point. The whole of Canada's involvement with the Inuit amounted to one big sovereignty exercise. In this, the survivors of the Resolute Bay experiment were by no means alone.

In 1880, Britain, having gained the prestige of finding the Northwest Passage and the realization that it was useless, gave Canada the High Arctic. An advisor in the Colonial Office wrote, "The object of annexing these unexplored territories to Canada is, I apprehend, to prevent the United States from claiming them and not from the likelihood of their proving any value to Canada." The Arctic was a kind of hand-me-down land and it would always be the case that, like so much else, the only time Canada ever found it really interesting was when the United States did.

Historian W. Gillies Ross has described the prototype of Canadian attempts to assert national sovereignty in the Arctic, the *Neptune* expedition of 1903. The ship, carrying a contingent of Northwest Mounted Police, was sent to Hudson's Bay to license the free-booting American whaling ships that considered the area open water. It was also to inform the Inuit that they were now under the authority of Canadian law.

To this end, the police chief, Major J.D. Moodie, devised a solemn occasion, swollen with pretense. He had the Inuit gathered together, gave them tea and tobacco, and explained that there was a big chief, King Edward VII, who ruled over them. The big chief had their best interests in mind and wanted them to do all that was right and good. Moodie urged them to travel to Churchill, 500 miles away, so that they might send happy messages to said big chief. Then, a witness wrote, "the Major ... with real ceremony presented a suit of woolen underclothes to each."

These people had been working for whalers for forty years and trading with explorers for 150. They had American repeating rifles and sewing machines. The men wore American overalls and sunglasses and the women had ball gowns. They were flabbergasted. Looking on, the American whalers were sickened. "Thus," wrote Ross, "in an atmosphere of incredulity, ridicule and disgust, was the new era of administration of the Arctic ushered in." The regulations and tariffs imposed on the whalers during the expedition finished off an already shaky industry and the whalers stopped coming to the bay. Having laden the Inuit with Canada, the *Neptune* sailed satisfied away, leaving their economy in ruins.

During World War II Americans working on Arctic military projects outnumbered locals three to one in some places and Canada again began to fret about its sovereignty. Complaints had been lodged with the Canadian High Commissioner in London by the Hudson's Bay Company. It was feeling, for unspecified reasons, a little crowded. As I read accounts of these times, it always seemed to me that Canada's problem with the Americans in the Arctic wasn't half so much their presence or — after the war — their constant demands to increase it, as their attitude. They were always so *American* about everything.

When they wanted weather stations to help guide their bombers — the first being at Resolute Bay — they just ordered up a couple of ships and readied them to sail north without so much as a by-your-leave to Canada. Once, Canadian diplomats were leaked a memo detailing plans for a USAF scouring mission over the Arctic islands to discover new ones they might claim. When their ships travelled in the Arctic, the personnel carried on like buffoons. "This observer," wrote a Canadian aboard a U.S. resupply ship in 1948, "had considerable difficulty in controlling his temper on several occasions." The Americans, he wrote, busted open historic cairns as if they were fortune cookies, shot seals in self defence and treated the Inuit like puppies. And generally acted as if they owned the place.

Mackenzie King had said it to High Commissioner Vincent Massey in 1943: "King said that Canadians were looked upon by Americans as a lot of Eskimos."

In the early Fifties, reports proliferated of disease and hunger among the Inuit. Not the least influential of these was Farley Mowat's first book, *People of the Deer*, published in 1952. Tuberculosis, for example, was rampant. By the mid-Fifties, almost ten per cent of the population had been evacuated to southern hospitals. One hundred per cent of the children tested tuberculin positive.

The resultant pressure from the public and its growing excitement over the Arctic's potential mineral wealth met the weight of U.S. demands and assumptions. The Canadian government was easily convinced it had to take greater possession of the North. The airstrips the Americans were building gave it the means.

Canada's dreams for the Arctic were all of a piece, as the government indicated in 1954 by naming its lead bureaucracy Northern Affairs and National Resources. Political scientist Frances Abele has argued that the government activities in the years that followed were a classically Canadian mixture of Tory paternalism and Liberal individualism. The government's whole effort in the Arctic, she wrote, can be seen as "a compressed reiteration of older patterns of Canadian development." It was bent on maintaining title to the supposed Arctic riches and determined, sporadically, to use its wealth to extract these; as it had to build the CPR. The Liberal mode was to see the Inuit as being just like any other Canadians only, *through no fault of their own*, not very good at it.

Contrary as they may be, both notions allowed most Canadians to believe Inuit would be only too happy to embrace southern society. Most believe it still. We cannot easily separate our personal (or national) ambitions from our cultural assumptions. Marshall Sahlins wrote, "Having equipped the hunter with bourgeois impulses and paleolithic tools, we judge his situation hopeless in advance."

Canadian sovereignty in the Arctic is generally considered a matter of legal proclamations and, recently, of guns. But by far, Canada's most prominent effort to be Lord of the Arctic has focused on getting inside, as it were, the collective skin of the Inuit. One measure of success in this is that their ancient title is now used to bolster Canada's 118-year-old national claim.

During the Fifties and Sixties, the government used inducement and coercion to corral Inuit from hundreds of camps into settlements built on the infrastructure established by the military. George Porter remembered: "Government said, in those days, 'We're here to help you people and to make an easier life for you fellows. So we will build you houses and stuff.' And people figure then maybe that's an easier way of living; to have a house, a nice warm place to stay. And send their kids to school. That's how they were asked by the government. And that's the way it started."

The easy life had its price. Some people, for example, were moved from bountiful hunting grounds to truly barren lands for administrative convenience. Thus consolidated, all that was right and good began to descend. Schools originally established by the missionaries were expanded, nursing stations were built, welfare and other benefits provided. Inuit found themselves in unheard-of concentrations and controlled by forces they could not, for the life of them, understand.

Sending Inuit to Resolute Bay was an early and extreme example of this kind of sovereignty assertion but it was unremarkable. Noah Adglak said, "Let the government understand what the Inuit wants. And not just be an experimental species to the government."

When the government made it clear that they were going nowhere fast, the people of Resolute Bay, as Inuit are wont, resigned themselves. And settled in for a long and turbulent stay.

Jack Hicks asked, "Do you notice anything about the houses?" Jack Hicks was the adult educator in Resolute, a man, by conventional standards, of extreme viewpoints ("Let's put it this way," a middle-aged acquaintance had said, "he is *more* radical than the NDP!") I took Jack Hicks' question to be pointed and thought of it as I wandered the village.

Arctic villages are of a standard mold. You could swap one for another in the dead of the night and no one would know the difference. On paper, they are cute miniatures of southern suburbs: four or six or eight strips of houses neatly set upon a little grid with the main service buildings handy among them. Reality is not so neat. The vagaries of terrain and prevailing winds often mocked the maps, building up, in all the wrong places, high, hard snowbanks that people trampled down as they could.

When I was a child there were neighbourhoods known as "the wartime housing." These were modest wood bungalows, stamped out in the late Forties, not to be confused with the stout little brick nests built in the decade that followed. They still stand in the poorer sections of some cities, usually around the ugliest factories. Arctic villagers live in wartime houses. These came, complete, as a kit, the size and shape of each dependent on the era when it was assembled.

The oldest ones — Eskimo Houses, they called them, or Max Pack Houses — are stubby wooden trailers. A few still have honey buckets and all are composed of tiny rooms lined with bulbous tin ductwork and restless chintz linoleum. Ivan Uvilluk, the electrician, went into many people's homes. He found this most depressing, especially when they were wrapped around old people. His complaint was that they did not keep the wind out. He said, "It seems they are for somebody who doesn't care about life." The newer versions of these are larger and neater of design. Expanding villages also have touches of the modern — homes that look like huge comfortable packing crates, with cedar panelling and high, steep roofs which lend them a certain Swissness. And there are bizarre bursts — Cambridge Bay had three geodesic domiciles, all boarded up — but the rule is uniform blocks of blocks: ten medium rectangles, five crates, ten small rectangles and so on.

The bill of lading for Resolute Bay:

Twenty-three houses on two roads.

One small visitors inn (private).

One boarded-up apartment building (failed government project).

One school (new).

One nursing station (new).

One village hall (old).

One co-op (desperate).

There were two kinds of houses in Resolute: old trailers and newer trailers. What Jack Hicks wanted me to notice, however, was something more obvious still. There were two kinds of houses in Resolute: brown ones and yellow ones. "That's just the way the outside siding came," said the woman who managed the housing. "It all just came in that colour. I don't know why."


During the first decade of the Resolute settlement, the military base produced a slag heap of wood and tin that swelled quickly and proved endlessly self-replenishing. "They throw," Herodier Kalluk said, "furniture and everything away." The settlers plundered this cornucopia of discards and crafted themselves houses. These grew as if organically, their relationship with families symbiotic. Rooms swelled when babies were born or a grandparent moved in; offshoots sprouted from a conjugal union or a fortuitous hunting season. They were painted in whatever colors spilled their way, most commonly in gaudy and safe International Orange. The base eventually became so stuffed that an avalanche of consumer products rolled down to the camp. Soon every home had a phone, washing machine, radio, record player and tape recorder. As was usual, the houses were arranged in a long line at the end of one arm of the deep bay, facing the sea, so people could see the whales coming.

Paul Amarualik said, "Gradually they built their shacks up into houses and gradually they built up comfortable homes." It was Paul Amarualik who had been born on the journey from Quebec. He and the village were both thirty-four. He was translating for his father, Simeonie, a man with dark eyes, a bushy mustache and an angry countenance. "Once they got well established and considered them home then the government started bringing in housing."

The first five houses arrived in Centennial year, like unsolicited mail. The families who got them were disappointed, finding them too small and too square. By then all manner of aid was arriving in the community. An administrator had been installed to distribute welfare, family allowance and old age pensions as well as to enforce hunting regulations and vehicle licencing. "The Eskimos of Resolute," a visiting inspector wrote, "are inclined to be independent and self-reliant but accept many forms of departmental assistance and advice." The department, Indian Affairs and Northern Development, advised that theirs was the only Inuit community without proper housing. So new homes kept arriving and the old ones became tool shacks.

The 1968 oil gusher at Prudhoe Bay in Alaska was the first real confirmation of the mineral wealth of the Arctic. A year later emboldened American oil companies sent the supertanker *S.S. Manhattan* grinding its hoggish way through the Northwest Passage on a trial voyage. A new sovereignty panic was created in Ottawa, this time tinged with fears of potential environmental disaster. And the gusher renewed the old lust for Northern riches. One of the results was an increase in all sorts of Arctic exploration. Resolute Bay's airport became one of the busiest in the country. The area's landing patterns were such that squadrons of huge aircraft were soon flying, low, right over the settler's heads. "We were afraid," Simeonie said, "one day a plane was going to drop right down into the village."

Consultants were hired and a village was planned that was to be a model for Arctic Canada. Whites and Inuit would live together, all wealthy from the oil boom. The plan called for a neat clutch of houses wrapped with crescents of apartment and service buildings — to keep the wind out — and tucked into the lee of a hill at the back of the bay. It was a concept.

New houses were shipped in and the villagers were moved. The now-old government houses were disassembled and dragged to the new spot. The houses the Inuit had built were destroyed. Levi Nungaq said, "These first houses were burned." We were sitting in Levi Nungaq's kitchen. On the wall were tacked, like butterflies, the feathers of two beautifully colored ptarmigans. He was wearing a Fruit of the Loom T-shirt and rolling dice incessantly. Now he stopped and said, "They just burned them. And the whole landscape was flattened".

Soon afterward, the oil boom busted and the model village faded away. Only one of the crescent-shaped apartment buildings was ever shipped and nobody wanted to live in it. Not the Inuit, certainly, and not the whites, who didn't want to leave the base at all. It was boarded up. Easy come, easy go.

Of course, the people had been consulted. Meetings were held, opinions solicited. They were even given the choice of two approved sites. What more could they ask? Yet, now they said, "We weren't too happy about it but we had to follow government regulations." Consultation to the Inuit means something quite different than it does to the government. One anthropologist wrote about the disappointment in a village when the promised consultation in the hiring of a teacher turned out to be the chance to scan applications, rather than, as people supposed, to invite prospective candidates to live among them for a time. The amount of say the Inuit had in government decisions about their lives had been steadily increasing, yet, even by their own definition, governments would never expect southerners to swallow what was often passed off as consultation in the North.

In one village, a cheery, young council official-in-training said, "We got a new school and a renewable resources office and a warehouse from the government last year. They just came in on the barge." *It was an election year,* I thought. "They are always informing the community that this kind of project will be coming. And they usually consult the people most of the time."

John Murray, an architect from Red Deer, Alberta who had often worked for the territorial government, told me about attending such a meeting. He said, "This government guy was talking 'auxiliary spaces' at them and using all this bureaucratese. *I* didn't know what he was talking about. The translator was having a heck of a time. They were just nodding their heads." The building under discussion was a community hall. "Of course, they were thrilled to get a new building. Later I asked the guy: 'What if this doesn't suit their needs?'" The polite form of the answer he got was that consultation is expensive. There were, for example, three types of standard-issue community hall available, depending on population: small, medium and large.

There is a housing shortage in Resolute Bay now, as in every other Inuit community. As planned, the village sits far at the back of the bay, beneath Signal Hill, so named for the communications tower at its summit. The main features on the beach now are a fuel-tank ranch and a large snowmobile graveyard strewn with cannibalized skeletons. Wind whips down the hillside and it blasts the village with cold air. It is no longer possible to see the whales coming.

A few winters ago, the village electricity failed. Houses began freezing. With a few exceptions, everyone jumped ship to the hotel at the base. The houses could glaciate and crumble for all they cared. "There is not," Jack Hicks said, "much pride of ownership." If repairs needed doing, people waited for the government to get to them. They said: Why should we do it? We built good houses. The government burned them down.


The officer in charge of the 1956 Eastern Arctic Patrol, J.C. Jackson, approved of what the natives, to that point, had managed. "Bearing in mind that we cannot expect an Alta Vista or a Manor

Park, the settlement at Resolute is well housed." This was in no small part thanks to the efforts of the presiding Mountie, who seemed "experienced in all the problems of raising primitive communities to a higher standard of living." He had brought the village to an "excellent intermediate stage of development." A consultant sent to Resolute a decade later also judged its native housing adequate "pending the development of the community and the possible expansion of tourism."

All government plans for the Arctic were based on assumptions of this sort. They saw standard of living to be a kind of concrete graduated scale to the top of which everyone *naturally* wanted to ascend. Like a staircase up a mountain side. Official reports rarely betray any inkling that Inuit would not want to live in a somnambulistic Ottawa enclave like Alta Vista or that the homes they built for themselves were congruent with their view of the world.

One sense of this view comes from the work of linguists, like Raymond Gagne, and anthropologists, such as and Edmund Carpenter, studying the Inuit language. Invariably, this work begins with the realization that what we call culture is a highly specific sieve for sifting our individual realities out of the infinite mass of possibilities the world contains. This is particularly apparent, of course, in language. Gagne, for example, notes that Inuktitut has no separate words for green and blue, so this distinction is overlooked by the Inuit. For them, there is no green and blue. But, as everybody knows, there are more than two dozen distinctly different kinds of snow.

Neither, traditionally, did Inuktitut parcel out time nor separate it from space. This is a fundamental of Inuit thought and language that is not easily grasped by us. We speak of time as a solid, as mass — a bit, a span, a segment. This is a way of thinking that has developed in Western culture since the the invention of the clock in the fourteenth century. The social historian Lewis Mumford believed the clock to be the key machine of our age because it taught us irreverence of the seasons and the sun. In doing so, it created an entirely new perception of the world and our place in it.

The English language is one in which nouns have primary importance and are indelibly fixed; verbs hang about like chauffeurs waiting to animate them. Inuktitut does something like the opposite, making little distinction between objects and actions. The names of objects sometimes change relative to their movement — their direction and speed — and to their relationship to other objects. Gagne has noted a dichotomy in Inuktitut word constructions dealing with objects of equal proportions — a box — and those of unequal — a rod. A caribou is called one thing when it is at rest or moving very slowly — and box-like — something else when running and giving a linear, rod-like impression.

Carpenter notes that Inuktitut evolved among people for whom all of the senses had equal importance; for whom more than seeing was believing. One's sense of space and objects is very different if it takes into account their sound and smell as well as their visible outline. These are perceptions no less tangible but potentially much more relative and dynamic, at once self-contained and mingling. This world, then, is not composed of things set apart from oneself and named — a world, that is, of nouns. Carpenter understood the Inuit use of language as a struggle to make comprehensible and thus life-sustaining forms out of the world. Most of the words for snow, for example, describe them not by type — hard snow, soft snow — but by what can be done with each, such as "snow that is good for *iglu*-building." "Words are like the knife of the carver: they free the idea, the thing, from the general formlessness of the outside."

This is the meaning of *sila*, the root word for both the outer environment and for states of mind. Sila, the goddess of the natural order and the goddess of thought. *Silakrertok*, fair weather. *Silatujuq*, intelligence. Nature has all the ideas, humans are its interpretors and mouthpieces as it talks to itself. To have a fixed thought, in a sense, is impossible. One's house, then, is neither finished nor unfinished. More accurately: it is alive.

The squeaky-clean suburbs that planners took to be the summit of Mount Standard of Living architecturally embodied the modern hope for a climate-controlled world. They assumed Inuit would also like such a world and most were indeed happy to get it. But, it seems to me, in sending the new housing the government was also delivering information. A message in a crate. This was spelled out in books and pamphlets distributed simultaneously. One such was called the *Q-Book*, which amounted to an owner's manual for the industrialized world. It was chock full of handy information on everything from housekeeping — "a good wife sweeps the floor every day" — to banking — even now hardly applicable, since there are almost no banks. Q stood for questions. But really, it was an A-Book. A is for answers. A is for assumptions.

The way these houses arbitrarily rained down was yet another lesson in the new power arrangements: the government gave, moved and destroyed at its choosing, in its time. God-like. People were no longer arrayed in a line, all turned toward the land, listening collectively to its declarations and laws. Now they stared out their windows into other windows. They saw roads, street lamps, neighbours. This could not help but reinforce the newly dominant civil law in which a person's behaviour was judged in relation to other citizens. And, ultimately, to the state.

Say what they might, the bureaucrats did, eventually, expect an Alta Vista or a Manor Park. What they sent the Inuit, as a consequence, were the grotesque skeletons of communities of a scale and style completely unlike anything the people themselves had ever made. What they got were southern neighbourhoods stripped of all embroidery, right down to the basics: houses and ground.

Gideon Qitsualik, who lived in Gjoa Haven and had travelled some, said, "We have two very, *completely* different environments. In Ottawa, there is a completely different environment. What they do there we cannot do up here. Same with Ottawa. They are the ones who make all the laws. They don't know enough about up here. That's why it is always so hard for us to live the way they want us to be."

Fr. LeChat, considering the whole panoply of government works in the past three decades, said simply, "In trying to help, they hurt."

The people of Resolute have had to deal with much more than this. Yet it was always the shell game of housing they spontaneously mentioned as a way of explaining their feelings toward government. It is no small irony that providing housing to the Inuit is something most Canadians would feel the greatest pride in; less still that Inuit feel they owe southern Canada a great deal of gratitude for the housing. The seeming paradox here, I think, cuts to the heart of many of our problems: Easier doesn't mean better. And nobody likes bombadiers.

Large crates were scattered around the Resolute Bay housing office, containing the materials for retrofitting creaky houses. Each had been branded for shipping by a big black dot, for quick unloading. The word from the housing office was that they would be sitting there until spring. The contractors who were to do the work had withdrawn and the territorial government was retendering. It would take some time to let the new contract and get the workers up here.

Southern construction workers were to the Arctic spring what robins were in the temperate zone. A dozen or so would arrive in May, be housed for roughly $150 a day and do the retrofitting. Well into autumn, Arctic hotels were still jammed with them while every other home held at least one man who longed for a little work. At the least, to finance his hunting. I never tired of asking officials why this was so and their answers never varied.

"We employ them as labourers," Stephen Bedingfield said. Bedingfield was a gentle bear of a man who ran the housing corporation in Cambridge Bay. "Sure. But we need journeymen carpenters. We have a couple being trained now." The head of a southern construction crew said, "If you need ten, you have to hire twenty." Just couldn't get 'em to work regular hours. Them Inuit. Sure, they could do anything. Just as good as us. Except: run the Bay, build houses, and show up for work on time. Anything else, no problem. Training was what they needed.

Among the most fundamental changes in Northern society has been the matter of who and what is considered competent. This goes beyond the simple, albeit crucial, question of who gets what jobs to basic ideas of knowledge and power.

Thirty years ago, and for thousands before, Inuit society was as close as could be to non-hierarchical. Herodier Kalluk, who was sixty-five, one day explained his memory of Inuit leadership. He said, "They just listened to the oldest and the wisest one, the one who knows the most. Maybe if they had a father. Or anyone who was wise. Whoever knows more." As with children, so with social organization. Orders, even unsolicited suggestions, were considered rude. They turned simultaneously to themselves and to each other to interpret the land's commands, checking intuitions with those who had been at this the longest. *Isumataq* was their word for a respected elder, from the root word for intelligence.

Anthropologists, as a rule, are loathe to compare hunting and gathering peoples for obvious reasons of academic rigour and human respect. Yet, certain notable patterns are unavoidable. Strongest of these — among peoples as diverse as the African !Kung, Australian Aborigines and the Inuit — is the belief in the collectivity. This is much more than what Inuit, tepidly in English, call sharing. Most aboriginal societies have few substantial divisions of labour within the sexes and only certain ones between them. Rarely, for example, are there journeyman carpenters.

The earliest southerners in the Arctic went more by the Inuit rules than vice versa. Proselytize or swindle as they might, they had limited power to mess with the basic social structure. Fr. Le-Chat, who was one of these southerners, said of the Inuit, "They were masters in their own land. White people tried other things. They always come back to the Inuit way." Technology removed this stricture from the modern bureaucracy. The power base began to shift.

An early example was the membership of the Eskimo Affairs Committee, created in 1952. The advisory committee's function was largely to dampen resistance from established Arctic interests to government activity in the north. Its membership included the Hudson's Bay Company, churches, Mounties and other bureaucracies. Nobody thought to invite the Inuit until 1959 when three — two from military communities and one from a mining village — were asked to join "on the grounds of intelligence, assertiveness and ability to express themselves clearly." Hunters and trappers need not apply. This quickly became the pattern. The men who were furthest from hunting were most in demand for the government job boom. "Because," said George Porter, who was one, "most of them were really good workers and had an idea of how a job had to be done."

Skills and patterns of community interaction started to become anachronistic. Of course people still use them, but no one really *needs* them. And they no longer run the community. It was as if you woke up one morning and found all of your knowledge — not just of accountancy or plumbing, but of manners, mores, value — had suddenly been devalued. To get by you had to take direction from Survivalists who were speaking in tongues.

Gideon Qitsualik was heavily involved in the church, cultural organizations and national politics and made his living as a hunter. He had been trained also as a carpenter. I never found out by whom but his house was ringed with the evidence in expertly built structures of diverse purpose. "The reason he never gets a job" — Thomas Anguttitauruq was translating — "is that he's told there's no job for uneducated people. He knows how to measure everything. He can count in English, he can count in Inuktitut. The only thing he doesn't know is how to read and write in English."

Gideon said, "Although the Inuit are told they are not educated enough, they know what is up here and they are educated in their own ways. Same with other people in other countries. They are educated in their own ways."

The problem Gideon complained of was obvious everywhere I travelled in the Arctic, as it is everywhere all the time. We confuse language and manners with intelligence and sophistication. We take those with whom we cannot easily communicate, materially and spiritually more than linguistically, as morons. Oh sure, the Inuit could take care of themselves *out there*. But *here*? Well, *morons*.

"It would be a lot better," Gideon said, "for the government to give northern people a chance to work for themselves, not just something they get for nothing, not just a handout. We are also willing to work. The government seems to be just giving us entertainment. Like, living in a luxury house, not living in a snow house anymore — fuel, electricity, all that. We would rather work for them first."

From the most profound and egalitarian participation imaginable, Inuit had become spectators in their own lives. Not qualified. As a result, of course, individuals become less able to participate. Anthropologist Stanley Diamond has argued, in general terms, that this process has been the course of civilization. Each aspect of life has been precisely defined and allotted. When we complain over the increasing complexity of life, I think, this is often what we are talking about. Life, of course, is unchanging. Only now, when no job can be done nor any decision made without platoons of experts, does this compartmentalization become obvious.

Now Inuit are expected to accept the dissection of their society into those who are qualified and those who are not; to believe only planners are allowed to plan, builders to build, experts to have expertise. Approaching old age, it is unlikely Gideon will ever be convinced that he needs a college diploma or the English language to know how to build a house. But, as a people, they have been given no choice.

It is not easy for me to imagine what it is to be a pioneer, but travel gives some clue. Travelling with women, I think, especially. In my experience, an entirely new environment often throws women into a state, they are dizzied by the bombardment of their senses. This I think is less true of men. Men only need to learn a few crucial rules, as if to spot the enormous boulders in a field, and then plough past them. Rules are empowering. In a few days you think you know the place. In a month you think you own it. From the identification of a few peculiarities — "alcohol is forbidden," "they take Tuesdays off" — and the confirmation of major commonalities — "they use money," "they sleep" — one can extrapolate a whole network of regulations. You can tell yourself that people are the same everywhere. Except: here, they get a few things wrong.

Bezal Jesudason understood this. With Terry, his wife, he ran the village inn at Resolute Bay. They outfitted most of the polar expeditions, every spring dispatching a flock of well-heeled adventurers who came from all over the world to have the Arctic make them famous. The affable Bezal had come to Canada from India. He had learned about cultural assumptions. The problem with pioneers, he said, was that they neither watched nor listened. To explain, he would make the bowed greeting of the East, with his hands fixed as if for prayer and ask, "What do you say for this?"

I think, in this vein, of the faintly amazing programme that renamed everyone. Early administrators, confused by the Inuit common use of a single name, issued them what were called disc numbers, dog tags, basically, to keep the records straight. Criticized for what some felt was the impersonality of this, they devised a more tender solution to the problem called Project Surname.

"The territorial government came along and said: 'We don't know anybody who's around here, because nobody has any last names.'" Paul Amuraulik, son of Simeonie Amagualik, was explaining a programme not known for its success. Into his teens, he had been called Paul Simeonie. This too was a flag of convenience, bestowed by teachers who found the disc numbers distasteful and unilaterally christened kids with a paternal surname. "Everything got confused," Paul said. "They started issuing last names by asking our parents how far they can remember their ancestors."

In Western society, names tend to be a mixture of prevailing trend signature — a Buck this year is a Joshua next — and patrilineal genetic labelling. To the Inuit, names *were* genetics. The Inuktitut word for name, *atiq*, is usually explained as meaning something more like a soul. The name itself, as it were, embodies a soul. It is the spiritual distillation of ancestors travelling through new bodies, a capsule of unquenchable light ever present in time.

A newborn is given the *atiq* of an ancestor, which imbues it with that person's being. The baby is considered to actually *be* both the child and the elder. So a woman named for her grandmother calls her mother daughter; the mother calls her daughter mother. In times past, the occasional practice of allowing a child to die when food was scarce could only be practiced against children without an *atiq*. The sense of it is something like what we recall in folk sayings like, "my child is my mother returning." And understand through physics.

When Inuit wrote:

"What we see from down here in the form of stars, are the lighted windows of the villages of the dead ..."

they knew whereof they spoke.

Names, then, were something very real. They were also used to connect children to characteristics of the land and even of other, living people. A child might be given five, six, seven names; taken from an ancestor, from a dear friend, from a place. Each was a loop in the sinewy thread that bound a child into the continuous weave of life.

Now along came the pioneers, using names like nails to tack them neatly into ledger columns. One of the off-handed side effects of this was to establish nominal reckoning by the law of the father. Another, among people who had neither masculine nor feminine names, was the creation of Mrs. Joe Inuk and friends, just when this absurdity was being jettisoned in the south.

Paul said, "When I heard Amarualik, I thought: 'Am I going to be an *Amarualik* for the rest of my life?' That was kind of hard to adopt. But gradually I got used to it. Turns out we are a big family."

As so often happens, things were lost in the translation. "The way they spell it is by the way it sounds. The way we do is by the way it sounds too, but our ears have different markings." Many families, as a result, ended up with a hodge-podge of surnames. "People have minds of their own so there was a lot of different spellings." Defiantly, Paul signs government documents with the name he hears, rather then the one they bear.

Aside from referring to the Inuk hired to oversee the project as "that fucking guy," people could hardly be bothered. For decades their collective and personal control had been draining away like blood from a wound that no one seemed able or willing to staunch. What was in a name? Nothing more than a little tattoo on the forearm. To keep the ledger columns straight.

In 1975, Hugh Brody wrote a book called *The People's Land* that lambasted the whites in the eastern Arctic as colonialists intent on ramming their value system down the throats of Inuit. "Whites in the north have always been intent on causing change," Brody wrote, "in realizing these changes they have dominated the Eskimos, and they continue to do so."

Brody had lived in the Arctic for some time; he was already an anthropologist with a considerable reputation and government financial backing. Nobody could doubt his legitimacy or integrity. Grudges were held nonetheless. "A lot of people," a school teacher said, "*really* hate that book." Later, a southern academic allowed that it was useful to give students a historical perspective, but added, "You know, it's not like that anymore."

But it was. It was just like that. It was as rare to meet a southerner who did not condescend to the Inuit as it was to meet one who did not attack others for their condescension. People are funny that way. Rarest of all was to meet an Inuk who felt in control of his or her life. Over the past decade the Inuit had, relatively, gained loads of political power. Everything *had* changed. And nothing had.

"In the early Sixties when teachers started coming up, that's when they started getting their own free will," Simeonie, of Resolute Bay, said. What was his idea of free will? The Mountie, then, stopped telling them what they could spend their money on and forbidding them to talk to the men at the base.

It would be some time yet before a more expansive notion of civil rights sank in. In the Arctic, the Sixties were much like the Fifties and even young people had only the vaguest notion of political revolt. In the late Sixties, Thomas Anguttitauruq went to Alberta. He had heard of hippies. People said they were strange. He asked the first guy he met with long hair, "Are you a hippie?" No. He was a peace worker. Would Thomas like to do some peace work? Thomas was rather unclear what peace work was, but he followed the guy back to his house anyway. "It was a barn." He stayed a month. "We were just hanging around all the time. *Doing peace work.* I didn't like it." Inuit weren't used to such politically justified lollygagging or the kind of organized complaining that is the stuff of political action.

Since the Fifties, Inuit could vote federally and be elected to local councils but neither meant very much. Until 1970, the Northwest Territories were governed entirely by Indian Affairs and Northern Development, which had grown rapidly through the previous two decades into one bloated outfit. Communities had an infinitesimal say in their own affairs, which was justified by the fact that they had no tax base. Only recently has it become common for villages to have elected boards of health and education.

Inuit were dramatically pushed into politics in 1969 when the federal government threatened to extinguish all "special rights" for natives. Over the next decade, young Inuit, like other natives, became increasingly activist, their work funded by federal government programmes that were sponsoring grassroots movements of all sorts in the name of participatory democracy. They formed organizations — the loudest was the Committee for Original People's Entitlement in the western Arctic, the largest was the Inuit Tapirisat of Canada in the east — and began petitioning for a few rights. The Berger Inquiry — "It is, however, the native people in the North that we ought to be most concerned about" — added the solemn baritones of a judge to their bright chorus.

The effects of this were several. Native representation has steadily increased in the territorial government. When the election that had doled out goodies in every village I visited ended, fifteen of the twenty-four territorial members were either Inuit, Dene or Metis. Federal bureaucrats, everyone agreed, were now much more sensitive to the wishes of the natives than they had been even a decade ago. And the demand for political participation within the villages had grown enormously.

"People grew up," Chuck Tolley said, "without knowing they could have a say." He was a senior education administrator for the Baffin regional board. He had lived in the Arctic for twenty years. Of the past, he said, "there are horror stories that would curl your hair." These days, he tried to be optimistic. He noted, for example, that the Baffin board is completely composed of people from the region's villages. "A lot of power has come back into the hands of the people who traditionally had it, away from the government representatives."

In the far western Arctic — the Mackenzie Valley area — and the southeast — northern Quebec — Inuit gained a good deal more power through land claim settlements, which allotted control over small parcels of land and cash. The federal government had been hotfooted into signing these by the desire to tap and ship oil from the Beaufort Sea and hydro power from James Bay. The majority of Inuit, in the eastern and central Arctic were still trying to get a settlement. Everywhere, the southern bureaucratic structures still ran things.

The Inuit most involved with community decisions were no longer necessarily people who knew the land. "They are those," Chuck Tolley said, "with the skills to communicate and who have a vision of what's happening." But most bureaucrats were the first to admit that they (the bureaucrats) still held the most sway in Arctic communities. The governments relied on them in formulating policy and the people relied on them in explaining the limits policy put on their decisions. "There is still power among the non-elected." Nothing was going to change, all agreed, until the Inuit were sufficiently qualified to be bureaucrats too. Southern laws are the permafrost. A bit of heat makes the surface mushy but just *try* to drive a shovel in. The foundations were pliable as granite. What southerners usually meant when they talked about Inuit taking over, was Inuit taking over the southern hierarchical system. Many Inuit had already gained rank in this system. But most also remained intimidated by the white bureaucrats, who were inevitably better at it.

"In those days," a man was telling me, "we were treated almost like the blacks in South Africa. We had to do whatever we were told. We were treated like dumb Eskimos." Those were the days, the Fifties and Sixties, when they had to ride in the box of the truck. No more, he was telling me, everything's different now. If the government wants to do something in the community, it has to ask the community first.

I reached for the tape recorder, to capture some reminiscence about the bad old days. Oh. He wouldn't want me to do that. This man worked for one of the communities. He was in maintenance. He had been working for southerners a long time. He had the skills to communicate and a vision of what's happening. What had happened to the two guys that held the job before him was they were fired for mouthing off about the shortcomings of the government to the local council. He tried to advise the council members a bit on the sly. But it would not be long until he retired and he had his pension to think about. He wouldn't want that to happen to him.

The administrators of the Fifties had found a comprehensible law, laid down by the earlier pioneers, already in place. Their task was to colour it in. But the spaces were so large they could not help but be confronted by certain questions, of which the Inuit recall them asking many. Even when they weren't working. This is much less so for younger bureaucrats and professionals, who now work in an established system and are so well connected to the south there is hardly a need for them to learn the language let alone the customs. Often I would think: *Imagine this — now — in Quebec.*

"Nowadays if you see a white person," old Simon Keanik said, "they walk right by you and you don't even feel you existed." The administrators and professionals I met — with a few notable exceptions — hardly walked at all. They swung, more like, convinced that their benevolent hearts automatically shot forth sticky strands of unimpeachable logic that carried them along like warmly dressed Spidermen.

One bright afternoon I bustled along a village road with a bureaucrat who had offered an introduction to a woman whose husband had long worked for the military. "He's dead now but I'm *sure* she'll speak to you .... Why, I'll take you over there right now ...." Within the comfy confines of his office, boots on the desk, he seemed a part of what I considered the sensitive elite of northern professionals, those attempting, at least, to work their way out of a job. He turned out to have the sensitivity of an anvil. Often I was fooled like this.

The old woman was alone with her granddaughter. The bureaucrat — who, as usual, did not speak the language — explained our purpose to the girl. Would she relay this to her grandmother? Shyly, the girl said, "I can't speak *Eskiiimo*." Sure you can, the bureaucrat said, with a friendly wink. *Give it a try.* She did as she was told and we went away thinking, if that is the word, that an appointment was set for later that evening. "You sure it's okay?" I asked. "Okay," the girl answered. Fine.

Returning that evening I saw the sad-faced, sack-like woman on her knees before the sink in a pool of hard light, scraping a skin with the half-moon knife called an *ulu*. Okay, I thought, let's get talking. With more accomplished interpretation, my request was relayed again. The old lady was mortified. No way, came the answer. Her husband, it turned out, was not long dead. He had, in fact, just died. "She wouldn't want to do that," her daughter-in-law said in a voice filled with dread "She *can't*."

Leaving, I thought to myself: you are an idiot; which, of course, I had been. What was surprising, however, was that a person whose job it was to make vital arrangements within the community had accepted the word wrenched out of a child as real consent. Variations on this, I thought, have happened thousands of times.

Without a sense of irony, you were lost in the Arctic; understanding the attitudes of the people became impossible. I could see this in a young nurse I met. He was clean and devout, someone who would not think of skipping a tooth-flossing or a Sunday service. He had always dreamed of working among the Inuit. Now, after only a couple of months, they had left him perplexed and not a little disdainful.

He was disgusted by Inuit homes, which were sometimes without refrigerators and where one might trip over a half-butchered seal in the middle of the living room floor, being plucked at like a bowl of peanuts. "You know," he said, in an *I-hate-to-say-this-but* half-whisper, "they're *dirrrty*." They were ignorant also. "It's right back to basics here," he said, meaning a preponderance of health problems that are considered anachronisms in the south. And, perhaps worst, he felt his concerns unappreciated. "You would think they would be grateful to us for taking care of their children, that we would even be a little bit special. But that's not it."

"To me," he said, "the Eskimo is dead." He meant the Inuit were not living up to their culture — as he had imagined it —

and were making a botch-up of ours. These people couldn't get anything right, no matter what you did for them. There was irony in the source of his frustration.

The government had ostensibly come to the Arctic because people were sick and having trouble feeding themselves. These were problems, in the first place, visited from the outside upon people who had provided for themselves for generations in a land Europeans unequivocally declared barren. But one of the results of the new bureaucratic and economic architecture had been to make even the task of feeding oneself properly very difficult.

Gideon said, "I will be going out tomorrow to pick up some caribou." Thomas laughed. "Its like he's going to the grocery store." Gideon went the next day. He travelled 300 jolting and vibrating miles across the corrugated tundra. He was slowed by a blizzard and a bad drive belt, stopped by a break in the sea ice. Intending to be gone for twelve hours, he returned after thirty-six with four caribou and the faintest smile on his face.

But for the neighbourhood comings and goings of the sports in orange vests, hunting is so far from the urban experience that we can not imagine, I think, how commonplace it remains for some peoples. To Gideon, harvesting a few caribou *was* as physically routine as going to the grocery store, though the metaphor degrades the cultural and spiritual profundity of the experience. What made hunting difficult, from the Inuit viewpoint, was the government's regulations.

Inuit can harvest as many caribou and seal as they please, but there are quotas and seasonal restrictions on many other species, including polar bears, muskoxen, whales and some birds. These were the result of the fears of government biologists that, without restrictions, the species would be hunted into oblivion, particularly since many were hunted by different groups and, increasingly, commercially, during their migrations. Until the last few years, the quotas were determined by biologists flying over the land, counting animals, and Inuit had had no say. "Frequently," said one report, "the hunter's only view of a biologist was a plane passing overhead."

Local hunting and trapping associations were now advising on the quotas but they were still ultimately determined by government. Elders, especially, bitterly resented this. "In the old days," Gideon said, "the Inuit looked after their environment better than the government does today. They maintained the level of the animals and had their own laws. The Inuit have been living up here for so many years. They will not kill what they don't need." He was certain the Inuit's own conservation strategies were being undermined by the government. This, he felt, explained the increasing instance of hunters, the young particularly, killing not only more than they needed but more than they could even carry. Killing, that is, just for the hell of it. Gideon would say: Out of spite. Inuit believe the more laws you put on people, the more you need.

Traditionally, the diet was almost exclusively carnivorous, livened with a few berries and edible plants. Contrary to popular suspicion, this provided all their daily requirements. Seal liver and whale skin, for example, are rich in vitamin C. Despite being long characterized as loving nothing so much as a good gorgefest on blubber, Inuit actually consumed half the fat of the average American.

The failure to recognize the worth of the Inuit diet contributed to the undoing of the many early Arctic explorers who perished from scurvy when they ran out of citrus juices and vegetables. This was most conclusively shown early in this century by the explorer Vilhjalmar Stefansson. Stefansson spent much of his career propagating the idea that the Arctic was a region of huge and unrecognized wealth. The Friendly Arctic, he called it. Among his vices, Stefansson was obsessed with a rather nasty desire to prove the ethnocentrism of the British — never any great feat — and did so by living on a diet of pure meat for a year, monitored by New York doctors, to prove the point. The demonstration, he wrote, had pleasant side effects. "I was more optimistic and energetic than ordinarily. To the best of my memory and judgement, I looked forward with more anticipation to the next day."

Between village life, wage employment and Coke, this happy diet was now being undermined at a spectacular pace. "At that time," Herodier Kalluk said of his early years in Resolute, "they never used to buy pop or sweets. Now they buy a lot of things that they never used to." Mostly they buy carbohydrates, which have replaced protein as the dietary staple. And most of these are sugars, to which many people are said to be addicted. During an eight-year period in the Sixties, one village quadrupled its sugar intake.

The changes wrought on the health of the Inuit are taking place so fast researchers cannot keep up. Certain patterns, however, have been emerging for two decades. One thing that happens to people habituated to protein who replace it with sugar, the research indicates, is that they start to grow at a phenomenal rate. This has changed the physiology of the Inuit and caused widespread myopia. Inuit also have one of the highest rates of dental decay in the world.

Until recently, children were breast fed for an average of three or four years. Now there is a reliance on bottle feeding which, combined with the reduction of meat in the diet, is blamed for the epidemic prevalence of otitis media — middle ear infection — and respiratory problems in children. Dietary change has also been linked to obesity, gallstones, acne, hyperlipidemia, arteriosclerosis and various cancers.

The impact of the diet changes also mix with those of other recent gifts to Inuit society — synergism, scientists call this — to bizarre effect. One study showed that vitamin deficiencies combined with incessant vibration from snowmobiles has resulted in the compression of vertebrae. Another linked repeated cases of botulism to the storage of untreated, rapidly decaying meats in plastic bags. And smoking among northerners is heavy and pervasive.

*"It's right back to basics here,"* he said. And I thought: if, in order to have a healthy diet, I had to rely on the nutritional information I had absorbed over my lifetime I would have already perished from scurvy. Most of us have a healthy diet because we

are surrounded by a variety of foods balanced by cravings and habit. Even if Inuit had a taste for brussel sprouts, which many don't, they are not easy to come by. The food distribution system in the north is such that, short of relying on a traditional diet, it is almost impossible for Inuit to eat properly.

Shopping for southern food in Arctic communities I was consistently and rudely reminded that none of it had been produced within a thousand miles. Vegetables looked as if they had walked from the temperate zone and were priced as if they had taken cabs. They had bananas, but they were black. They slumped between a $7 bunch of gray asparagus and a single, brown, aerated lettuce, moldering into the likeness of a brain. Yours for $3. An Arctic Vegan is an inconsolably miserable person. A litre of milk costs $3.69, a dozen eggs the same and a chicken costs $12. Carbohydrates, which arrive in bulk, are comparatively cheap. Otherwise, the more remote the place, the more occasional the air service, the higher the prices. The only exception to this was liquor. Price-controlled in the NWT as it is elsewhere, booze cost the same in Resolute Bay as it did in Yellowknife, a fact that outraged everyone but the outright drunks.

Southern workers receive various subsidies for their isolation that allow them to circumvent the problem by ordering food in bulk by arrangement with retailers in Montreal and other cities. This takes planning and money in bulk. Inuit, on the other hand, do not have the wherewithal to get around the exorbitant prices. Few are ever burdened with a bulk of money. "Everybody," Thomas said, "spends their money as soon as they get it."

George Porter, who was half-white and lived as southern a lifestyle as any Inuk, said, "It's the way most of us were brought up — buying from the Bay and the Co-op. So if you don't really know which is cheaper that's what you do. It's easier for white people because they save all their money. And they have enough money by next year that they can afford to pay for the freight and the food they order from the south. But, if you don't have money, how you going to pay to have food shipped? And it's kind of hard to buy if you don't see, unless you have some kind of catalogue and you can read and write and understand it."

In a thousand places around the world, the most basic of human abilities — to feed yourself and your family — is breaking down in similar ways. Dietary habits are appalling, land turns to dust, people grow crops they cannot eat. We tend to ascribe all of this, in a blanket, self-assured way, to ignorance or material poverty or impossibly fickle nature. This is sometimes true. More often true, however, the fault at least partially lies with economic or political meddling by the Western world. Land is defoliated by war; export crops are grown to pay debts; junk food, powdered baby's milk and cigarettes rain down as if from heaven.

Obviously, health care in the Arctic had increased life expectancy and decreased suffering. Infant mortality, still higher than the national average, is one-eighth of what it was thirty years ago. Still, within a couple of generations, the Inuit had begun to mutate. The short, thick and astoundingly keen hunters with the eyes of hawks and teeth of pearl are growing lank and stooped, myopic and partially deaf; and their famous smiles are now as black and windy as charred forests.


The times never let up on the people of Resolute Bay. Throughout the Seventies a steadily thickening flow of explorers, resource workers, builders, inspectors, soldiers, students and bureaucrats, ninety-nine per cent of them men, passed through the base and the village. A bar, the Arctic Circle Club, was opened. There was no end of money or alcohol. But neither could buy people back their sense of power or purpose.

The stories people tell make the whole village and base sound like one great brawling party, racing, as if fated, toward a bad end. Marriages disintegrated, friends and spouses fought, there were rapes, accidents, deaths. Often as not, come sunrise over the base, an Inuk was prowling the grounds with a rifle, looking for his wife. Eventually, the problems became so bad that the bar was closed down, but that only forced people to buy hard liquor, which is cheaper to fly in than beer. The rancour and wrangling just went on. The year before I visited Resolute, several families — thirty people in all — had just packed up at once and moved out. "They were," a newspaper report said, "fed up with their lot and with the drinking."

Next to the angels, the best witnesses to anything are always children. Their gaze is silent and mercilessly lucid. One day, after school, I talked with a boy and a girl, both twelve. They had seen a great deal.

The girl said, "When alcohol comes up, there's lots of fighting. Sometimes, when everybody's not drinking for a while, all of a sudden their orders come in from Frobisher. They start having parties and there will be kids staying up late, scared to go home. We used to see a lot of our parents getting beaten up. That was when the bar was open."

The boy said, "When my parents used to drink, I wouldn't go to sleep until early in the morning. When they stopped I went to sleep. I slept well."

The fights were over little things, the kids said. Petty jealousies. They could see straight through their parents. They had mixed feelings about who was at fault for all the unhappiness. Their parents didn't have to drink, they said. But they weren't the ones who brought booze to the Arctic either.

The girl said, "Why did they bring alcohol in the first place? That's what I always wonder. Same with drugs. I don't know why they brought up drugs. Sure don't make you healthy. Same with alcohol. Doesn't make you smarter; doesn't make your troubles go away. I don't know why they drink. They go crazy, that's all I know. Sometimes they are a lot of fun to be around when they are drunk, not too drunk, feeling high. You laugh a lot with them. Sometimes when they're drunk they teach you a lot. They talk a lot." "What about?" "What they been through in their life. They been through hell. I think our parents are finally learning what happened in their lives."

The people of Resolute had been jerked about by the grand puppeteers a bit more than had most and had developed a harder edge. But their problems were universal. I heard these kinds of stories everywhere.

It is generally held that women have been better able to cope, psychologically, with the changes in Inuit life. Their work within the home was less dramatically altered and more easily incorporated the dominating culture. They learned English and southern work habits faster and assumed many of the organizational functions within the new communities and, later, political organizations.

Comparatively, men floundered. The encroaching society made them into children — *and not even Inuit children.* This has been worst for the many young men who have found themselves caught between two worlds and unable to fully enter either. The seeds of their ability find no ground at all in this twilight and grow only into a terrible, howling anger. As in every place where the world burns, the sudden exertion of an outside power damned the river of their energy but could not stop its flow. A shit-tide of violence began to back up into their lives.

We never know where the reverberations of power will find their level. After listening to the kids in Resolute, I thought it is incredible, really, that the weight of a forty-year-old undeclared, intransigent war between two feuding empires thousands of miles away should ultimately shake down onto the heads of these children; having to wait out an Arctic night until their parents were exhausted from beating the hell out of each other. But I was just being soppy. It happens all the time.

In every village I saw the scars: A pretty, twenty-five-year-old girl limping across a restaurant on a wooden leg that was the petrified remnant of the night she collapsed dead drunk in a snow bank. An old woman, who had had the same sort of accident, sitting on her couch, quietly smiling, her hands reduced to two small balls wrapped in Crown Royal bags. Man after man shuffling sheepishly and trying to explain where his wife might be without having to admit that he beat her or threw boiling water at her or summarily booted her out into the snow during a drunken rage. A woman, mentioning her brother's death, casting her eyes away and avoiding the details: that, drunk, he tried to rape her and she shot him.

The World Health Organization (WHO) has called alcohol abuse the single most important health problem in the North. Northerners of every background drink a lot and alcoholism is rampant right around the pole. Per capita, Inuit drink less than other Northerners, but alcohol's effects are always worst in native communities, where there is binge drinking, less tolerance, more repressed anger and a higher proportion of income spent on alcohol. Many communities in the Canadian Arctic have tried to grapple with the problem by banning alcohol outright; others allow it in only under special permit. But needs find a way of getting filled. Bootleggers are everywhere and lots of people make moonshine. Eskimo Drink, they call it: mix raisins, yeast, white sugar, brown sugar, water and leave it stand for twenty-four hours. "It tastes okay," said one who knew, "but it gives you a hangover for two days."

Even in the tiniest communities drugs can be purchased at wildly inflated prices. Dealers, most of them transient southerners, accept the fruit of the land in exchange, trading hash oil or cocaine for polar bear skins. And there are always glue and gasoline, the drugs of preference amongst young native Canadians. Who sniffs solvents? "You can go as young as you like and old as you like," a grizzly of a Mountie said. In some villages there are seventeen-year-olds who have been addicted to glue since they were nine. "They've got nothing to do and all day to do it in."

You have to watch a kid inhale a tube of airplane glue to quite imagine what this means. With difficulty, he splatters the contents of the tube into a plastic bag and wraps the bag's fluttering lips around his face. As he sucks inward, the bag collapses and his eyes begin to gawk wildly. Little bits of plastic stick to his chin and fly up his nose. And then he slumps grinning like a lunatic, but not a happy one; compulsively ramming his fingers up his nose to claw at the coating in his nostrils and talking like Donald Duck. Glue sniffing is one ugly addiction to be saddled with. The toluene in the glue attacks the brain's cognitive capacity. There are many glue sniffers in the neighborhood where I live. Whenever I have looked into one of their faces, I felt I could actually see the brain disintegrating.

As much as ninety-five per cent of crime in Arctic communities is attributed to alcohol and drug abuse and most of it is violent. Inuit have twice as many drunken, fatal vehicle accidents as non-natives. The suicide rate among young people, particularly men, hovers around three times the national average and has been called, by WHO, a "clearly discernible epidemic." Since the Fifties, there has been a steady increase in the abuse of women, to the point that Inuit women's groups were now trying to organize shelter programmes in their villages. Talking to women about wife battering was some measure of the general recognition that there was a terrible illness abroad in this society, an imbalance cut loose. They did not necessarily blame the men. Girotti Morgan, a thirty-seven-year-old teacher of Inuktitut, said, "It always seems to be the men who end up in court. Sometimes it can be the woman who beats the man. They should try to teach both to get along. It's always the man in trouble."

The impulse to violence is like a possession, and so indiscriminate that it turns even on the most revered of Inuit society, children and elders. Once I tried for days to interview a respected elder in a village and finally learned that I was being spurned because he had been beaten during a family celebration. An acquaintance who went to visit the man shuddered to describe him, as if he had seen a ghost. "His face was *completely* black and blue."

Many young men blamed the old for their situation. Simon Awa, the CBC reporter, said the young found it incomprehensible that the old people had, it seemed, given in so easily. "I guess it seemed to them like this great big white man who had so much power. And our people just went along. They were stupid. If they had tried harder it might be different."

Often it was said by southerners that Inuit had grown accus-
tomed to blaming all their problems on the whites and government. These were people who had been around for a while; who
had listened for years to academics, reporters, governments,
Inuit and themselves repeating the same old litany of crimes.
Many were in no position to make things better now, but they
felt guilty nonetheless. As did I. Their comments, thus, seemed
something of a protective shield. But I listened to the Inuit more
carefully afterward for the sound of whining. I heard little. In
fact, Inuit did not complain much at all. They frowned on it.

Jobie Weetaluktuk said, "We have complainers. But we live
in a difficult environment. You have to work hard and you
shouldn't have to complain. The environment requires discipline
and you have to keep at it. So in the long run it does not pay off
to protest."

"There is nothing but ice around me," said an old poem, "that
is good!... My country is nothing but slush, that is good!"

I asked a man in Resolute how he felt the place had treated
him, all in all. More than once in his life this man had been hit
full in the face by the regurgitations of the sewer of violence,
which had spilled several tragedies upon his family. He said,
"Sometimes it's not too good. But if you try to think not too good
about something it can be very bad all the time. But try not to
think too much about it, and try to be happy about it, and it's not
too bad."

Inuit had always been able to endure a great deal. Healing
themselves was something else again. Given the present situation, the elders felt this was impossible. They had fallen too far.
"Now the families don't seem to get along within the families,"
Abigail Kaernak said. "There's more conflict. The only way it
could be prevented is with help from the white people, in white
people and Inuit people helping each other more, understanding
each other more. Understanding the way life is. "

One of the lies about travel is that you cannot visit people such
as these. People forced to the margins are always thought to be
as welcoming as a pack of Rotweillers toward members of the

dominant group. As a white Western male, I was always prepared for this. But it was rarely the case. In my experience, people welcomed anyone they thought willing or able to bring a message back. The message was always the same: you probably don't realize this, but you have made a mistake here. Nobody wanted to believe they had been deliberately oppressed.

Once, in England, I spent a few days interviewing young men from inner-city Manchester. Like all northern Britons, they had been explicitly written off by their government. They spent their days beating a track from Job Centre to dole office to the human filing cabinets the British are pleased to call Estates. At twenty years old, their future was desperate. What I found extraordinary about them was the evident lack of anger. They all detested Margaret Thatcher, but mostly for her haughty airs. Even in the most politically polarized country in the West, they could not fathom that their misery was deliberate. Part of the problem was the lack of understanding in the south: "They think we're flat-cap wearing, beer-swilling, fish-and-chippie people." And there was something more mysterious — a car crash, a twist of fate— that they felt no one understood. But that no one would admit to not understanding. "They're trying to coover oop now," a pugnacious lad named Robert said of the government. He raised one eye-brow. "At's 'ow I look at it. They may have made a bloonder soome'ere, a big mistake soome'ere."

Inuit elders, like Abigail, felt sure that their problems stemmed from gaps of this sort. They assumed governments were confrontational, insensitive or just plain domineering because of cultural and linguistic misunderstandings, perhaps also fear. Napatchie McRae, translating for Simeonie Kaernak, said, "He would try to make the white people understand that the Inuit are not trying to fight against the white people. But they are just trying to open up their feelings about the treatment they are getting." Noah Adglak said, "Inuit cannot do whatever they want to do anymore because the government doesn't understand what the Inuit culture is all about."

Much of what they said, of course, was true. It was also a product of their own cultural misunderstanding. Gideon said once, "It would be impossible to completely live the way Inuit wants it. But it should be fixed the way it would be more comfortable to the laws we have. We would like to see the Inuit and the white governments work together, understand each other. And not one bigger than the other; not one smaller." Even after decades of having their lives run by the south, older Inuit had not really absorbed the idea of utilitarian domination. They could see it and feel it, yes. But it had not sunk in. It was for this, I think, that many of the young felt their deep and secret anger. The young had been born into a cynical world. Like babies addicted to heroin in the womb.

The elders were also animated by a profound sense of gratitude. "In a lot of ways they are very much better off than in the old days," old Simon Keanik said. "He's very pleased with what is happening. But a few things are less than better. A few things he disagrees with." They all said that. They appreciated the warm houses and the medicine and the television sets. They were thankful for old age pensions. They were relieved to be assured of food.

These things had come first as trade and then proliferated as gifts. Only then did the elders realize what price would be paid and then it was already too late. Gideon said, "The governments are giving us these little things — just like, as a child, when you are crying for something, you get warm mitts or something like that. You get a house nowadays. That cannot go on forever. We have to stand up for ourselves."

Strange as it sounds, of all people Inuit reminded me most of Berliners. In the old people of West Berlin one also perceived a core of resentment circumscribed by layers of indebtedness. They too had been handed a ridiculously easy life after the war which they too had paid for with their freedom and with their children's futures. Both had made a Faustian bargain, though of very different sorts, and both had inevitably lost. Both now felt haunted by that loss and hopelessly caught up with impossible forces. Both, too, as a result, were enclosed by the bitterness and violence of their own children. Yet they embraced life with a kind of huge, hungering passion the heat of which you all too rarely feel wandering in the Northern Hemisphere. Their lifestyles, of course, could hardly have been more different; they were antithetical, virtually reverse images. Yet what bound them finally in my mind was the way they pursued their lives. They both had a certain knowledge of the darkness and the light. Both, in their own ways, lived close to the ground.

Paul Amuaralik spent his days at home charting the known roads and remembered journeys of Resolute Bay's hunters. The main room where he worked was lined with wood panelling, warring fabric designs, Canadian flags and the Coke-can detritus built up by he and his son, a couple of guys in baseball caps. But when he worked, his huge map, covering most of the floor, predominated. The map was an unlabelled image of the Queen Elizabeth Islands on which Paul overlaid fabulously intricate, colour-coded renderings that detailed the steps in the eternal minuet of the hunters and the hunted. Tiny polar bears, fox, seals, walrus and whales were clustered at the junctions of waterways, surrounded by arrows pointing in the directions each would flee. A dozen solid black lines ran from heart-shaped Cornwallis Island across the channels. These were the large arteries that carried hunters over the ice for nine months of the year. The island coasts were speckled with the dots of common campgrounds and hexagons marking ancient Thule ruins.

Paul had been working on these maps for months, collating a mass of details gathered from many hunters and meticulously plotting them in different scales on perspex. Eventually, the maps would be shipped south and fed into the maw of the government's planning process for the Lancaster Sound region, which promised to sort out the competing demands of oil tankers, ice breakers, submarines and lone hunters travelling the Northwest Passage. Paul said, "We are trying to let them know where we stand by indicating where we go. Hopefully the government will understand what we are trying to do." In other words, they were getting their dibs in.

The composite map created by Paul, who was thirty-four, represented the contemporary Inuit approach to the land. As such, it was very different from the map that Simon Keanik, who was eighty, had tacked up in his main room. Simon's map had been a gift from one of the many anthropologists who had come to him in recent years, as if to the summit of a mountain, begging knowledge everyone knows will soon disappear. It too was a basic chart of the land for hundreds of miles. Simon had added his own overlay by running his finger across the map, tracing the paths he had walked, sledded and boated in his time. These were so many and diverse that the greasy tracings had blended into a single grey-black splodge that eliminated his home of Gjoa Haven entirely and spread, gradually lightening, like an aerosol spray to the furthest edges.

Thomas Anguttitauruq translated as Simon explained this map. He said, "Travelling and knowing the country is so important to him. For a long time now he's been having maps." They were useful primarily in describing to outsiders where he had been. Men of Simon's generation needed no maps for picking their way across the land that strangers have always found confusingly monotonous. "If you have never been there, but you are told, say, to go that way, Inuit always knew which way it was. If someone explained it to them it was so easy for them to travel." This was an ability that had astonished visitors to the Arctic for generations.

"They have a very clear conception of all the countries they have seen or heard of," wrote Franz Boas in the late nineteenth century. He described how a map would be drawn in the snow to guide a man setting out across country he had not seen, that he would then and evermore hold within his head. More remarkable was the Inuit facility for rendering these maps on paper for explorers with stunning precision, charting as much as 1,000 miles of coast line *from memory*.

One of the differences in the appreciation for their maps between the old man and the young, was their notion of completeness. Simon had travelled some distance beyond the edges of his map, yet he had no real clue of where it would fit into a larger projection — a map, say, of the circumpolar region, much less one of the world. He could not recall having ever seen either. Paul, of course, knew precisely where his chart fit into the larger territorial mosaic. And he knew that claims encroaching from all sides threatened constantly to overwhelm those he was meticulously staking out with tiny, cereal box-like animal stickers.

Walking Resolute Bay one morning I was surprised by a demonstration of this. Winter was setting in. The bay was a solid, corrugated field filled with translucent boulders and the sun listlessly rolled along the horizon, as if it couldn't be troubled to get up. Against it, a ship appeared, a small red wedge slowly creeping west. I was so startled at first that, momentarily, I forgot that I had heard it was coming, that I even knew its name. The ship was the *M.V. Arctic*, an oil tanker with a load from Panarctic Oils' Bent Horn well at Cameron Island bound for the south. It was heading for a rendezvous with the *Louis S. St. Laurent*, most powerful of the Canadian Coast Guard's icebreakers.

The ships would be the last to sail the Northwest Passage that year, clearing Lancaster Sound just as it became impassable. Neither had the strength or power to navigate the passage in the winter. Under the Arctic Waters Pollution Prevention Act, created after the voyage of the Manhattan, neither was legally qualified to do so either. The federal government, however, had exempted the *M.V. Arctic* from the law in 1985, allowing Panarctic to transport oil in a ship that, theoretically, was too fragile to withstand the ice it might encounter. After the American Coast Guard icebreaker *Polar Sea* sailed through the passage in 1985, the government had announced that it would build an icebreaker capable of sailing the passage all winter, for reasons of national sovereignty and potential resource extraction.

I thought of this as I watched this ship clawing its way across the horizon. The day before I had been out there with a pair of the village teenagers. Ostensibly we were seal hunting. But the kids were really more interested in racing their snowmobiles on the ice. Far from shore, it can be as flat and smooth as the surface of a bowl of milk. Every so often, usually in the spring, it happened that an icebreaker came along at just such a time. Without warning, the pressure wave radiating outward could transform this surface into a heaving plate of shattering glass. This had happened the year before near one of the villages. The man who was broad-sided had escaped with his life. But he had lost both his snowmobile and, later, the suit for damages that he brought against the company involved.

The lines and arrows on Paul Amarualik's map indicated the streams of life that stood to be severed by icebreakers and oil tankers and, in a broader context, other military and industrial projects to be erected in the name of national sovereignty and wealth. He said, "If the ice is broken up then the animals are going to say: 'where am I going to settle now?' Probably they will have to move away from the conflict of the ships and that's going to disrupt the hunting very much. Shipping year round is just going to hurt the animals, hurt the hunters and disrupt the whole pattern of way of living on both sides."

Biologists tended to agree, but no one was sure. Knowledge of the migration, breeding and feeding habits of Arctic animals is, to be generous, spotty. For some species, the bulk of research amounts to little more than the results of annual aerial inventories. It is known, for example, that the 400,000 caribou of the Bathurst herd, one of five major herds in Canada, treks northward every spring. It happens as if by clockwork, but no one knows what the clock looks like or how it ticks. It is the same with every Arctic species. We do not know what governs the cycles of their proliferation or the peculiarities of their behaviour. We know less still about their interactions with their environment and each other. No one can predict their natural responses to biological and climatic changes, much less to pollution, alterations in the terrain, mechanized movement or noise. Of all Arctic animals, we know the least about those that live in the sea. What is known about Lancaster Sound is that forty per cent of the Beluga whales, eighty-five per cent of Narwhal and one third of all the breeding seabirds in eastern North America spend time there.

Inuit knew the habits of the animals intimately, but accepted and paid infinite respect to their mysteries. Theirs was to follow. The greasy splodge on Simon's map was a testament to a life of doing this, to both his and the animals' ability to wander freely across the country, unchannelled and unaware of any artificial divisions within it. No more than the caribou did Simon recognize borders. "He travelled along all of those areas and nobody ever tell him, 'We own this land, this is our territory'; no one ever tells him not to go in *that* area or not to hunt in *that* area."

"Owning land means living on the land and dying on the land," someone said. I nodded, earnestly and politely. I always nodded when they said something I thought made sense, even if I could not quite grasp it whole. This was one of our culture's forms of unconscious lying to which the Inuit had long ago twigged. In time, I came to find the truth inherent in their genuine confusion embarrassing. Simon simply *did not understand* the concept of owning land. Rifles, snowmobiles or boots, yes. Children, animals or land, no.

"For him, he doesn't feel that anybody owns this land, it's here to be used. Like, he's not greedy over it and he wouldn't want to be, you know. But it doesn't make sense to him if somebody says this area is mine and this other part of the land is yours. It doesn't make sense to him."

This was not to say that all the land was the same to Inuit. People were attached to specific communities by birth, dialect, usually kinship and also by an intimate knowledge of a particular territory. Before the settlements began, more than 125 separate groups lived in the Arctic, each designated by a name with the suffix *miut* which means, roughly, "the people of." Each was what anthropologists call a deme, a kind of molecule of social organization made up of nuclear families; a tiny mobile village, as it were. They were named after the most prominent feature of their home area. North to south along Somerset Island and the Boothia Peninsula, for example, lived: the Kuuganajurmiut — the fast, large river people; Ikirisangmiut — people of the narrows; and the Arvirturmiut — Bowhead whale-eating people.

These were places where they lived, had lived or might live again. In the *Inuit Land Use and Occupancy Project*, Thomas C. Correll described the territory of each deme as defined by the simple names it gave to individual features in the land: the river, the lake and so on. The territory in which a man lived was said to be the land possessed by him through intimacy and attachment, not exclusive rights. In this way, a person might be said to have had land in many places during a life. The *miut* suffix, Correll wrote, reflected something more like a state of mind, something you carried with you. This was what the Inuit meant when they said they did not own the land, but rather that the land owned them.

Thomas said, "Simon doesn't like this idea of authorities nowadays saying its better to have boundaries. He doesn't like that idea at all." He paused, and then added: "There is no real proper word for boundary. But we learned that later on."

Paul's map was a measure of how well they learned; the realization that their traditional attitude was getting the Inuit nowhere. Authority insists on boundaries. Land use and occupancy studies have become a common and necessary tool for the Inuit in the past twenty years. Developed by sympathetic outsiders such as Hugh Brody and Milton Freeman, they were originally intended to counter the convenient idea that Inuit and Indian lands amounted to no more than enormous, disused spaces. They sought to document the regularity and logic of the lifestreams and thus show that hunters were not aimless wanderers who could just as easily prosper on any old large hunk of land. Collectively, the studies amounted to an extraordinary schematic of a web of communications in the Arctic as intricate and established as that of Europe. And all of it invisible to the eye. It was a breathtaking demonstration of the amount and complexity of the information hunters carried within their collective memory.

The studies were an integral part of the land claims process, intended to demarcate certain crucial areas. To say: This is where we stand, because this is where we go. The irony was that this undid the Inuit view of the land as seamless. The lines on the maps were borders in-process that correlated to southern demands but to nothing in the land or the Inuit consciousness. In the end, they would be used to fragment the land and fence the Inuit into certain pastures, as had happened to the Indians through rather less sophisticated means.

Inuit saw it the other way around. They felt they were fencing the intruders out. Paul said, "Whoever wanted to look around up here, we took them openly. If they needed help, then we started to help them. It turns out that some of them backstabbed us." This would not be allowed to happen again. The anger that the young least tutored in white ways had released in beating up their elders was now channelled, among the most tutored, into a fury of fence building.

This is a reaction we can understand. The notion that only real estate can confer genuine power is deeply embedded within us. Our legacy of delineation is so long, that our base conception of life begins with an earth divided from the cosmos and segmented from there by countries, provinces, cities and so on right down to our houses. In an agrarian society, land *is* power. The French political philosopher Michel Foucault has written that the words and associated concepts of geography itself are intimately bound up with the military and ideas of domination. Region, for example, comes from the French *regere*, to command. "To trace the forms of implantation, delimitation and demarcation of objects, the modes of tabulation, the organization of domains meant the throwing into relief of processes — historical ones, needless to say — of power."

This was how school children were taught to read maps, as line drawings of history. When I was in school the studies of history and geography were considered interchangeable, different perspectives on the same process.

In *Arctic Dreams*, Barry Lopez examined the difference between ideas of place and of space. The former is the landscape of the familiar, the realm of calm and memory. When we travel into the open spaces beyond we extend the boundaries of our place into the foreign space. This is a means both of understanding and of conquest. In a foreign place, Lopez writes, "the observation that it is merely space that requires definition before it has meaning ... betrays a colonial sensibility." This was what Justice Thomas Berger was saying when he called his Mackenzie Valley pipeline report *Northern Frontier, Northern Homeland.*

Thomas said, of Simon, "He knows how to survive up here in all the ways you can survive up here." It was this that made the land his home. It was the many maps in his memory that gave his freedom flight. Yet the very intangibility of these things and their inaccessibility, had let outsiders believe, more easily in the Arctic than most places, that this was just space — mere *territory* — waiting for a little ingenuity to come along and whip it into something discernible.

"We need borders now," Inuit said. This was a kind of final defeat, a conquering of their most fundamental beliefs. Here the ironic became the insidious. Inuit could only protect themselves from assimilation by assimilating, by using the tools and rules of industrialized culture. As with economics, education, health, families, their only route to regaining power underscored their ultimate powerlessness. But they said, look: It is this or outright genocide.

Gideon said, "It is hard to live a certain way and there is only a certain way of living nowadays. If you have no land you can't survive very well nowadays. Governments and people from other countries, even from Canada, are coming in and pushing us into a corner. And one of these days if we don't own the land we are going to fall off the cliff."

Borders and maps it would be then. They knew the outsiders would only respect the things they could hold in their hand.

Inuit want what they call *Nunavut* — Our Land. This would be a homeland for the people of the central and eastern Arctic, run by an Inuit-dominated government. They had been working on plans for Nunavut for more than a decade. Politically, the territory would comprise roughly half of what is now the NWT, the other half being designated *Denedeh*, which means roughly the same in Dene. Nunavut would amount to something slightly grander than a land claim, giving the Inuit some runoff from resource exploitation and a voice in the management of most aspects of life in the territory in addition to exclusive use of a percentage of the land.

If the Nunavut settlement roughly equalled the terms of the agreements signed with the Quebec Inuit and with the Inuvialuit in the west, Inuit would end up with outright control of about twenty per cent of the land and an equal voice in decisions concerning the rest. Over some matters, such as military installations, they could count on no say at all. When land-use planners working on Lancaster Sound asked the military about its intentions for the region, the reply was a list of areas where unspecified experiments were being done, which "must continue to be used for some years, with or without a formal reservation." Lesser bureaucracies are similarly reluctant to give up their perogative in the Arctic, though not so inviolable.

Constitutionally, the notion of aboriginal rights is vague in the extreme. The 1982 Constitution Act "recognizes and affirms" existing aboriginal rights, but did not say what they were. The first ministers' conferences that followed the constitution's proclamation were continually unable — read: unwilling — to agree on the question and to therefore define what aboriginal self-government means. Pending amendments to the Constitution, agreed upon at Meech Lake without native participation, only make matters worse. The eventual hope is that Nunavut will be a province but the constitutional changes make the chances of this seem dismal, because they would require 100 per cent consent from the other provinces, some of whom will not be so willing to share the pie.

In Canada, our sense of ourselves as jolly good fellows prevents us from consciously acknowledging — as, say, the Americans do — that the territory has been taken by force. Ownership of land by the federal and provincial governments, in a sense, has the stature of myth as the critic Roland Barthes uses the word: something so commonly and unthinkingly taken for granted that it seems *natural*. What governments call land *claims* are really a kind of fancy, formalized begging. The governments already own everything: the land, the resources, the villages. They can afford to negotiate until walrus learn to fly. It is up to the Inuit to niggle back, bit by excruciating bit, the rights and freedoms they had before the wind of metal swept into the Arctic. Moreover, the federal government is well known to cheat on claims agreements.

The younger Inuit whose job the negotiations had become long ago realized that the Canadian government's greatest fear was the creation of another Quebec, even as they themselves had been inspired by the French struggle. "I guess they consider the Inuit presence and the Inuit ambitions in the Arctic to be somehow taking away from Canadian sovereignty," said John Amagoalik, as if that was the craziest notion in the world.

Amagoalik was among the most senior Inuit politicians. For years, he had been involved with the Inuit Tapirisat of Canada and the Inuit Circumpolar Conference. He was a needle of a man with a gaunt face and pin-point eyes. His family had been among the first settlers in Resolute Bay when he was six. "I remember in the fall of '53 landing in a boat on the beach. It was just like landing on the moon."

We sat now at the shiny council table in the municipal chambers in Iqaluit. Like most indigenous political bodies in the Arctic, the council attempted to adhere to native ways of decision by consensus. "It's slow," an official said, "but it works pretty well." As he spoke, Amagoalik stared absently into the glare of the table. Like many an experienced political activist, he seemed tired of explaining his position. He was grappling now with questions of sovereignty he claimed to find confusing. One was why Inuit were, as a rule, loyal Canadians. The other was why the Canadian government seemed not to recognize this.

He told me this story: In the mid-Seventies, when he was working for the territorial government, an official party was stranded by a blizzard at Hall Beach. They sought shelter at the radar station. There, they were kept waiting at the door while the supervisor checked with his boss in the United States. The government officials were blasé about this, Amagoalik said. He was incensed. "I reacted as a Canadian Inuk." He could not, however, say quite what that meant. "For some reason, Inuit are very loyal Canadians, I don't understand the whole reason behind it."

In the villages, people often spoke of the omnipotent one — *Government* — with bitterness and suspicion and of its foot-soldier — *Mountie* — with unqualified contempt. But *Canada* was something else again, an entity of better stuff than its agents. Canada gave things. Government took things away. Canada was the Marshall Plan. Government was tanks in the streets.

But there was something more: "Sovereignty" had become a mantra in the Arctic. Sovereignty and oil were the only magic words the Inuit had left. They were only things southern Canadians could give a good damn about as far as the icy wastes were concerned. It was thought in the North you could get most anything you pleased if you could work out a sovereignty angle. At the least, you got attention.

The people of Resolute Bay were trying to solve their problems by having the government declare the village a "sovereignty town" and recognizing the price they had paid for the national claim. This they reckoned, retroactively, worked out to about $100,000 per person plus free trips back to Quebec plus a house there. The government had more or less accepted this, though the back pay was still being negotiated. It had only agreed, so far, to the trips and a few houses.

When the Inuvialuit Development Corporation, in partnership with ITT, bid for the North Warning System contract, Roger Gruben bolstered his argument with the sovereignty line. Inuit, he said, had been upholding Canadian sovereignty in the Arctic for eons. The least Canada could do in recompense was give them a little military contract. In the eastern Arctic, Louis Tapar-duk, director of the Baffin Regional Inuit Association, used the same argument talking about land claims, but took a more clever approach. "During our land-use planning we want to give the feds some additional tools to claim sovereignty over the Arctic islands. Settling land claims will help the government claim sovereignty."

Forty years ago, there were still many Inuit who knew nothing of Canada. Now they were indelibly Canadians. And that was that. They would make of it what they could. Embracing Canada's reign, they felt, was the best way to get back some semblance of their own. The egalitarianism of hunting societies, above all else, is based on logic: Inuit know well that most people, most of the time, are motivated by self-interest.

"As far as I can see," John Amagoalik said, "the Inuit presence in the Arctic strengthens Canadian sovereignty." Nunavut, everyone said, could only help Canada's Arctic dreams. Comes a time when the only way to save your own skin is by becoming somebody else's.

A few days after I watched the *M.V. Arctic* pull itself, slug-like, across the white horizon, I was flying low along Lancaster Sound. I was with an ice-reconnaissance crew whose job it was to find, by means of observation and radar, the *St. Laurent* an easy route. The sound was a clogged, mottled plain of many types of ice. The thinnest, nilas, formed in panes of opaque, silvery sugar-glass which rode up on each other. Where they overlapped a fringe of perfectly cut square "fingers" formed and interlocked. Old ice lay in roundish, creamy white patches pocked with craters. At 1,000 feet, they looked like scum on the surface of old paint, though each dimple was ten feet high and denser than tempered steel. And there were sheets of grey brackish ice broken by irradiant, blue-green pyramids.

Due east we flew. The land rose up from the sound, became the craggy coast of Devon Island, and then rolled away forever, hard-soft, yellow-white and gently rough. Like a plate of bone. The exposed skull of the planet. "Sit beside the guy with the heaviest parka," someone had said of Arctic flights, "and hope that he dies on impact." What did it mean to reign over this? Incredible resourcefulness or infallable machines. I had the latter on my mind.

One of the crew members, a barrel of a Quebecois zipped into a blue jumpsuit, told me about the time, a few years ago, that he spotted a submarine in the western Arctic. He roared, "I weesh I had said nothing. Nothing!" That was because the Canadian military had locked him up like a defecting spy and grilled him for hours, desperate to scrape out every atom of knowledge he had accidentally ingested. Of course, it had been an American submarine. The Americans didn't give the Canadian military much in the first place, and they gave nothing at all about submarines. The Soviets, the experts said, never came anywhere near Canada.

It was complex and it was relative, this sovereignty business; a matter of fish chomping fish with ever more mechanical abandon. Theoretically, the sovereignty dispute between Canada and the United States had mostly to do with this strip of variegated ice beneath us, the widest of the channels through the Arctic archipelago. The issue was straightforward: Canada said that, legally, the channels were internal, like rivers. The Americans said they were international straits, meaning anyone could sail through them whenever they pleased. Aside from their hope to ship oil through the passage, the Americans' prime motivation is to keep the area safe for their nuclear submarines and to avoid setting bad precedents. Pentagon strategists worry that if Canada is allowed to close the Northwest Passage other countries will also get uppity about their waterways. Pretty soon its gunboats might find themselves without any strait in a storm.

Each time the United States pushed its claim, Canada was thrown into a fit of delineation, scribbling lines on its maps of the archipelago and just daring America to cross them. There was the twelve-mile Territorial Sea line, the 100-mile Pollution Prevention Zone, the 200-mile Fishing Zone and, finally, something called Straight Baselines that hugged the outer coasts of the islands like a cotton toque pulled tightly down on a pointed head. Cross them, of course, the United States always did.

Volumes of legislation had been drawn up to explain and justify these lines and Canada went to some trouble to have the pollution zone included in the Law of the Sea Convention. While arguably contributing something to the theory of international jurisprudence, this meant nothing. Canada, for one, is not willing to submit its case to the International Court of Justice. And the United States has shown time and again that it regards international law as useful for scoring debating points, but not something one ought to live by. It would not even sign the Law of the Sea Convention, let alone observe it.

Roughly seventeen countries protested Canada's lines in the Arctic, only the Soviet Union unreservedly promising to respect them. Only the Americans, however, had the gall to keep sailing over them, as if they weren't even there. The Manhattan had been through the passage in 1969, the Polar Sea in 1985 and, it is presumed, nuclear missile submarines in between.

After the voyage of the Polar Sea, Canada and the U.S. began negotiations over the use of the passage. These had the same unreal air as land claims negotiations. Canada was fancily, formally begging the United States for control of the Canadian Arctic. The document so produced is loaded with unctuous platitudes of friendliness and an American undertaking to ask permission before sending icebreakers through the passage. However, no mention at all is made of sovereignty, commercial ships or nuclear submarines.

In the end, Canada's laws in the Arctic gained the same respect from the United States that Inuit laws did from Canada. It was the same old story. Power rules.

In 1987, the Canadian government showed how well it had learned this by announcing a new military policy that gave the Arctic high priority. "The military role in sovereignty," it said, "is that of the ultimate coercive force available when the capabilities of the civil authorities are inadequate to enforce Canadian laws and regulations or when Canada's right to exercise jurisdiction is challenged by other states." To this end, the government white paper planned a whole new line of ultimate coercers.

In addition to the fighter bases and radars — "Canadian sovereignty has been enhanced" — it would buy a dozen nuclear submarines — "essential to our security and sovereignty" — and build an Arctic warfare base — "an assertion of Canadian sovereignty." Billions of dollars were to be spent building lines of steel. Who were these to ultimately coerce? The Soviet Union. Sovereignty is an elastic concept. It means whatever it has to mean.

Part of the reason for the voyage of the Polar Sea, according to strategic analysts, had been to conduct a variety of military experiments. In its wake, someone in the Canadian defence bureaucracy leaked several studies on Arctic military development that had been done for its Operational Research Establishment. They were compilations of the obvious but rarely admitted. One, for example, concluded that every major military development in the Canadian Arctic since the war had been initiated by the United States. Canada, it said, had always acquiesced out of fear. "If Canada did not go along her sovereignty might be endangered by unilateral American actions on Canadian soil." It was this sort of sovereignty expression that was contained in the government's plans. Comes a time when the only way to save your own skin is by becoming somebody else's.

Certainly none of the new weaponry will be any threat to the United States. Effectively, America will be running most of it. The air forces are already under American command. Government ministers argued that the submarines would enforce Canadian sovereignty, letting hang the assumption that this meant chasing American submarines out of the Northwest Passage. But no one intended they would do any such thing. The Navy made clear that it had bigger plans than the picayune duty of playing traffic cop there. The submarines are intended to work with American and NATO subs facing off against the Soviets. They would be another block in the submarine wall stretching from the Norwegian Sea to the Bering Strait. Sure, the Navy talked sovereignty. But, like the Air Force before it, what it really had in mind was the wearing of leather jackets and the sniffing of plutonium.

The plane banked over the northern tip of Baffin Island and swooped low at Strathcona Sound, dropping a canister of maps to the idling icebreaker. At the end of the sound was Nanisivik, the mining community that is to become Canada's Arctic warfare base. The village of 300 was built in 1974 atop a lead and zinc seam that is now almost exhausted and soon to be abandoned.

The base is the most independent of Canada's Arctic military projects. It is to be a permanent home for wargames. Several of these had been run recently under the name Operation Lightning Strike. In Iqaluit, for example, paratroopers and loads of their gear had dropped in for a couple of weeks, delighting the merchants but upsetting the men in municipal works. The cleated treads of their vehicles were murder on the gravel roads.

The exercises are predicated on a war that would begin with a force of Soviet paratroopers known as Spetsnaz attacking Arctic villages and installations. Canadian defence minister Perrin Beatty has described these Spetsnazians to reporters as if he knows several personally. "Spetsnaz are basically world-class athletes, whose role it is to disrupt things by causing havoc and assassination." No one bothered to explain why the Soviet Union would fritter away its time making a stylish World War II movie in the midst of a conflict of nuclear titans. This was because the idea was absurd. Everybody knew the Canadian paratroopers were really, symbolically, pointed at the Americans. But it was rude to say so.

Traditionally, this part of the Baffin coast was the land of the Tununiarusirmiut, "the second shaded place people." Twenty miles away, in the next fiord, sat Arctic Bay, a village of 500. The mayor had declared himself in favor of the base, though he had to admit there were others who were against it. Beatty had declared there would be a full study of the impact the 600 soldiers were going to have on Inuit culture and the environment. I assumed this meant the usual round of consultation, as it was part and parcel of the announcement of the base.

Of all development in the Arctic, Inuit were most careful about criticizing the military. The strongest anti-military voice came from the Greenlanders within the Inuit Circumpolar Conference. They were still smoldering over the American expropriation of Thule for a bomber base. Alaskans tended to be American nationalists. Canadian Inuit fell in between, voting against military development at the ICC but speaking softly at home.

"We are not necessarily aiming at preventing any sort of military presence," John Amagoalik said, "we just want to make sure it doesn't go mad." They could hardly afford to give the impression of not holding up their end for defence. They could not be perceived as unpatriotic, as *disloyal*. That was the sort of thing that could get you pushed right off the cliff.

Nanisivik and Arctic Bay shrunk away to two tiny dots, stuck with each other in the middle of a big blank page. We flew toward Resolute Bay. Sovereignty town. I thought about its history, about the base there, about the base that would come to Nanisivik, about the people of Arctic Bay. What was going to happen to them?

The reigns in the Arctic are like a a human pyramid. Only: inverted. The people get more numerous and fatter towards the top.

But the skinnier people, on the lower levels, feel they have no choice but to keep the rest up. If they relax, they will be crushed.

The creation of the Inuit Circumpolar Conference in 1977 reawakened in Inuit the knowledge that their world spanned national parochialisms. Lateral air routes and satellites had helped them to leap across the yawning synoptic gaps in the neural web of their ancient memory. Yet, simultaneously, the people of the borderless expanse now sat, like everyone everywhere else, in their anchored boxes surrounded by a concentric array of boundaries. And these, to varying degrees, had been internalized.

The earnest and bespectacled Jobie Weetaluktuk, television producer, said, "As Inuit we have family members in the Soviet Union, Greenland and Alaska. They are a part of us. So as Inuit we don't have enemies. But as Canadians we do — those dictated by Americans or the NATO alliance. We have enemies as Canadian citizens."

The image of the institutionalized Other is buried as deeply in our psyche, and right alongside, the concept of territorial borders. For the Inuit, the idea of hating and fearing a whole group of people, of being in constant conflict with them, is something very new.

The Inuit way of being was to avoid confrontation at all costs. Jean Briggs has documented the signs and processes through which this was done in the camps where she has lived with the people. When conflict did occur both sides backed off. The weak were smart enough to fear the strong. The strong considered the conflict demeaning. Inuit myths were full of confrontations so resolved. In one, a fly and a water beetle have a fight. The fly buzzes the beetle and taunts it for gutlessness. The beetle promises the fly "a sharp reply." Then he turns around and walks away. "But he didn't make the slightest attempt to answer him, for he was not good at thinking up answers."

Inuit were neither angels nor innocents. Archaeological evidence shows that territorial warfare was apparently quite common among the settled and wealthy whaling communities of the Bering Strait. Nor is the history of contemporary Inuit exactly lily white. Family vendettas amongst themselves and skirmishes with Indians were common 100 years ago, although they were often consciously designed to keep casualties low. Caribou Inuit of the central Arctic staged "battles" in which opposing groups would send forth an individual at a time for a fight to the death. After a few died, peace was negotiated.

Still, Inuit maintained a fundamental belief in the stupidity of conflict. Like all of their ideas about how people ought to live together, these grew out of their iron land. They were the original pragmatists. The significant Others for them were not of this world. Like ancient peoples, the Inuit perceived their inversions, their enemies, in the dark spirits that threatened life. It was the struggle against them that united their collective, just as struggles against other peoples unite ours.

For people to fight amongst themselves, then, was just begging for trouble. This was the root of the problem elders had with the tenor of land claims negotiations. The white way of negotiating, they said, was nothing of the kind. What was the sense of negotiating if it amounted to nothing but each side trying to grab something from the other? Surely one, and probably both, would end up resentful? Surely the whites realized that resentment was a dangerous thing.

Given the behaviour of southerners, though, some felt they at least had to put up an antagonistic front. If only to be taken seriously. Noah Adglak said, "The government has taken over the land and is telling the Inuit how to control it. That's why they seem to be bitter. That's the only way to act now. Even though they are not angry they seem to be angry."

Most Inuit were first tutored in the concept of national enemies when the military arrived in the Arctic. Old Simon Keanik said, "He heard about the other white people, like Russians, who were from Europe; he was told that they were savage and that they wanted to take over the country after they kill all the white people in Canada. But he is not quite sure. And, himself, it's not his enemies."

None of them felt the visceral hatred that is meant to be part of the fun of having enemies, but the military had instilled a certain fear that some elders found hard to shake. Bezal Jesudason told me of taking an Inuk to Europe. It was this man's first trip out of the Arctic and he was nervous. Slowly it dawned on Bezal that he was more nervous in Germany than he had been in England. He was remembering all the things he had been told. And seen in the movies.

John Amagoalik said, "We understood that we had three enemies: the Japanese, the Germans and the Russians. A lot of people used to get very nervous when they saw a Japanese person. And if they heard that someone had a German name they became very suspicious. All of this was suggested to them during the Cold War, during the Fifties. I don't know why."

Many people had grown wise to the national propaganda. Gideon Qitsualik, said, "Even after the war he knows that the Russians and Americans, they are not very friendly to each other. For most of the Inuit, they talk among themselves, they are not against the Russians. Because the Americans hate them we have to hate them too. But it's not that way for us at all. And we were told that the DEW lines were built to protect us from the war, which made us feel a little bit safer in those days. But nowadays we don't feel so sure about that."

Yet the stubby remnants of the early fears remained, albeit obscured now by the mists of the continually conflicting information whites provided. Elijah Qammaniq, who worked at the Hall Beach radar station, had been hearing rumours of war for thirty years. For everyone, these had been given new force in the past decade by the arrival of television. Yet, in the absence of a translating voice — he understood virtually no English — Elijah could not make out the good guys from the bad. He would like to assist in the national enterprise of standing on guard, he said, but he could not be positive to recognize the offending face.

"He's not too sure who the enemies might be. If he was told he would try to keep an eye out too."

In its new military policy, the federal government declared its intent to increase the number of Inuit keeping an eye out by improving the equipment and training for the Canadian Rangers. Created in 1947, the Rangers are basically an army reserve unit, cousins to the khaki-clad misfits who gather Saturday mornings in southern cities. There are about 600 Rangers in Arctic communities. One can join for the asking and instantly receive an old, bolt-action rifle, a year's worth of ammunition and an armband emblazoned with the Ranger insignia, a rifle crossed with an axe. Baseball hats and T-shirts are also available, for an extra charge.

Government ministers and the media have developed the habit of calling the Rangers "sovereignty soldiers." According to military briefing notes, their main purpose is training soldiers in Arctic survival but they are also expected to perform duties such as reporting "unusual or suspicious activities within their area" and aiding "in the discovery or apprehension of enemy agents in time of conflict."

Pending the outbreak of war, Ranger staff apparently have their hands full with the onerous task of trying to whip the Inuit into soldierly form. "We certainly attempt to gradually acquaint them to basic military rules (timeliness, orders, team work, etc). However, we can only accomplish so much in each community. The training package continues to be improved and amended to keep astride the quickly changing assimilation process in the north." This had not been entirely successful. When a contingent descended on Resolute Bay for a major exercise, planned long in advance, there was not a Ranger to be found. Polar bear season had just begun and they had all gone out on the land, throwing timeliness, orders, team work etc. out the window.

When I asked Rangers what they did, the initial response was always a slightly puzzled look. No one ever asked that. I felt a little guilty doing so. I knew that once a year the army came to the village for an exercise and then the men earned $400 for a few easy days on the land teaching soldiers how to build an *iglu* or skin a seal. I knew, also, that they could pick up an extra few hundred dollars renting out their snowmobiles to the forces and that they usually found the time during these romps to get a caribou each. And I knew, most importantly, that the rifle and 200 bullets brought in food. Still, it seemed important to ask. Sometimes I got rather vague answers. "They told us at the meeting that if Queen is asking for help that we are supposed to be involved in that," a man in Resolute said. "I'm not too sure."

John Komak, of Cambridge Bay, had joined the Rangers for something to do. "I was unemployed at the time and I felt like to get out of town and practice rifle shooting."

"What do the Rangers do?"

"We look after some strange people there. We have to report them to the military service here at the DEW Line station."

"What do you mean by strange people?"

"People that you've never actually seen before. We have to talk to people and find out who they are. If they have some strange language, we have to find out who they are. We had some Russian visitors last year but they already knew who they were so we didn't have to report it. Basically it's the Russians that we have to watch out for."

"Why?"

"It's important for the people of Canada and the United States. We have to look after sovereignty. That's what they stressed. And we have to look into those situations."

"Do you worry about the Russians?"

"I think I have to worry about them because I have read about Russians there and I don't particularly care for their way of life. I like my freedom and they don't have any freedom .... I like to be on my own rather than listening to anyone talking to me or anything like that."

"Do you worry about war?"

"Not exactly. They say that eventually if they do attack we have to be prepared .... We have to be on the front line; and to encourage people to go into that kind of state if we have to go to war .... I don't worry about it. If you have to fight you have to fight .... If there are Russians there you pretty well have to fight them."

"What about the Inuit on the other side?"

"If there are Inuit people there it would be hard to identify the Inuit people. They are on the other side, we are on this side"

"Would you fight Inuit?"

"I don't think that would be necessary. I don't think Inuit should fight the other Inuit people. They should be together I would say .... And who knows what's on the other side?"

"You think there will be war?"

"I don't think so. I think people are civilized now and I don't think war will be that important nowadays."

"You think the Rangers take their role seriously?"

"Very seriously .... We look after our country here for Canada. And I guess that's what the Rangers are mainly for, for sovereignty."

"Why is that important to Inuit?"

"I don't know. Maybe because the Americans are coming into Canada as well and we have to set it up so that we keep it for Canada rather than any other country."

I edited the conversation for length. In its full form, it circles round itself in tight Kafkaesque rings of nonsensical paradox. On the face of it, I was never the slightest troubled knowing that the Canadian government puts several hundred-thousands of dollars and hundreds of serviceable weapons into the northern economy annually to keep up an Arctic brigade of Keystone Kops. I was happy to see money spent this way. But amid my little chuckles more disturbing aspects caught in my throat.

Inuit are proud of their skills and quite happy to teach anyone who wants to learn. Only the military ever asks. But there is a deep cynicism in the asking about which Inuit are not wholly disingenuous. The Canadian government employs them, for southern consumption, as flagpoles crowned with baseball caps. Meanwhile, the military attempts cynically to convince the Inuit that they are contributing to the material defence of the country.

This is the same cynicism that sends soldiers on their massive and expensive annual Arctic exercises.

But the Inuit are rather more sophisticated than the military would believe. They know their creaky old Lee Enfield rifles are really pointed at the Americans. They know, too, that in the interests of patriotism they are bound to support the rhetoric of enemies and war. They are not being paid to actually do anything, but to simply say something which none of them believes.

Until very recently, intellectual integrity was beyond question with the Inuit. Belief and existence were inseparable. They were a people among whom lying could be fatal and speculation was pointless. There were times — after my conversation with John Komak was only one of them — when I thought that the final power that the Inuit were losing, always among the last to go, was their instinct of *how* to believe. Life and philosophy had been differentiated and thus mutually obscured. The verifiable and logical had been replaced with the caveat. The weight of the caveat had replaced the genuine weight of life and the legalistic had become its artificial philosophy. There was ever less room to move and power was the only dictate of direction, the only available route of self-preservation. In this, an indelible boundary is being drawn within the culture and within individual minds. What was being lost was the purity of their inquiry into life, the closest any of us comes to something that may be called truth.

I can never think about boundaries without, by one road or another, arriving at a memory of the Berlin Wall. The quintessential border. Just our side of Checkpoint Charlie was a museum that housed a strange, eclectic collection of artifacts and art work documenting the history of the wall. There was the gondola of a hot-air balloon someone had escaped the East in, there were photos of people shot using lesser means. What I remember most clearly is a painting. It depicted a woman, neither old nor young, who was lying naked and unconscious, riven at the pelvis with a concrete wedge. She was, of course, Berlin; perhaps all of Germany. She could have been many places. She could have been the Arctic.

If the painting were to depict the most indelible border of the many that have been drawn there in the name of sovereignty, it would be a slab of iron, stamped from beneath to raise a faint impression of this woman on its face. She would be called Sila. This iron wall might be splattered with the colourful graffiti hedgings of traditional fellow-feeling, *isuma* and comical doubt. But it would be virtually unbreachable. It would be sealed with concrete arguments about the inevitability of borders and power. It would be mined extensively with national obligations. It would be a kind of iron floor which lifted the people up off the land and severed the strands of their ancient intuition. It would be the wall between nature and thought.

# Chapter Three

# Systems

I waited in the cab of the four-wheeler, parked overlooking
Iqaluit, while Chuck Tolley went inside to collect his two young
boys. On the high land across the bay, the black smoke from the
garbage dump was dispersing into a pinkening sky. Lights were
going out in the office building and coming on in houses up and
down the hillsides. Kids were horsing about in the schoolyard.
Houses were being built. The air resounded with the clat-clatter-
ing of hammers.

James and Charles were just piling into the back seat when the
radio emitted a tinny fanfare to warn that the five o'clock CBC
news was about to march through. The announcer's voice was
cheerfully urgent: "The North Warning System works! It has
detected two bombers over the Beaufort Sea. More later." More
was drowned out by the trundling of the truck as we started out
of Iqaluit along a steep and rough road. Chuck Tolley wanted to
show me what was known as the Upper Base. On one side of the
road we passed an old U.S. Air Force barracks, that now housed
college students. On the other side there was a sloping pile of a
thousand empty fuel drums that had rusted into one massive iron
blob on the hillside.

The base was at the end of the road, just beyond the crest of the hill, on a plateau of several dozen acres, overlooking the town. It was surrounded by barbed wire, but its gate sagged wide open and fresh sets of three-wheeler tracks ran through. Chuck said, "The kids come here to play and fool around." I could see why.

It was a large military base in the usual Arctic configuration: a dozen wood and tin buildings were huddled around a greying radome. There were offices, storage rooms, a kitchen, a mess hall, radar rooms and living quarters, all connected by aerial walkways and riveted to the ground with short stilts. There were a pair of candy-striped radio towers and two tropospheric transmission dishes. All of which, apparently, had come under air attack.

Walls and whole parts of buildings were ripped away, revealing white tiles, shower sockets, heating pipes, electrical outlets, water tanks, lockers, miles of piping and wiring, furniture. The mid-sections of raised walkways had been blown out; their ragged stubs creaked and drooped. Twisted metal, splintered wood and bunches of knotted cable were strewn in the snow. The mute transmission dishes still stood but the building that housed their brains had been smashed. Dynamite had felled the radio towers like a pair of giant oaks. They were crumpled to the contour of the land across a frozen lake which fed the river which fed the town.

Thirty years ago this had been a Strategic Air Command base, the fueling stop for bombers headed north. In 1959, the American military spent $6 million upgrading the airstrip on the bay below. By 1963 the whole operation had become technologically obsolete and was abandoned. It was a routine security precaution, in such cases, to blow the place to smithereens.

James and Charles gawked and said nothing. Chuck asked, "What do you think boys?" No reply. Charles offered, in a languid voice, "I don't know, Dad." Then they both stared out the window again, in silence. It was almost evening. Magic hour. The base looked like some monstrous dead animal sprawled on the plateau. Someone or something had started to gut it but got bored and strode off. Slowly, the remains were being picked apart by the big Arctic ravens with the long sharp beaks.

There are about fifty installations like this across the North. Most of what was built in the Fifties, designed for a war starring bombers and fighters, fell out of fashion when missiles came along. Canada's formal permissions for the sites had been suitably sprinkled with promises to keep the Arctic tidy — "There shall be no disposal in the north of supplies or materials of any kind …" the DEW Line agreement said — but, when the time came, everything was unceremoniously dumped.

If you didn't know better, you would think of these places as monuments to pointlessness. Chuck Tolley was like this. He had been teaching in the North for twenty years and he knew all about government claims of impecuniosity. As we left the ruins of the Upper Base, he said: "Yet we had all this money to spend on this. I don't suppose it ever really accomplished anything." I agreed, but I also knew it was not the way to the meaning of this place. Short of war, the only accomplishment anyone expects from a nuclear weapons system is that it be better than the one which preceded it and that it lay the foundation for the one which follows.

Analyst David Cox told me about working on a massive study, in collaboration with the Swedes, into the testing of nuclear explosives. Many experts had been involved. They had concluded that banning nuclear tests was the key to strangling weapons development because new missiles required constant warhead refinements. When he told me about it, the study was just about to be released. Already Cox was gloomy about the reception he felt it would — and eventually did — get. Frankly, he said, the military finds the idea of such retardation repugnant. For them, each new weapon is an evolutionary step.

The nuclear weapons system is like a great steel snake: constantly growing, and busting out of its old hide, but never going anywhere or doing anything. Just waiting. The detritus littering the Arctic is obviously an indication of incredible waste. But, more importantly, it is an indication of growth. The more bits of snake skin you saw laying about, the bigger you knew the thing had become.

At Hall Beach, if I stood in the right place, I could see three layers of electronic sediment as clearly as if I were looking at the cross-section of a rock. In the far distance, at the shore, were the 120-foot-high black monoliths that towered above the Thule ruins. These had been replaced by two microwave dishes in the middle distance, that were big as billboards and clad in grey steel. Nearer still, were two shiny, octagonal aluminum platforms, the size of school trampolines. These were the foundations for the latest step. The North Warning System was being built west to east and winter's approach had stopped construction. In the spring, new satellite dishes would be set upon the platforms. The radar stations were being rewired in preparation for a war involving the nuclear weapon of the Eighties, the cruise missile. The development of the cruise is behind much of the new military development in the Arctic. And that story is a perfect example of why the snake cannot be sated.

The Germans invented the cruise missile in the dying days of World War II and they might not have come out so badly if they had done it sooner. The missiles were basically small pilotless planes, all engine and bomb. The British called them "buzz bombs" but the Germans called them V-weapons. V was for *vergeltung*, retribution. Prominent among their inventors was one Dr. Merkwuerdigichliebe, the original Dr. Strangelove. The Nazis put a lot of hope in V-weapons but took ages to get them to work properly. Once they did, the missiles were a terrifying force because they were extremely difficult to shoot down. During two weeks in 1944, 5,000 rained on London and Antwerp, killing 1,600 people and damaging 200,000 houses. The British were so daunted that they made plans to evacuate London.

After the war, the Americans and Russians gradually refined the German handiwork. In the early Seventies, the USAF began seriously concentrating on the cruise, trying to perfect it. This work had all the horrific momentum that is characteristic of nuclear weapons production, developing as it did out of the neat coincidence of technological, industrial and bureaucratic needs. Since the Fifties, bombers had been steadily declining in strategic importance. In 1960, SAC had more than 2,000 bombers and nine intercontinental missiles. By 1970, it had 600 bombers and more than 1,700 missiles. Bomber bureaucrats did not have to be prescient to read the trend line.

At the time, the ever busy technologists working in military industries were making breakthroughs in miniaturizing electronics, jet engines and nuclear warheads. It is a truism that weapons technologists will build whatever they can imagine, simply assuming that a better weapon will find a place in the stockpile. Weapons strategies, scholars argue, are matters of capability. It has always been this way. When scientists see a possibility that is "technically sweet," Robert Oppenheimer said, they go after it and worry about the consequences later.

The combination of these imperatives produced, in three years, a weapon that was expensive, technologically unique and deadly enough to make bombers worth having once again. The final burst of enterprise came from a sort of down-home nuclear arms race in which Boeing and General Dynamics were pitted in a "fly-off" to see which had the better weapon. Boeing won and began churning out cruise missiles adapted for air, sea and land. It was the ground-launched version that later became a public relations nightmare when it was installed in Europe.

The German V1 could fly 250 miles and hit the city it was aimed at twenty per cent of the time. The American cruise could fly 3,000 miles and be almost guaranteed to hit within 100 feet of a specific building. Some claimed it could fly that far and sweep between the goal posts on a football field. In 1987 a new version was developed that was said to be able to hit the crossbar. The missile is guided by a system, manufactured in suburban

Toronto, called terrain contour mapping, which takes radar readings from the ground and compares them to the flight plan in its digitized brain. This allowed the cruise to fly at 500 miles per hour fifty feet off the ground in wide S curves around obstacles. Like a cataclysmic hummingbird. On a radar screen its image was barely visible, one-thousandth of that produced by a B52. And it was vastly superior to the comparable Soviet technology.

The original justification for the American cruise was that it could get past Soviet air defences — radars, missile bases and fighter jets — that could stop bombers. Once the Soviet technology began to improve, the Americans became nervous about their own defences. Thus began the momentum to rebuild the Arctic radars and fighter bases. The Reagan administration provided the decisive push for the Northern rebuilding programme, but, by then, it was really a forgone conclusion.

So these things go. It takes twenty years or more to develop a nuclear weapons system. Politicians are usually around for about half that. Bureaucracy and industry endure. In a study of the way nuclear weapons decisions are made, the Oxford Research Group concluded that politicians have little say in the matter. They know nothing about weapons development and routinely defer to military experts. They are well paid rubber stamps. This is true even with a programme as publicly tied to one politician as, for example, Star Wars was to Ronald Reagan. Virtually all of the research for the project was begun years before Reagan ever began jabbering about atomic astrodomes. His infatuation merely resulted in bloating the budgets and bureaucracy tremendously.

Whatever their other human attributes, people who work in the nuclear weapons system have little sense of irony. No one saw anything special about the circular cycle of developments in the Arctic. It was tediously routine. Nor did strategists smirk when they explained that the North Warning System will be obsolete by the time it was completed — as the DEW Line had been. In the early 1990s, the new imaging technology will be replaced by *new* new imaging technology, which will be mounted on satellites. There will also, by then, be a new bomber, the B1, capable of evading the new radar. It is to be followed by a newer bomber, called Stealth, which will be capable of evading the new, new radar. A line of stealthy cruise missiles is also being developed. Etcetera. Etcetera. Etcetera. Ad infinitum.

The 132 stealth bombers on order, which cost $300 million each, were being built in a town called Palmdale. "Once a small rural town with no industry to speak of," an American magazine reported, "today the fastest growing city in California."

"He's very pleased that the governments are spending so much money on the radar system and subs to protect our country," Gideon Qitsualik said. Inuit always began to answer the question like this. And then, inevitably: "But, up here in the North, if something happened to these nuclear powered submarines or weapons, if accidentally some radioactive materials happened to leak out, well we have no gardens, we have no farms, we have no trees up here to survive with. You know, gardens would be affected for a few years, it wouldn't last that long. It would not be as bad as it would on what we have up here. It's so delicate.

"Up here, whatever grows, the animals that we eat, will eat. Caribou eats plants and rabbit eats them. Seal swims around in the water and eats fish. And then, with a nuclear submarine, if something happens, a lot of them would probably die off. And then we, the Inuit, would completely die off. There's no way of surviving. Because everything we need we can't afford to buy from the Bay. If we try to live alone from the food that we buy from the stores we wouldn't be able to survive."

On this subject, Gideon was more passionate than most, but his intuition was dead common. Inuit, as I have said, did not want to be seen as unpatriotically grousing about the weapons system and most were not very worried about war. But everyone realized there was good reason to fear for the environment. Only now was it emerging that the junk piles scattered across the Arctic were not just ugly. They were poisonous too.

Forgotten within the wreckage were hundreds of electrical capacitors and transformers, some as big as desks, that had been smashed in the retreat or cracked by the cold. They were filled with thousands of litres of polychlorinated byphenyls. PCBs are a chlorine compound in clear yellow, glutinous oil that became popular with industry in the Thirties because they are fantastically resistant to heat, oxidation, acids and bases and electrical breakdown. Doctors studying mysterious illnesses in electrical workers in the Seventies found PCBs were also excellent at producing weight loss, hair loss, eye problems, jaundice, acne, intestinal damage, impotence and cancer of the liver. Only in the Eighties was a way of destroying the chemical found.

Leaking equipment drip-fed the land with PCBs for more than twenty years. Environmental bureaucrats suspected the blight but could not get the defence bureaucrats to fess up about what was actually on the sites. Between them, they mewed and memoed on the subject for several years. Finally, when plans to expand the radar system were being completed, then-environment minister David Crombie wrote to then-defence minister Robert Coates and said the chemicals had to be cleaned up immediately "if we are to avoid a major controversy." Crombie's people had warned him that the government could expect a big public hassle over the new radar system if Northerners learned the legacy of the old one.

The deal between Canada and the U.S. was signed the following year. That summer, an officiously urgent clean-up began. Two fifteen-member crews working for three government agencies collected 7200 litres of PCBs and hundreds of kilograms of soil from twenty-four sites. "The PCBs and contaminated material," said a wire story, "were packed in absorbent material, sealed in sixteen gauge metal drums and then sealed again in large metal crates." They were then flown to Hall Beach, from where the USAF transported them to Alaska. Okay, they said, wiping their hands: Pristine again. Just like it used to be. Three years later it was discovered that buildings in the villages of

Igloolik and Hall Beach, fashioned from military waste, were still contaminated.

The image of Northerners gratefully mining piles of lethal military junk as if they were naturally occurring hardware seams has great resonance. I think, for example, of Brazilian Natives prying open a discarded radium capsule and being so amazed by its luminous splendour that they passed it around their village for days before its true and awful nature was discovered. The meaning of such stories, however, is not just that the understandable ignorance of aborigines puts them in greater danger from the murderous side-effects of modern technology. The real import is that these effects are proliferating and scattering without anyone, including their inventors, knowing or understanding them. Among the contaminated buildings in Igloolik was a federal government scientific research station.

In 1985, scientists were shocked and amazed to find PCBs, heavy metals and pesticide residues in the livers of polar bears, in seals and in fish. As this became widely known, Canadian government spokesmen fell all over themselves denying the contamination could be blamed on local military or industrial operations. Probably they were right. Probably the majority of poisoning was from chemicals migrating to the Arctic from the south and slithering up the food chain in increasing concentrations. But scientists can never be sure. Only very recently have they begun to understand the vastly complex connections between plants, animals and their environment. As it happened this work was largely pioneered in the Arctic by scientists tracing the pathways of the most insidious by-product of military technology. Everything Gideon instinctively knew about the land's sensitivity and about the pathways of toxins, scientists confirmed twenty years ago by following the bright trail of radiation poisoning.

In Resolute Bay I met a man called Wayne Davidson, who had made an obsessive hobby of studying radioactive contamination in the Arctic. Davidson was a weatherman — an Upper Air Technician, to be precise. He exuded what I came to think of as the Arctic Upper Air Technician's Righteous Indignation about the treatment of the Inuit. He lived in the Resolute base in a room claustrophobic with clutter and pervaded with the steady hum of electronic equipment. When I arrived, his bed and bureaus were piled high with reports, colour-coded graphs from his computer and bulletins from sympathetic accomplices in Scandinavia and Alaska. He said, "Have I got a news story for you!" From a journalistic viewpoint, it was not particularly new. It was his, though; if only because of the passion with which he told it and the fact that he was one of few who could be bothered to do so.

Scientists have known for decades that the Inuit took the brunt of the radiation poisoning from most American and Soviet atmospheric bomb tests. These totalled more than 300 explosions before they were banned in 1962. Only people who lived right beside test grounds swallowed more of the fallout. Seven years after the ban, Inuit had radiation concentrations twenty to 200 times greater than those in southerners. What was extraordinary about the numbers was that they were not a measure of fallout, but of sensitivity. The circulation of radioactive particles through the earth's atmosphere is such that the heaviest fallout in North America came down roughly along the forty-ninth parallel. The Arctic received about one-quarter as much as southern Canadian cities. But that had a much greater impact because of the way the Arctic ecosystem works.

The humble foundations of the Arctic food chain are the rootless mosses called lichen. These survive in the frigid, arid climate by lying dormant in the winter and becoming extremely efficient sponges during the three summer months, sucking nutrients and moisture from the air. Like all plants, they crave potassium. Among the radionuclides prominent in fallout is Cesium 137, an analog of potassium. Clever as lichen are, they can't tell the difference. Consequently they suck Cesium out of the air as voraciously as if it were the real thing.

Temperate zone ecosystems have a rapid growth rate, because of their wealth of rain and sunshine, which constantly renews life. Pollutants wash out of plants fairly quickly and are moved onward through the soil and water. And warm climates are flexible. The multitude of species of plants and animals disperses the effects of pollution. The sound of life in the temperate zones is a cacophony of racing heartbeats. In the Arctic, it is a strong, slow thumping. Arctic plants and animals are resilient and adapted to the cold through a variety of ingenious strategies, but the paucity of water and sunshine makes for an extraordinarily languorous rate of renewal.

And the ecosystem is a model of simplicity. Which means it is also a house of cards. The Arctic supports relatively few species but often in great abundance. Life is painted with a broad brush in few strokes, here and there, on a canvas of almost unimaginable size. Wild, though cyclical, fluctuations of growth and death are the norm. Pollutants or other stresses striking a population at the wrong point on the wave may thus send it crashing irrevocably downward.

So: lichen cling like the starving to whatever they get hold of and retained ninety-five per cent of the radioactive fallout. Cesium 137 is a long lasting radionuclide, taking thirty years to decay to half of its strength, all the while emitting penetrating gamma radiation, similar to x-rays. Caribou live largely on lichen, exclusively so during the spring and autumn when there are no fresh grasses. Because it takes as long as five months for Cesium to be worked out of their systems, the great tawny herds migrating northward in springtime during the Sixties practically glowed in the dark. They had ingested as much as ten times the amount of Cesium now considered "acceptable" as well as other radionuclides, like strontium, which built up in their bones.

Inuit, of course, live on caribou. The more than two million caribou drifting on the Arctic plains are to that land what wheat is to the rest of the Northern Hemisphere. At each stage in the chain, the radiation was concentrated and passed onward, in ever more lethal amounts. Ultimately it passed to the next generation.

In the late Sixties, scientists found the breast milk of women living in Baker Lake was as much as 100 times more radioactive than that of women in Montreal.

Fallout decreased when the Soviets and Americans starting blowing their loads underground, but it didn't stop. Radioactive discharges from power plants found their way to the Arctic as did the fallout from Chinese atmospheric bomb tests. Then came Chernobyl. The background radiation in caribou meat was already as much as forty times higher than in southern beef before the Ukrainian reactor came unhinged and the explosion pushed the levels up by as much as one-third. Inuit got off easily compared to other northerners. The irradiation of reindeer in Scandinavia was so severe that the Sami culture, already imperilled for all the usual reasons, was pushed to the brink of collapse.

"But if these levels had been found in southern beef," Wayne Davidson said, "people would have screamed murder." He was a man who spoke so quickly and excitedly that he was always on the verge of hyperventilation. What came out was a torrent of accusation backed up by a flurry of papers, document after document to substantiate his arguments. Every one of the dozens of studies since the Sixties had noted the persistence of the problem and called for more study, but no one ever got around to warning the Inuit of the seasonal contamination of their food.

"The government was more interested in the pathways of radiation. They wanted to know how long it stayed in people, and whether they got more from eating this or that. They studied native people for a long time, but they never told them to avoid eating the spring caribou."

After Chernobyl, Davidson badgered government officials to do so. In this he was joined by Dr. Rosalie Bertell, one of the world's leading experts on low-level radiation. She argued that, when all the numbers were crunched, Inuit were being exposed to levels of radiation that were both intolerable and illegal. The government responded, as it had for two decades, by arguing that the levels were within "acceptable limits." Disinterested scientists have been saying for at least twenty years that there is no such thing. Every increase in radiation exposure adds to the illnesses within a population. Nevertheless, the debate over the fitness of the spring caribou became a media battle of numbers. Davidson's side lost. It is the way of the Media to believe that the government always has the best numbers. Also to bore easily.

People around the Resolute base thought of Davidson as an eccentric. They called him Wacky Wayne. When I went to pick up some documents from him at the weather station, his boss gave him hell for talking to me during working hours. As I left, the boss stopped me in the hallway. He tried to explain that, frankly, he sort of admired Wacky Wayne for trying to help the Inuit. He just didn't think it should be done on government time.

And Wayne said: "There's been a cycle of radiation into these people since the Sixties. Nobody has ever put this together before for a very typical reason. Which is that nobody cares about native people."

This is true, of course. Particularly so when the military is involved. I think, for example, of the people of the Marshall Islands in the Pacific who had their homeland blasted to bits by American nuclear weapons tests and were deliberately contaminated to provide "valuable ecological radiation data on human beings." They now give birth to a form of life the women there call "jellyfish babies." Or of Mururo Atoll invaded by the French military for the same purpose with the same result. Or of American Navajo reserves that were exposed to the dirtiest atmospheric weapons tests and now have four to five times the national rate of birth defects. Or the Innu of Labrador with NATO fighter jets screaming over them at tree-top level, scaring, so the people say, caribou calves right out of the womb. Or the Serpent River Indian Band in northern Ontario with their water supply contaminated by uranium tailings. Or the Metis and Dene in Alberta whose land was expropriated for a weapons testing range. To name a few.

Convenient genocide, though, is not the whole story. I think there is a more profound reason why governments are reluctant to make the kind of admission involved in telling Inuit they cannot eat caribou anymore, even for half the year; the kind of admission that Rosalie Bertell's work demanded. After fifteen years of assembling global data on various kinds of fallout, Bertell had arrived at the conclusion that some sixteen million people, in every region of the earth, had been affected by radiation poisoning. Military development was to blame for most of it. This, she argued, was the true cause of the increasing incidence of many illnesses — from cancers to children's hyperactivity to male impotence — that were routinely blamed on bad genes or bad faith or God. "Thus," she wrote, "a death process is underway."

Bertell is a diminutive, soft-spoken Grey Nun with a masters degree in biology, a doctorate in mathematics and an extensive background in epidemiology. She has been lauded by groups around the world. She could hardly be more credible. But governments, particularly in Canada and the U.S. where she has worked, don't want to know. To accept what she says would be to admit that the system by which they ostensibly protect their lands and populations is off the rails. And the most they can do about it is advise people not to eat.

The protection of a country's territorial sovereignty by military means, by attempting to build walls, is the highest priority for most governments. This is obvious both from the amounts of money spent and the fact that the military is given a carte blanche accorded no other department. Nothing is ever too much to protect the nation's lives and livelihoods. Nowhere in Canada is this as obvious as it is in the Arctic. Nor anywhere is it more obviously a mug's game.

Radiation is not the half of it. The structure of the air and water currents of the northern hemisphere are such that the Arctic is becoming one huge pollution sinkhole. Fresh water rivers around the pole, the Gulf Stream and the North Atlantic Drift combine to drive a steady torrent of chemicals, oils, metals and plastics into the Arctic Ocean. There they become locked in time, the low temperatures and ice cover preventing them from breaking down. "The Arctic Ocean Basin," said a 1987 Canadian government report, "is the ultimate depository for the unwanted persistent chemicals produced by much of the world's industry." Actually: the penultimate depository. Last stop before the people. Some of the Inuit of Thule, for example, have levels of mercury in their blood that approach the point of poisoning. Seals wash up on northern shores in increasing numbers, either killed by pollution or because they become entangled in plastic garbage and drown.

The same sort of thing is happening with air pollution. In winter, the Arctic air mass extends southward as far as the fortieth parallel where prevailing winds pick up a fine mist of sulfates, soot and hydrocarbons from Europe and the Soviet Union and carry it north. In winter and spring, the region sits beneath a pall scientists call Arctic Haze, a ghostly smog so dense it can reduce visibility from 200 kilometres to twenty.

The Greenhouse Effect — the gradual climatic warming caused by carbon dioxides shot into the atmosphere from burning fossil fuels — is thought to be potentially self-reinforcing in the Arctic. The water produced by melting ice will retain more of the sun's heat, possibly making the warming trend three to four times as severe in the Arctic as elsewhere. The depletion of the ozone layer is worst over the polar regions. Both poles have severe ozone holes above them, caused by chlorofluorocarbons (a.k.a. hairspray propellents). A joint Canadian-Soviet polar expedition in the winter of 1987 found itself being inexplicably fried, apparently because of the ultraviolet light now drenching the region. Among other things, the bombardment is known to threaten marine life by killing off the lowest rung on the chain, plankton.

As devastating as all these trends will likely turn out to be for the people of the Arctic, they will not, of course, suffer alone. For more than 100 years it has been well known that the climate of the Arctic has a profound impact on that of the rest of the world. The reduction of ice cover, for example, and the attendant warming of the Arctic atmosphere, is thought to decrease the circulation of the planet's air masses. The impacts of this are felt around the world, from the reduction of rain in Europe to the worsening of drought in the Sahel — and thus the promotion of starvation in Africa.

Scientists first began studying these effects in 1882, when the First International Polar Year was held. One hundred years later, they freely admit that they have only a vague idea of the processes involved, let alone of their effects combined with the toxic impacts of modern military and industrial technology. This was abundantly clear at an international symposium called *Arctic Heritage* held in Banff in 1985. After listening to the presentation of papers on various aspects of the Arctic environment, Fred Roots, chief environmental scientist for the Canadian government, summarized: "Our knowledge of natural arctic processes is very uneven. Although we have heard many times that data on arctic characteristics and phenomena and populations are incomplete, or too few, or unrepresentative, on the whole it appears that, except in some areas of marine biology, where data are very sparse indeed, *we know more about what is there than we understand how it works.*"

Some know more than others. Two years later, in a report to the federal government, Roots wrote that the military, with its endless resources and technology, was hoarding much of the physical knowledge about the Arctic. "It has moved many areas of important scientific arctic research away from the influence of organizations and interests primarily concerned with the north to that of interests and organizations concerned with military power and global strategies .... Much of the most sophisticated and significant arctic knowledge has become 'closed' and inaccessible to exchange among northern peoples and northern scientists at large."

This went beyond irony, really, well into the realm of the surreal. With the First International Polar Year, every national government around the pole acknowledged that the importance of the region was global, that what happened in the Arctic happened to everybody. More than 100 years later, they still made occasional and cursory bows to this idea. All have signed a modicum of agreements for mutual scientific study of Arctic environmental and climatological issues and all talk a good game of cooperation. But the main enterprise in the region remains the construction of military walls.

The very essence of the power of national governments is derived from their maintenance of territorial sovereignty. Their walls are the limits to their reign but from them the power flows inward. To admit that those walls cannot hold back the most serious of threats, cannot really protect, strikes to the core of that power. The problem is, more or less, pathological.

In many of her works, historian Barbara Tuchman has documented the relationship between the desire for power and the efficacy of judgement. This was her specific subject in *The March of Folly*, where she analyzed six cases of leaders willfully refusing to change course as they charged toward certain disaster. She wrote, "Folly is a child of power. We all know ... that power corrupts. We are less aware that it breeds folly; that the power to command frequently causes the failure to think; that the responsibility of power often fades as its exercise augments."

Gideon Qitsualik said, "Building all these things that they are building right now, nuclear submarines and things like that, he figures it's not protecting our country at all. Because it just makes everything worse."

Captain Larry Pauling was eager to talk about sovereignty. This I found rather surprising, until I got to know him a little. For Captain Pauling these questions were bound to have a double edge. He was a U.S. Air Force quality-control officer who worked out of the radar station at Cambridge Bay on Victoria Island. He was the only American military officer who was involved with the operation of the radar line full time, but he had the power to tell everyone else what to do. He was well liked nonetheless. You just could not help but like his exuberant, black, Texan how-the-hell-are-yaness. Call him Larry. Everyone said he was a huge improvement over his predecessor, who was the sort of up-tight nit-picker people did want to find themselves stranded with in the middle of nowhere. Larry was happy to talk about anything. He had the conviction of his arguments.

He said, "You know, Kevin, there's a lot of this sovereignty talk right now. And not just in Canada. I've been all over the world and I know in a lot of countries people would like to run things for themselves. Like in Greenland now there's a lot of this sovereignty talk. But what people don't understand is the threat. You have to be prepared for the threat" — a big smile now, like a burst of sunshine — "and that takes money. The U.S. has a lot of money."

Larry talked and talked in that vein and I enjoyed it immensely. Then he took my tape away. "I just have to check it out with my boss." I never got it back. It was strange. I kept trying to figure out what he had said that his boss would have disagreed with.

Hardly anyone I met in the Arctic didn't understand the threat. Inuit may not have considered the Soviets enemies, but everyone was clear — in an amorphous way — on the general nature and weaponry of the conflict. Everywhere I went the nuclear weapons system was on the move in a way it had not been since the Fifties. The developments were well-publicized. People in the Arctic were used to seeing weapons hardware and their reactions to it were local ones — about the environment and noise mostly. And many people found the military exciting.

Submarines, for example, always caused a real stir. One afternoon, a few winters ago, weather technicians working at the extremely remote Mould Bay station on Prince Patrick Island found themselves inexplicably shrouded in a thick fog, which meant to them a break in the ice. Soon they picked up the radio chatter of a surveillance plane overhead. The seismologist's machine detected a wave form with a steadily increasing amplitude which he took to be a submarine propeller approaching. Peering into the fog and straining to hear backchat through the static, the fellows of the station were thrilled. One said, "You actually hope someone's going to invade you. You know, make the news, make the TV." They never found out if it was really a sub. But it was a great story to tell.

In some coastal villages, like Pond Inlet, sub sightings are fairly common. Every once in a while a couple of hunters will look up and there, just offshore, will be a black, eyeless whale of a boat as big as a skyscraper. People got a kick out of this sort of thing. Especially kids. Once I was having tea with a couple when their six kids burst in for lunch. In the lead were the two youngest, six-year-old twin boys. It was Halloween and there was a costume party going on at the school. The twins were dressed as cowboys with identical Gary Cooper mustaches. They were apoplectic with excitement. A jet fighter had just ripped the sky in half and done a barrel-roll right over the village.

"Kids like weapons," Jobie Weetaluktuk, the reporter, said, "because weapons are toys." We were watching video tapes the Inuit Broadcasting Corporation had shot of a public demonstration day during Operation Lightning Strike in Iqaluit. In one clip the town boys were being taught to fire machine guns and were pretending to shoot each other. In another, the little heads of a dozen kids stuck out through the open turret of a tank, forming a kind of Jacobean frilly collar for the green- helmeted driver. Village men quizzed the soldiers on their dried rations, which they allowed would be handy for hunting. Others ran about being Rangers. It was a carnival, livening a Saturday. "This helps the military," said Jobie dryly, "to be more acceptable."

About what the military was actually doing, people had no idea. Even men who had worked on the radar line for years did not really know what it did. They felt constrained talking about this, but they really didn't have much to say. "It supposed to be guard, Russian guard. They watch the screens all the time, watch the planes go over there." They said things like that. "We're not supposed to talk to the people about it," Alan Ayak said, "anyway I don't know." When I asked Mathew Ehaloak what the military was doing, Joe Koaha, who was translating, listened to the answer, smiled and repeated: "It don't matter to Mathew." Jonah Anguilianuk said, "It protects everybody in the north."

Sometimes southern men living in the Arctic intimated a certain knowledge of these matters. "I'm just interested," a town official said one day on the subject of fighter bases, "because I think the whole thing's ridiculous ...." I perked up. I always enjoyed anti-weapons tirades from people who did not make them for a living. ..."Because, I mean, from a strategic point of view, if you want to interdict, the locations are all wrong ...." I was disappointed. Moreover, he knew nothing of substance. This was the adult equivalent of pretending to shoot machine guns.

Even the soldiers and technicians working in the military sites could not *really* say what was going on. Of course they knew the basic scheme, but there were huge, intentional gaps in their information. Major Bob Stephens was the Canadian commanding officer at Cambridge Bay. Down the hall from his office was an American government bureau called the Defence Mapping Agency. "They really have no DEW Line function," Major Stephens said. "What their job is I have no idea." Among other things, according to analyst William Arkin, it is to collect electronic data on the size, shape and features of the land which is converted into digital information and used to programme cruise and other nuclear missiles.

Military security relied on the compartmentalization of information. Despite his rank, there were commands, for example, that Major Stephens was not allowed to know. These were encoded in what was called crypto and for the eyes only of American nationals, who were hired for the purpose. At one site the man who guarded these was a swarthy Hispanic who seemed to have convinced himself that I intended to make a grab for his official decoder the minute he unfolded his arms. I gave him the berth I usually reserved for sled dogs. What sort of codes did he guard? "Codes," said the major, "to identify planes, particularly in a wartime scenario."

I had pressed this issue from a sovereignty point of view with the commanding officer in Hall Beach, Major George Sykes. It only annoyed him. He leaned forward of the enormous Canadian and RCAF flags on the wall behind his desk and said, "This is North American defence we are talking about. This isn't Canadian defence. The sovereignty portion is really not an issue here. We are partners with the United States in the defence of the North American continent."

Major Stephens said, "I am not supposed to know and therefore I don't know."

Even if you wanted to, even if you were supposed to, *knowing* the breadth and complexity of the nuclear weapons system is essentially impossible. It involves consuming a mountain of figures and details. The only people who even approach the task — the strategic experts — tend to be locked within the system by their very knowledge of its arcane and inexpressible mysteries. They are a kind of high priesthood; their pronouncements intelligible only to one another.

From the viewpoint of the people who run the system, the fewer that *know* the better. The history of secrecy, suppression, lying and laundering of information about nuclear weapons is older than the things themselves. After studying this history, the American journalist Robert Karl Manoff wrote, "It is a system that maintains deterrence by mobilizing science, technology, industry and politics. But it is also a system that maintains itself by organizing the knowledge that all this other activity requires." In the radar stations there were signs warning people to be careful with their two cents worth. "Other People Slyly Eavesdrop Continually," they said.

There are complex reasons why most North Americans do not really concern themselves with the possibility of nuclear war. One is that most of us have never known war and cannot quite imagine what it must be like. We are not dogged by the memories that haunt Europeans of a certain age nor even surrounded by the landmarks that give these memories some force among their children. Most of us have not endured the savage proxy butchery taking place in a dozen southern countries. We have been inordinately lucky. Uniquely so, historically speaking. Another, perhaps paradoxical, reason, offered by psychologists, is that nuclear war is so awful to dwell on that people cannot stand even to fear it consciously. "Psychological numbing," they call this.

My feeling most often is that people think nuclear war is impossible. This is what we have been told for four decades and what the vast majority of us believe. We have absorbed the political rhetoric that the weapons are irrelevant given the presumed force of human unwillingness to consent to — even to imagine — their use. *Unthinkable* we call a war that we know is not undoable.

The political climate of the Eighties created a whole school of popular writing that attempted to explode this myth. Gwynne Dyer in Canada, Thomas Powers in the United States, Duncan Campbell in Britain all come to mind for their careful explanations that the nuclear weapons system is not merely set up to threaten, it is set up to fight. "Everything we have done is consistent with preparation for war," Powers wrote in *Thinking About the Next War*. "When the war comes we shall fight it with the weapons at hand, and these prominently include nuclear weapons." The proliferation of this sort of opinion helped to create the public fear that has made a rapprochement between the superpowers popular. Yet, there remains, I think, a belief deep in the public mind that the whole system is one colossal bluff. Military men take a different view.

In my limited experience, they are not a great deal more ideological than most people but they are of course professionally committed to the efficacy of arms. "I don't want to categorize all enemies as Soviets," Major Sykes said. His tone made me feel presumptuous for the way I had phrased my question. "I'm not going to say who the enemy is because I don't know who the enemy is. Under today's world conditions anyone is a potential enemy." This was practically the eve of the 1987 Washington summit between Ronald Reagan and Mikhail Gorbachev, so Major Sykes might have meant that anyone in this world is a potential friend. But that was not what I understood him to be saying.

Younger men seemed to need the fire of anger more but they were no less business-like discussing their duties. Take Captain David Chausson. Talking with him about radar capabilities I happened to mention "the KAL accident." In a tone that let me know I was the gullible sort, he said, "A lot of people don't think it was an accident." He did not resort to name-calling when he spoke of the Soviets, but his opinion was clear.

Captain Chausson was an Air Weapons Controller. "A good comparison," he said, "is an air traffic controller. Everybody knows what that is. He keeps aircraft apart. My job is to bring them together." Specifically, through the use of radar, he guided jet fighters to attacking bombers. Normally he worked from a command post in North Bay, Ontario, the Canadian NORAD headquarters, which is hardened to withstand a nuclear blast. He and two female assistants had been sent to Cambridge Bay to conduct tests on the North Warning System radar, which had just been installed. The object was to determine how well he would be able to do his job from the station. It was a two-week assignment, half way through, and the women were already dying to get home. They couldn't *stand* being out in the middle of nowhere with nothing to do at night, though it wasn't quite Armed Forces to say so. In the evenings they amused themselves playing video games which, they said, wasn't really all that different from work. Sometimes, say, you would be working — practicing with a couple of planes on your screen. And all of a sudden one of the guys would key on without saying anything and start coming at you with another. Just to freak you out. *Guys.*

The premise of their tests was that the shit had hit the fan — "Increased tension or world events," was how Capt. Chausson put it, "that when analyzed by our leaders indicate perhaps hostilities are imminent" — and the North Bay post was in danger of being cut off from the Arctic radars. Teams of Air Weapons

Controllers would be fanned out to the northern sites to guide CF18 fighters against attacking bombers. No one knows these things for sure, but the chances are pretty good that by the time that was necessary we would be on the brink of a general nuclear war. Given the porcelain fragility of the radar sites themselves, Capt. Chausson would only be able to do his job if it was a war started by our side. "The function of the North Warning System," David Cox wrote of a Soviet attack, "would be served when it was destroyed immediately prior to the arrival of hostile forces."

Captain Chausson had, of course, considered the potential product of his work. "This is just a personal opinion but if one thinks of a nuclear conflict it's something that I think to any rational person is very frightening. Something like that is horrific on any scale. I personally hold a belief that there are too many rational people in this world to let something like that happen because there could not possibly be any victors in a conflict like that."

Mind: "When you sign on that dotted line you are signing the ultimate liability, which is to give your life for your country .... It's just something that you live with, something that you have committed yourself to do .... You have entered a community, a military community and they are paying your salary in return for your services and if it is a true commitment when you sign on the dotted line you know that you will carry through with it. You have to."

I have met another kind of soldier whose personal axioms drew rather less on such canons of duty and valour and rather more on comic books. The major who briefed me on the Spetsnaz operation was one of the these. "It wouldn't be a shoot-'em-up sort of a thing with a massive number of troops," he said. "What you'd do is just send in a bunch of your fighters with some napalm and bomb their supply base and let them freeze to death." I spoke to this major in downtown Ottawa, late on a Friday afternoon in January. Afterward, I waited for a bus outside the Department of Defence building, in a queue with military bureaucrats and schoolgirls. Both, in their respective uniforms, were a-titter with the weekend. The streets had the soft, woolen edge particular to Friday afternoons in the wintertime. The windows of pubs were steaming up, people were bundling their provisions homeward, the yellow lights were coming on along the Rideau Canal. It was snowing lightly. *You'd just send in your fighters with some napalm and bomb their supply base and let them freeze to death.*

The funny thing about this major was that he was in the department's public relations directorate. Euphemisms, the asbestos tiles that keep military theory from burning up in the atmosphere of common sense, were apparently unknown to him. He was sort of heinously refreshing.

Late one afternoon I arrived in Yellowknife for an interview with Brigadier General Patrick O'Donnell, who, kindly, had agreed to stay late in his office. Brig. Gen. O'Donnell was commander of the Canadian Forces Northern Region. Ostensibly the headquarters for the Canadian military in the Arctic, the office in downtown Yellowknife really amounted to a combination public relations firm and travel agency. The real action, command-wise, was in Ottawa, Washington and Colorado. Brig. Gen. O'Donnell had a meticulous and gentle manner and I could imagine him in many other professions. Medicine, perhaps.

We talked of the various facets of the weapons system, of the growth of the military in the Arctic, of strategies. "It is not technically what you could describe as a grand militarization of the north," he said. More accurately, it was an improvement of capabilities. Toward the end of the interview, as always, I asked his opinion of the prospects for war. He had faith, he said, in deterrence. But what if it failed, as all military planning assumed it might?

"The response is very scenario-dependent," he said. "If you were to have an all-out, no-holds-barred nuclear holocaust, right from minute one, from ground zero, then there might not be very much left to respond with. Let alone there not being a whole lot of value in it, I suppose. But if you start at the other end of the spectrum and consider a much more limited attack, then, of course, your capability and the effectiveness of your response could be extremely telling."

He assumed it would never come to this. "You hope not; but you feel confident that you can respond."

The soldiers I met in the Arctic all shared this view. They believed, with the public, that there would be no war. But they still had to set their workaday minds to the business at hand. They were neither heroic nor hot-headed in this. When they spoke of their Soviet counterparts it was usually with more professional respect and less rancour than one hears among businessmen discussing competitors. Theirs was a quiet confidence as they went about attending to the myriad logistical details of preparing for a general nuclear war.

The weapons exist in a netherworld. The idea that they form a wall across the Arctic is, of course, an abstraction, an anachronistic metaphor. Politicians and journalists speak of lines of defence and seem to imagine something from World War I, like a trench filled with machine guns. This is a product of maps — on which the weapons look like barriers or armies coiled to charge — and of our intentions — which we take to be wholly defensive. Everyone recognizes that these are crude, inaccurate metaphors, but they are easy. They do not, however, give a sense of how the thing works.

As one unaccustomed to weaponry, when I walked around a radar station, certain details resonated: the green trucks, the segmented radome, the obelisks, the administrative voodoo; a fighter jet ripping straight up off the horizon, leaving a vapor trail that splits the sky. They gave you an unpleasant feeling, but nothing you could use in an argument.

For the Inuit the netherworld was the province of the spirits who contained within themselves the possibilities of life and death. When Inuit were disrespectful of life, they believed, the spirits reacted by unbalancing their world. Hunger or illness or bad weather visited a camp. Then it was the job of the shaman to travel to the netherworld and attempt to mediate. The Dorset made a carving of a flying polar bear, its arms straight back along its body. Soaring. An intricate skeletal pattern was engraved on the outside, like a three-dimensional x-ray image. The figures are believed to represent the shaman's embodiment in the bear's form, which carried him or her to places not given to normal humans to visit. There negotiations were conducted with the spirits to restore equilibrium.

Say we were to go on such a journey around the circumpolar Arctic, a kind of commoner's spirit inspection tour. To make the abstraction real. Consider the big picture.

Flying north of Hall Beach, you veer toward Greenland, with the intent of circling the Arctic Ocean. If you were high enough you would look down upon a sea that is almost entirely enclosed. It is a climactic mirror image of the Mediterranean, but five times larger. There are only a few places to sail into it: the Bering Strait, between the USSR and Alaska, the Davis Strait, between Canada and Greenland and the chasm in the coast line between Greenland and Scandinavia, across the North Atlantic. In winter, the entire surface of the Arctic Ocean would be covered in ice that pushes out from its centre and jams every crevice in the coast line, encasing every island. Between spring and autumn, this recedes slightly but most of the ocean remains beneath the polar cap, a continent-like table of ice an average of five metres thick. Skulking beneath it would be American and Soviet submarines carrying intercontinental nuclear missiles.

For decades, submarines were seen as the spoil sports of nuclear weaponry, preventing either side from thinking it could ever win a nuclear war. When they put to sea they became virtually invisible. Even if either presumed itself certain of destroying the other's land-based missiles and bombers, it could never be so sure about submarines. Missiles fired from submarines were not very accurate, but simple murderous revenge doesn't take much accuracy. Flying over the Soviet Arctic coast, just east of northern Finland, you would pass above the Kola Peninsula, the only part of the Soviet coast that is always ice-free. Most Soviet submarines are berthed here and rarely leave, whereas the Americans let theirs roam the world's oceans. Until recently, if war came, Soviet strategy was to disperse their submarines into the North Atlantic. The corresponding American plan was to station attack submarines between Greenland and Scandinavia to stop them. Technology changed all that.

Anti-submarine warfare is a matter of listening. Every sound made in a submarine, from the whir of engines to sailors chatting in their bunks, radiates outward through the hull. Sound travels five times faster in water than air and vastly further. Submarines scan the sea with hydrophones and process what they record through computers, to separate the cries of whales from the churn of propellers. The technology has become so advanced that talking is banned on submarines when they are in sneaking mode. The Americans brag they can discern individual Russian submarines by their audio scent. The paraphernalia of being able to wage a submarine battle, then, includes elaborate networks of hydrophones, computers and torpedoes operated from submarines as well as ships, planes and helicopters. But none of it works very well in the Arctic Ocean.

The Arctic pack ice, which seems as immutable as land from above, is a surface in constant turmoil. Enormous plates, driven by wind and current, continually jam against each other. Ridges are suddenly driven upward and dagger-like keels thrust as much as fifty metres down into the sea, creating a terrific racket of growling and explosion. It is, in general, a bad place for a submarine war. Submarines can be trapped or have their hulls ripped open or lose the several mile-long radio antennas they drag or be stuck beneath ice too thick to surface through. And they can have an extremely tough time finding their enemy in the shifting, roaring seascape. To take advantage of this, the Soviets have developed technology to fire accurate missiles from their Arctic bases and a strategy of keeping their submarines there. The Americans responded with a plan to send fleets of their submarines into the Arctic to attack the Soviets. But they don't intend to wait for a nuclear war to do so.

The American Maritime Strategy is a great example of what people mean when they talk about nuclear war fighting plans. Plan A is not to fight one if you can help it. Plans B through Z involve exponentially more complex manoeuvres which fall under the rubric of what nuclear theologians call "escalation dominance." This means being dominant as the war escalates. It is a fancy way of saying winning. The idea is to keep upping the ante without causing so much damage that the Soviets launch a desperate and massive *vergeltung* attack. One plans to smash a command post here, obliterate a missile base there, until they get the point. What strategists really hope for is something like the scenes in cowboy movies where the bad guy gets the drop on the hero, only to find that the hero's lame sidekick has the drop on him. This is called "extended deterrence." It means creating a long, long string of lame sidekicks to effect a corresponding chain of stupid-faced bad guys.

Nuclear theologians put a lot of store in good luck and weak bellies. The American Maritime Strategy is this: The Americans want the Soviets to think that, at the first sign of war, they (the Americans) are prepared to sink their (the Soviet's) nuclear missile submarines, thus destroying much of their ability to fight a nuclear war. The Soviets are meant to reason further that this threat is more likely to make them (the Soviets) so afraid of losing their submarine missiles that they would want to launch them immediately. Just to be on the safe side. This, of course, would initiate the Holocaust. The Soviets are *therefore* expected to back down. Because: who wants to initiate the Holocaust? This is one kind of "extended deterrence" — convincing the other guy that you will make him blow up the world if he so much as looks at you the wrong way. The nuclear theorist Thomas Schelling defined this kind of thing as "rocking the boat." The Americans reckon that once the Soviets see all those U.S. Navy submarines swarming beneath the polar cap they will reach for the sky. This is the game the Canadian Navy hopes to join with its planned nuclear submarines.

Both sides are now refining gadgetry to help them fight despite the ice — hulls that can break through it, hydrophones that can drill through it, radio systems that can transmit through it. And both are constantly patrolling, mapping and trailing each other around, trying to determine what the other knows and what each can get away with; the Soviets advancing possibly as far as the edge of the Canadian Arctic islands, the Americans going as far and brazenly toward the U.S.S.R. as to have entered Soviet ports.

So: as you flew over the Arctic Ocean, you would see black tubular shapes beneath the opaque ice cap, advancing toward each other and then receding. As if on a single pivot.

Above the ocean the sky would be even busier with traffic of a similar sort. Periodically you would encounter planes like the Canadian Aurora, sweeping low over the sea, trying to spot submarines. There would be spy planes, also, AWACS radar planes and planes carrying troops and supplies. But mostly there would be bombers and fighter jets, each side sending its bombers towards the other to see how far they can get before fighter jets show up to turn them around.

Asking the military about these interactions is like posing the optimist/pessimist query with half a glass of water. One cannot be sure whether they consider this play or war or whether they can tell the difference. A happy young flyer described Soviet bombers meeting Canadian fighters over the Arctic islands as if it were an airborne, nuclear-armed frat party. "Sometimes, the crews wave at each other. You know, they will hold up a *Playboy* or a can of Coke. It's a bit of a game ... uh ... of course ... it's a *serious* game." Brigadier General Patrick O'Donnell spoke of the nuclear confrontations — "we respond to these incursions as though they're the real thing" — in a tone that suggested these were just so many memos being faxed back and forth — "it is just a very standard quid pro quo if you would."

Taking this trip on certain days we might also spot the slender shape of a cruise missile, the length of an old Buick, flying with strange, articulate movements on a circuitous test path over the Arctic archipelago. Fighters would be flying alongside, practicing at tracking and intercepting it, pretending they were fighting a nuclear war. Directly opposite, one might chance to see an intercontinental ballistic missile arcing above the Soviet Arctic coast from the far west to the far east. Also just testing.

And on china white cliffs and slate plains around the entire coast of the Arctic Ocean you would see military sensors of every sort: radar sites, listening posts, communications transmitters. Overhead, military satellites spin in polar orbit. Beneath the sea, in the gaps between the continents, strings of hydrophones bob at anchor. If you could see across the electromagnetic spectrum, the entire Arctic would appear wrapped in a dense smog of radar energy.

They all look north, these sensors, gawking toward the pole, and are as sensitive to light or sound or heat as an eyeball is to a finger. The radars can see a plane 2,000 miles away and 20,000 feet high; the satellites can photograph the licence plate of a car.

Some of the sensors, too, collect pure data, the sort of thing Fred Roots complained about the military hoarding. They record information on the movement of vibrations through the land and of electromagnetic energy through the air; about the the lay of the tundra and the behaviour of ice; about the sun, the atmosphere, the northern lights. About anything, that is, that has to do with the control of weapons. No one has ever shot a missile over the North Pole, with its unusual and shifting magnetic field, and no one can be precisely certain what will happen when they do. The military is constantly updating its information to improve the accuracy of its weapons and prevent nature from interfering with them. Bizarrely, it also uses nature to learn about the weapons. A system of sensors across the Arctic, for example, studies the northern lights. The huge amounts of electricity dispersed by the lights into the atmosphere roughly simulate the effects of the electromagnetic burst of nuclear weapons. This, in turn, can be used to design communications systems that will survive nuclear explosions.

Communications strands shoot southward from the sensors. Some of these are homely cables lying in the turf of forests or strung between telephone poles or resting in the silt of the sea bottom; some are beams of energy that zap through the space, ricocheting, say, from the Arctic up to a satellite, down to suburban Toronto, up to a satellite and finally down in the western United States. In seconds. Like corridors filled with tiny, scurrying spies, the strands carry messages about the movements of missiles, planes, submarines and troops; about the contours of the environment; about launches and explosions; about what the Russians are saying on their radios.

In Canada, the strands all run to North Bay, Ontario and from there to Colorado, to the base of hollowed-out Cheyenne Mountain in the Rockies within which is a command centre mounted on shock springs. There strands converge from thousands of other sensors: a radar complex on a windswept English moor; a spy station on the northern tip of Ellesmere Island; a radio tower on a Labrador seacliff; hydrophones off southern Greenland. And so on. And on. Inside the mountain the information is processed through banks of computers which are constantly mulching millions of bits of information, attempting to construct from them a single, moving image of the world. From there, headquarters for the portentiously named U.S. Space Command, the computers zap commands back out to missile silos in the American prairies, bomber bases in upstate New York and submarines under the polar ice. Etcetera.

Day in, day out and all around the clock, the sensors are telling the mountain what is going on out there. And the mountain is telling the weapons what to do about it.

The military has become obsessed with the wiring of the weapons system. It is the key to being able to fight with nuclear weapons. For a decade, the worst nightmare of the nuclear theologians has been an attack that destroyed the nerve centres — command posts, key radar installations and the like — and left the nuclear giant flailing about blind and dumb. For example, the Arctic radars have been sold to the public on the basis that the cruise missiles could fly through the old ones. This the thinnest of truths, even though the new radars are more powerful. Much of the work, however, is in rewiring the sites to speed and secure communications through the system. This is part of a massive programme that will gird the North American continent with more powerful sensors of every kind and completely overhaul the communications system. In every instance, the key word, the touchstone in all military plans, is *survivable*.

At Alert, on Ellesmere Island, for example, the military has conducted experiments on two satellite systems. American government documents dug up by William Arkin said that one, called Navstar, would carry sensors to provide "nuclear trans and post attack damage assessment information" and "force management" — telling where missiles have hit, what has been blown up and where to aim the next one. The other system, called Milstar, is to be "more capable of operating in a nuclear environment ... so we can better manage our forces in a protracted war." The military wants to be able to collect more information, process data and issue commands faster and do so in a world where the ground is exploding, cities are on fire and the air is charged with electromagnetic energy. It wants to make damn sure that when it finds itself in that world it can keep talking and thinking and shooting its way through the cosmic mess of a nuclear war.

In recent years, historians have consistently pointed out that the nuclear competition between the superpowers is nothing new in the history of the world. It is, rather, something brutally old. In *The Causes of Wars*, for example, Michael Howard examined the competition of states from the time of the ancients. From the conflict of Athens and Sparta onward, he argued, wars have been justified with a thousand arguments but had a single impetus: "The causes of war remain rooted, as much as they were in the pre-industrial age, in perceptions by statesman of the growth of hostile power and the fears for the restriction, if not the extinction, of their own."

Arms races, Howard argued, are just the material reflection of this jostling for advantage; attempts to gain the technological upper hand. This is obvious throughout the Arctic. Every new permutation on one coast per force begats one on the other. One of the most common notions about the nuclear arms race among scholars now is that it is not really a race at all. It is more a gigantic game of push-me-pull-me in which either side provides the force that enables the other to expand. And vice versa. Etcetera. They argue that the superpowers tailor their forces, like their rhetoric, to what they see in the mirror. In theory this is true. Practically, the history has always been that America cuts its forces to what it thinks it sees, or pretends to see, in the mirror. Then the Russians cut theirs to what they read in American pattern books. Thus fulfilling American prophecies.

The 1988 edition of *Soviet Military Power*, published annually by the American military, said, in a rather accusatory tone, that the Soviets were building new radars, communications systems, fighter jet bases and ground-to-air missiles and deploying AWACS radar planes, all to stop a cruise missile attack. Doing, in other words, exactly what the Americans are doing. Except, that is, for the ground-to-air missiles — which some analysts believe will be the next American project in the Canadian Arctic as part of a miniature version of Star Wars.

The Russian cruise missile is so similar in design to the American that Canadian military officials have begun to admit that testing the weapon in the Arctic is not just, as has always been said, to know how it would fly in Russia, but also to know how to shoot the Soviet cruise down in Canada. Their superpower symbiosis has become so absurd that they share an international weather satellite system that each uses to help target missiles on the other's homeland. In its study of nuclear weapons decision-making, the Oxford Research Group found that the military research and production bureaucracies in the East and West varied slightly in detail, but that their imperatives and operations, essentially, were identical. That they amounted, that is, to a closed loop.

Edward Thompson is a British historian who is given much of the credit for sparking the European peace movement of the Eighties. He did this initially with the publication of a furious essay called *Protest and Survive*, which was a reaction to the decision to install cruise and Pershing missiles in Europe. This was followed by an outpouring of writings on the nuclear confrontation which were, one way or another, the culmination of decades of thinking, in different contexts, about the competition of powers. In 1986, he wrote that he had come to realize the problem was not just that the two sides hated each other's guts, but that there were *two* sides. "Like wrestlers in combat, the hostile posture must be maintained with every nerve, since any weakening would lead to overthrow."

The competition has become so big, so many people on both sides — military bureaucrats, industrialists, politicians, technologists, strategists, theologians and a ragbag of hangers-on — are getting so fat off it, that they desperately need each other. "Out of their two opposing social systems the opposed blocs have made something like a *third* system in which they are simultaneously antagonists and partners: the Cold War."

The changes in the political leadership in both superpowers at the end of the Eighties have obviously altered the tenor of the rhetoric somewhat, but everywhere you looked in the Arctic — as in a hundred other places on the planet — the physical systems were entrenched, growing and inseparable: The bombers and fighters danced wing to wing; the submarines trailed each other trailing each other beneath the ice cap; the sensors sensed each other and the computers, through their myriad tentacles, commiserated.

Paul Bracken, of Yale University, wrote a book about the control of nuclear weapons in which he argued that their "coupling" has been "cemented" by the warning systems so commonly regarded as benign. "If the situation were not so potentially grave," he wrote, "we could dismiss this as science fiction." Even in the lowest state of alert the system reacts to "very small technical stimulus" and as tension heats up it becomes an ocean liner tossed to and fro by baby's breath. What really tightens things down is that both sides monitor the other's warning systems as well as its weapons. *I am listening to you listening.* Thus they hear each other going on alert and react, naturally, by doing the same; scaring themselves like children camping in the backyard making ugly faces at each other in the lantern light.

In heady times, Bracken concluded, the warning systems can "interact ... in unusual or complicated ways that are unanticipated to produce a mutually reinforcing alert. Unfortunately this ... is not a totally new phenomenon; it is precisely what happened in Europe in 1914." He illustrated his point with a diagram that showed the route from warning to weapons to warning and so on: a circle.

Military and civilian experts alike tend to sniff dismissively at this sort of analysis. They regard the system as one fine piece of machining and argue that the risk of it going off by itself is *virtually* non-existent. Yet, as they have to admit, the system screws up almost every day. The weapons — ships particularly — tailgate so closely that they regularly collide. Three times, for example, American subs have bumped into Russians vessels while spying in Soviet harbours. And, as everybody knows, the data processing computers register hundreds of fake warnings a year. Mathematicians who study statistics and probability note dryly that this will not always happen. The system operates solely on the basis of predetermined patterns that computers, generals and politicians recognize. And it is programmed to go from peace to nuclear war *in minutes.* Sooner or later, the dice will fall in a way no one has anticipated, in the wrong place, at the wrong time. Then it will do what it has been built to do.

From the window beside my desk I can see workmen putting the finishing touches on Toronto's newest office tower. During the construction, two workers were killed and several injured when a faulty shaft in the building's elevator snapped and it suddenly plunged *upward*, smashing them into the roof. At the inquest, engineers testified that the industry safety features had always concentrated on preventing elevators from falling down. It never occurred to them that an elevator might crash upward. Once, at a convention in Europe, someone had suggested this was possible. But, conventions being what they are, no one took him too seriously.

We just never know the way things will happen. And systems, cut loose, tend to follow their own course. Recently, this has become the essence of analysis of World War I. Yet many could see what was happening even at the time. In an anonymous memoir called *War Nurse* a woman who was part of that conflict recalled: "At the beginning I'd taken it as natural that I didn't know what the war was about. I was a woman, I wasn't very bright …. But I also took it for granted that *somebody* knew what it was about. That back of all of us … there was someone who understood the situation and had it pretty well in hand. But all of a sudden we found that we had lost that feeling. We didn't feel a soul knew anything about it. We didn't feel the governments of the different countries knew what was going to happen any more than they could foretell the weather; and that they had just about as much control over it. The thing was just going ahead and no one could stop it."

Say you ended your journey by heading straight up over the North Pole, to hover in the icy magnetic darkness and to see what Polaris sees. From each coast, you would observe the thousand black and spindly branches of each weapon system rising up and northward, like two gigantic mechanical trees. Straight beneath you they meet and their branches lock one into another with such force that they weld together. Not walls at all. Not even two belligerent systems. One.

Many times flying low over the Arctic I would imagine the moment had come and gone. One afternoon flying over Victoria Island at sunset, in a DC3 packed to claustrophobia with planks, a new dining room suite, cigarette smoke and children, I chanced to look out a port-hole and glimpse a world from another time. A bank of heavy, pitch black clouds raced high across the southern sky, like a herd of charging whales. Riding their backs was a gauze of glistening white mist that gambolled and flared into the deepening blue. Below, piled all the way down to the creased and silvery tundra, were cumulus clouds in great soft undulating folds, like pleated layers of skin. A deep red glowed in their centre, diffusing into the surrounding tufts in gentler, shifting shades of pink. The allusion of the light was unmistakable. Beyond that opening was all of life's mystery and through it came all of life's gifts. The primordial.

It lasted no longer than a gasp. The clouds shifted slightly and the sun emerged beneath them to sit squat on the tundra. This was a dull burning rock of a sun, presented as if on the tongue of a dark, frightening face. But for the rampaging herd of blackness, everything — the tundra, the clouds, the sky — was washed over in scarlet. I felt as if I were seeing the inverse possibility contained within the power of this twilight. I thought of Wells' traveller at the end of time: "It would be hard to convey the stillness of it. All the sounds of man, the bleating of sheep, the cries of birds, the hum of insects, the stir that makes the background of our lives — all that was over."

This was the landscape I had always envisioned of the aftermath. What I could see below was what the scientists predicted in their reports of the nuclear winter: an ice encrusted, featureless cold red forever. This was the way the planet would die. Not blown up, as children and video games imagine, but pathetically choked off from the sun by the smoke of its own debris and frozen into a lifeless mass.

The theory holds that as little as 100 megatons of nuclear explosives — two per cent of the bombs — would ignite fires in forests and cities from which would billow immense clouds of dense smoke. They would fill the atmosphere like black ink in a glass of water. The planet would be shrouded and the sun blocked out. Any green plants that survived the blast, fire and radiation would perish, starved of light. And their demise would send an inexorable wave of death crashing up the food chain. The smoke would persist for weeks, perhaps months, and might become self-perpetuating by reversing the convection currents — warm air rising into cold — that normally clean the atmosphere.

The Arctic, it was thought, might fare better than most places — there was little to burn and the plants and people were adapted to the cold and dark. But no one could say. The land would be easily devastated by its absorption of radioactivity. Or if the climatic change happened during the calving season, the caribou and migratory birds could be instantly wiped out.

The world has already seen these effects on a tiny scale. In 1815 an Indonesian volcano called Mount Tambora erupted blowing twenty-five cubic miles of debris into the stratosphere where it remained for more than a year. The dust belt cooled the earth's surface by a mere six-tenths of one degree but the consequences were terrible. Crops froze in July throughout Europe and eastern North America, producing famine and contributing to outbreaks of cholera and typhus. The following year Byron wrote,

The bright sun was extinguished, and the stars
Did wander darkling in the eternal space.
Rayless, and pathless, and the icy earth
Swung blind and blackening in the moonless air.

No end of variables have been attached to the nuclear winter theory but dozens of inquiries over a decade have all come to more or less the same conclusion as did a 1983 American study: "The extinction of a large fraction of the earth's animals, plants and microorganisms seems possible ... and the extinction of the human species itself cannot be ruled out."

Governments have not taken this seriously. The Canadian government commissioned a report which substantiated the theory and went on to adopt a policy of further study. The American government said the findings only bolster its belief in planning for nuclear war to ensure the impossibility of nuclear war. Among its many sterling contributions to the United Nations in the past decade was voting against a resolution calling for further research on the theory.

In that brief glimpse of a Stygian landscape I thought also of the images I had often seen in advertisements published in high technology weapons magazines. These are to the military what the Eaton's catalogue was to suburban families when I was a child. Their illustrations are indistinguishable from those painted on the covers of colour comics and the sides of arcade video games: Jet fighters shoot bursts of laser-light at guided missiles which bob and weave with infinite cleverness. Invariably, the backdrop for the weaponry is a denuded expanse of violet tundra. They are depictions of the plain of lost possibilities; the landscape of the exhausted human imagination.

When trying to explain the *why* of the current militarization of the Arctic, the experts do not speak in generalities. They draw elaborate charts in which fine black lines separate the different types of nuclear weapon, the unique technological and bureaucratic history of each and the precise strategy for its use which is so much the product of the weapon's capabilities that it might be found in a plastic envelope tucked into the packing crate.

A comprehensive view, however, is possible. There is, for example, the explanation offered by Ursula Franklin, a wise physicist who was one of the founders of the Voice of Women. She has argued that the superpowers have run out of room and credibility everywhere else in the world they might like to plant new weapons. In the West, Europe bristles; in the East are the Chinese; the South is a swath of fire fueled by warring surrogates. And everywhere the people daily grow more hostile towards having new bombs placed in their midst. The wide open white spaces of the Arctic, however, are a tabula rasa; on the Northern front one finds gaps, opportunities. Like the monster in Mary Shelley's *Frankenstein*, the "filthy mass ... shunned and hated by all mankind," escapes into the Arctic, "most savage of places," where it can get some space to howl.

Dr. Frankenstein's monster was abhorred and driven from the villages of Europe, but it was also compelled northward by the involuntary growth of its own obsessive capacity for murder. Likewise the nuclear system. The superpowers are not meeting to fight in the Arctic. Like the clever, but proud and stupid Dr. Frankenstein, they, and everyone else, are being dragged into a battle there with their own collective, repulsive creation: "My reign is not yet over .... Follow me; I seek the everlasting ices of the north, where you will feel the misery of cold and frost, to which I am impassive .... Come on, my enemy; we have yet to wrestle for our lives. But many hard and miserable hours must you endure until that period shall arrive."

Jobie Weetaluktuk, said, "We say *noongnusutuuk*, which just means they last forever, and they are called *qaatujugraak* which means big bombs. So if you combine the two you have *qaatujugraak noongnusutuuk*: Big bombs which last forever. They go off and Boom! but the effects will go for many years. So we just say forever."

And then he said: "I know people want to have power. And that they will say things to get elected, they will use things, the fears that people have. But when they point nuclear weapons at the other one and threaten to attack, this I don't understand. It doesn't make sense."

I had gone to the Arctic frankly assuming and hoping that their proximity to nuclear weapons installations would give Inuit a profound sense of their danger. I believed this because I had read it in the publications of their political organizations, written by people who now lived in the south and had gained such an understanding from what *they* had read. Perhaps I hoped for it because it would make easy copy. It was a foolish idea. Living beside a nuclear installation, as I have noted, meant no more and no less than living beside a mine.

Yet those Inuit who did speak of these things tended to do so in much the same terms of genuine puzzlement as had Jobie. They did not know or care about the details of weaponry or strategy, about minute calculations of the probability of disaster. They knew only about consequences. *Qaatujugraak noongnusutuuk.* We just say forever.

Gideon Qitsualik said, "He figured everybody would be a lot happier if their governments or people decided to work, make a good living, instead of getting ready for the war or creating weapons all the time."

These are the sorts of arguments that people who believe in weapons and borders long ago learned to dismiss. Naive arguments. Artless, innocent, unsophisticated, amusingly simple arguments. In part, this is an easy way of silencing uncomfortably obvious criticisms. This is how *motherhood* came to be a pejorative term, a label for social desires that everyone ostensibly, common-sensically shared but which anyone with half a wit could recognize were unattainable. Peace is a motherhood issue.

This is not only the reflex of the powerful. For hours I would sit at kitchen tables and listen to the old Inuit explain their value systems and I would continually and automatically nod my head. Like an enthusiastic toy dog. Trudging back to my lodgings, I would look around at the village, a tiny bundle of votive candles alone in a black universe, and think: *Easy for you to say.* Clustered together, all by themselves in this land, no threats, no competition, everybody in this together. Clearly the Inuit were in no position to understand the complexity of systems of global power.

In time I came to realize that this was just the point. It was the lack of analysis, an absence of the calculation which passes off as sophistication among us, that was at the core of their understanding. Inuit were neither disingenuous nor judgemental. Of course they understood power and the competition for it; they were quite clear that wars were projections of visceral human impulses, matters of greed and blood revenge, as common as the feuds in their own history. What Jobie meant when he said he did not understand nuclear geopolitics, was that he had not, even in the deepest part of his gut, an appreciation for the sophistic elevation of this over life itself. Inuit were willing to tell the government what it wanted to hear; they were willing to put up with what Canada considered essential to its survival. They knew this was necessary for their own. But there are many things it is not given to their culture to understand.

When he reached Igloolik during the Fifth Thule Expedition, Knud Rasmussen met a shaman named Aua. For days, the Dane questioned the Inuk about his culture. To each explanation of the specifics of a particular attitude or taboo, Rasmussen responded by asking: Why? Finally, the shaman left the house where they were talking and Rasmussen trailed him around the camp. They saw men returning from the seal hunt empty-handed, they saw a woman dying in her *iglu*. Aua swept Rasmussen from one intractable mystery to another, each of which pointed to the most intractable of mysteries. All the while, he turned the Dane's question back upon himself: "Why?" Rasmussen, of course, could not answer. Aua said, "You see, you are equally unable to give any reason when we ask why life is as it is. And so it must be. All our customs come from life and turn towards life; we explain nothing, we believe nothing."

Inuit did not see themselves as victims in this. Rather they took responsibility for the totality of their world. This is best reflected in their myths of creation. The central figure in these is Sedna, who lives beneath the sea. In one version of the story, Sedna as a young woman refused all suitors until she was one day seduced by a dog disguised as a man. He carried her away to live with him on an island from which there was no escape. Once, when her family came to visit, she tricked the dog and attempted to make off with the family in its boat. The dog-husband, as they will be, was easily enraged. He attacked the boat. To save themselves, the family threw Sedna overboard and when she tried to cling to the gunwale her father cut her fingers off. She sank to the bottom and the joints of her fingers became the mammals of the sea. There she lived still, beneath the sea, guiding the fortunes of Inuit. If they were disrespectful of life, she could wreak starvation upon them.

The interesting thing about the story, and this is true of all Inuit stories, is that the responsibility for the situation ultimately traces back to them. They recognize their gods to be created in their own image. Not vice versa.

When I would crouch at the doorway of a Thule ruin, this was not an easy myth to understand. Compared both to those who came before and after them, the Thule had it easy, living at a time of relative abundance. Yet, here on the shore of a gravel plateau against which the ice ground and buckled and across which swept a bitter, cutting wind, these tiny homes of skin and bone and turf seemed wedged into a crevice at the vortex of implacable natural forces. How they could take responsibility for *those*? How could they blame themselves for the possibility of starving in such a place? My world had raised me to think this way.

The answer, I think, was in the question. Blame was hardly the issue. On the contrary, theirs was a world with neither guilt nor innocence. There was only the continuum of reality. The boldly polarized realms of the Arctic — the totality of light and dark, of abundance and destitution, of life and death — taught them about the dualism inherent in all of life's possibilities.

You had to look closely at the land to understand this. The first time I walked out on the tundra I was overwhelmed by the cruelty of the place. It stretched out in every direction beneath a vault of a sky, an expressionless immensity of slate. I saw nothing and heard nothing but the crunching underfoot of frozen, crushed rock. A sharp wind came from the northern distance. But it was the apparent absence of life that froze me within. My eyes had not adjusted.

I came to a tiny pond, a metre square perhaps, which was covered with a thick layer of transparent ice. Air bubbles were trapped in the ice, like frozen milliseconds. Otherwise, it was as clear as the glass of a museum display case. Beneath was a mat of deep green and yellow and rust lichen, with spongy, cauliflower heads. So bright and joyous against the grey. Dormant but still beaming. As I peered into the case, something ex-haled. A single bead of air rose from the miniature garden to rest beneath the ice. Dormant but alive. Excited by this, I was strain-ing to see another when a sound overhead made me rigid. It was an Arctic raven. They are huge and thuggish birds to begin with and this one was positively threatening. It hovered straight above me, dangling its big orange claws and cawing. It eventually decided, I think, that I was just too big. A few feet beyond the pond I noticed a splattering of blood. There were no signs of what this animal had been or where it had come from. Just a num-ber of distinct, bright red concave depressions in the snow.

I had already seen all manner of evidence of the animal wealth of the Arctic in the villages. Muskox heads out back of a house and beluga parts lying on the beaches; flippers, antlers, rib cages and spines as thick as my leg. Still the unyielding petrification of the land was such that these small signs of a chain of life were startling.

Walking some distance, it was possible to discern this chain extending in all directions, into the past beyond memory and into the future beyond reckoning. Possible also to feel that it was not a chain at all, but a web with threads of gossamer delicacy. I came upon a bed of stone and bone, where a home had been 300 or 3,000 years ago. High tufts of brown grasses sprang up through the snow, scattered patches of nutrient wealth in the places where animals had died and where they would feed again. These were the footprints of the living history of these people as they walked in place through time; phantoms of the umbilical cords through which they were nourished over generations of life on these stone flats.

These were also the threads of Inuit intellectual culture, the scattered notes taken over centuries as the land taught them how to be. This was a place where the powers enveloping people had such force that they inevitably brought out the best and the worst in them. To survive, people had to find a balance, to take respon-sibility for equilibrium, to have a profound respect for life. Pure life. Theirs was a world too close to the edge for motherhood issues.

Other footprints bespoke another way of looking at the land, formed by a different intellectual history. I think not even of the tumult of wreckage around the old military bases, but of much subtler things. Tire tracks, for example. There were places where the land was gullied, like a furrowed field, but the ridges were ragged and encrusted, more like unhealed wounds. Heavy vehicles driven on the tundra had destroyed the vegetation which, in turn, reduced the insulation of the ground. The permafrost melted and the soil eroded, deepening the scar and altering the drainage pattern. Among other things, this dries up the surrounding top soil and also forms barriers which change the movements of animals. It can take *hundreds* of years before a tire track disappears from the tundra. Meanwhile, an ecological system which has taken thousands of years to develop is irreversibly altered. This had happened, for example, on Cornwallis Island during military exercises in the Seventies.

Paul Amarualik said, "There were exercises and they were running and driving around a lot and that can affect the land a lot. They kind of rerouted some of the rivers."

It is not likely the soldier driving his armoured truck across the tundra had any idea he was rerouting rivers, displacing animals and causing permanent damage. To outsiders, the tundra seems so huge and ferocious it is difficult to imagine we have the power to make on it any mark at all.

I asked Noah Adglak, "Do you think white people understand the land?" He said, "A white person might think he understands about the land. He might be wrong. It might be just from the landscape."

Of course, individuals for whom the Arctic is not home sometimes develop a keen respect for its forms of life. "It's not bad, it's a different environment," said Major Stephens, who had not chosen to be in the Arctic. "It's quite a surprising place. The colours up here in the summertime are quite astounding. The flora in the area, it's very very tiny and you have to go looking for it. But to see these delicate flowers growing out of bare rock — it's sort of amazing. They say we're above the tree line but there are trees all over the place. Unfortunately they are about an inch and a half high. There are willows all over the place. You put your foot down and you are stepping on about a hundred trees."

We were talking over drinks in the radar station lounge. Outside it was frigid and black. The wind howling across the tundra funnelled into a jetstream as it passed between the station trains. The lounge felt like a basement joint or a well-appointed suburban rec room. There was dark wood and imitation leather. Country and western played through a speaker beside a television on which it was a warm sunlit day and the Edmonton Oilers were womping Winnipeg. There was a pouting Vargas girl on the wall. From the next room came the sound of pool balls clunking.

Perhaps Major Stephens was not up on the full ecological significance of those tiny trees, but I instinctively felt he was careful about where he placed his boot. Still, for most of us, our respect for the natural world is filtered through the inherent knowledge that we have already subdued it. Our immediate intellectual ancestors in the Arctic, the explorers of the nineteenth century, also thought they were impervious. They realized too late that they were wrong.

The explorers were a different sort of men than the missionaries, fur traders and even whalers, who, as I have said, lived with and learned much from the Inuit. As a result, the explorers did the worst by the place. In circumstances where the frontier exploiters usually survived, the military expeditions, nearly all of them British, were often crushed.

The personal ambitions that drove the British naval explorers who ventured to the Arctic had much to do with prestige and their personal quests for adventure. The impetus for the exploration, however, grew out of the Enlightenment and the wedding of science, technology and politics. Sir John Barrow, second lord of the Admiralty and an ardent geographer, promoted Arctic exploration for thirty years. When his bosses demanded he justify the grandest voyage, which was to complete mapping of the Northwest Passage, he invoked the name of Queen Elizabeth and her ministers. "With their enlightened minds they sought for 'knowledge,' the result of which, they need not be told, was power." His words launched the third expedition of Sir John Franklin, the most famous and disastrous of the Royal Navy's Arctic excursions.

Franklin, who had led two previous Arctic expeditions, set out in 1845 loaded with the best of everything the Victorians had to offer. His 129 crew members were the cream of the navy. His ships, the Erebus and Terror, were heaped with scientific gadgetry and the first to be equipped with modern steam engines. The provisions came from London's prestigious Fortnum and Mason's and included eighteen oxen. Among the amusements on board was a library containing 3,000 books. "I really do not think," a young sailor wrote home, "that if I could be in London for an hour or two, I would want to get anything." The expedition's gear, however, was not enough. The young sailor's letter was carried on a supply ship that accompanied the explorers as far as Greenland and returned bearing the last words ever heard from the men.

The men set themselves the task of bravely going where no whites had gone. Franklin had done this before. In the first of his two earlier expeditions over land to the Arctic coast, he had pushed his small band of officers and Indian voyageurs toward the completion of their mission despite conditions — a dwindling food supply and fearsome landscape — that made the Indians plead for him to turn back. The third and fatal expedition intended to close the 300-mile gap remaining in maps of the passage. Ultimately, it became hopelessly stuck in the near-permanent ice north of King William Island.

The men were bound and fortified by their discipline and the kind of military loyalty that later brought twenty British and

American navy expeditions into the Arctic searching for Franklin and company. During the long dark winters when they were inevitably blocked, they kept the constant and wretched spectre of scurvy in abeyance with citrus juices and kept their manners with amusements that ranged from recitals and revues to building shooting galleries and elaborate cairns to taking "pleasant picnics on the ice." The diligence of their scientific purpose is evident from Franklin's earlier expeditions, which gathered detailed descriptions of the Arctic's geology, climate, topography, solar radiation, sound propagation, almost 400 types of animal and more than 600 plants in addition to charting 1,750 miles of coastline.

Their science, of course, was imperfect. Franklin's expedition was stranded because he took a wrong turn, guided by a faulty map. More important, it exacerbated an attitude towards the land and its inhabitants that combined condescension and foreboding. Watching a wolf stalk deer during this first voyage, which was already short of food, Franklin wrote: "We were amused by the interesting spectacle .... The pursuer being alarmed at the sight of our men, gave up the chase ... much to our regret, for we were calculating upon the chance of sharing his capture." They considered the Inuit "lively and agreeable" but their lives, in Barrow's words, "a most cruel and wretched lot."

Comparatively, of course, the explorers considered their own society the furthest advancement of civilization. They examined the Hudson's Bay Lemming and the Large Ringed Plover in minute detail but paid so little heed to the Inuit as to learn nothing from them. They stuck to their uniforms instead of fur and knew little about hunting or the value of fresh meat in preventing scurvy. In overland journeys they refused to use dog sleds and instead exhausted themselves pulling overburdened sleds thousands of miles by hand across the tundra while Inuit zipped past them. When their ships were crushed or sunk or hopelessly moored in the ice, when their food ran low, they became helpless and destitute. Many starved or froze or died wretched with scurvy.

Franklin died during the second winter of the expedition. A year later, their ships still locked in ice, the 105 surviving men set out on foot, dragging a boat mounted on a sled. Their load weighed 1,400 pounds and was made up of what they presumably considered essential to their survival. Among the contents: walking shoes, several types of silk handkerchief, a set of cutlery engraved with the officers' crests, slippers, nails, four heavy cooking stoves, curtain rods, a four foot high pile of extra clothing and forty pounds of chocolate. "In short," wrote Francis McClintock after finding the remnants, "... a mere accumulation of dead weight, but slightly useful, and very likely to break down the strength of the sledge-crews."

Historians have argued over the men's circumstances ever since. Stefansson outright ridiculed them. Others have maintained that they were probably fated to starve in an area where there were too many men and too few animals. It is clear, however, in retrospect, that their doom was ensured by their ignorance of what the Arctic demanded for survival.

The difficulty of understanding and appreciating lands of which we are not part is profound and deeply rooted in all people. Like most, Inuit had little curiosity about distant places and a blanket assumption that all would be inferior to their home — the very same sort of assumption, that is, that explorers always brought to the Arctic. A boy who lived in a village of 200 said he found Montreal "boring." In Ottawa once, by chance, I ran into an Inuk I had met in the north. This was in January and, while I was finding Ottawa bitterly cold, I thought my friend would be enjoying the reprieve. Are you having a nice time here? "No. It's too hot. No snow." One evening in Cambridge Bay I was sitting with Joe and Susie Koaha in their living room. Susie had been telling me about going to the world's fair in Vancouver with the territorial government's pavilion. She had been homesick. "I found it was too moist there." The television flickered in the corner as we talked. An image of a forest came up. Joe said, "You know, that's one thing I really can't stand. *Trees.*

I always feel that like they're picking at me, that they're going to eat me."

The explorers felt something similar about the Arctic. Quite reasonably. But the tragedies that befell many of them were not inherent in where they were as much as in their belief that they could outsmart it. They were not stupid men. But they were thoroughly the product of their times. Theirs were the days of the Pax Britannica, when the British believed they had the highest of destinies. More important, now, they were the days when the belief in the power of science and technology to give men dominion over nature, and over each other, was approaching its apex.

Our modern scientific paradigm is the result of the revolution of thought during the seventeenth century and primarily that of Rene Descartes. It was Descartes who developed the theory of absolute separation of mind and body and the concept of the material universe as a machine and nothing but. This belief contributed to the collapse of the reverence people had long had for life. American academic Carolyn Merchant has written: "As long as the earth was considered to be alive and sensitive it could be considered a breach of human ethical behaviour to carry out destructive acts against it." But one can do anything one pleases to a machine. The Cartesian world view was the basis of the Enlightenment and fused with the contemporary notion of history during the nineteenth century to create the belief that man could overcome nature with his intellect and that, inevitably, he would fashion it into immortal perfection. The belief, that is, in what we call Progress. This, of course, is what Mary Shelley was on about.

As they trudged across the ice, the heaviest load on Franklin's men was their ideology. They believed themselves to be in a battle with Nature, nowhere more fierce than the Arctic, not unlike the one they had recently fought with the French. And they believed it would be won by the technology their refined intellects had produced. Looking back from the elevated position of a superior science and a more liberal ideology, we are easily tempted to condescend to their ignorance of the Arctic and their attitudes towards the Inuit. But we hardly question their premise. Our chuckles are drowned by the explosions of splintering timbers around us. When, rarely, we acknowledge this awful noise, we are overwhelmed with despair. The systems of power and technology now seem to have become so big and unwieldy we feel helpless before them. Another god for whom we do not take responsibility.

Few places is the sound louder than in the Arctic. There we confront a culture that has not yet completely undergone the spiritual and physical fracturing which has become the engine of our own. Inuit could only have survived and flourished in the world's most difficult land by maintaining a fundamental belief in the whole. That is what makes their attitude towards life different. We can now see the paradox between our understanding of the land and the landscape. This harsh place, as it turns out, is the most sensitive barometer of change on the planet. As we learn to read it we realize it is telling us that we will not be able to survive unless we find a way to understand the world as the Inuit do.

When we stare into the crystal clarity of the Arctic ice, the face that looks back is, I think, something like what the Germans call a *doppelganger*: the double that appears as an apparition on the cusp of death. It is identical to our own, but instead of flesh, it has a skin of carbon-carbon. It is what the Italian fascists, who called themselves Futurists, imagined when they wrote, "War is beautiful because it initiates the dreamt-of metalization of the human body." This face is our double, but it is only half of what we are: one side of the polarity of nature and humanity, technologically separated, given form and now concentrated, with symbolic irony, in the land of twilight. There it awaits our final battle with ourselves. Reaching into one of the darkest corners of our past and assuming the consequences in advance, we call this battle the Holocaust. Thus we imagine ourselves making a "whole burnt offering" of life itself, of making a sacrifice of ourselves to ourselves.

"Many Dewliners," Major Stephens said softly, "are quite intro-
verted. They stay within themselves." We were padding along a
dimly-lit hallway in the radar site, so narrow that I had to walk a
little behind him. The passageway was painted a depressing yellow and filled with big exposed pipes and a low, incessant hum.
"They try to keep the lights down," the Major whispered, "people
are sleeping here all the time." It felt like we were in a submarine.
It always felt like this. People behaved as if the exterior atmosphere was composed of pure nitrogen. They wore short sleeved
T-shirts, sweat pants and running shoes. "The only reason we
have Arctic clothing here," a supervisor said, "is to give people
when they go to Winnipeg." Stiff formalities were necessary to
maintain privacy. Voices were muted. Movements silent. You felt
like blood in the plumbing.

We came to the computer room, beneath the radar dome. "This
is the brand new radar, the FPS 117," the Major said, "a very tidy
installation." The room was filled with shiny blue metal cabinets.
"There are the transmitters." (A row of blue cabinets.) "There
are the receivers." (A row of blue cabinets.) "It's all a computer
driven system, everything is computer controlled. The data is
processed and transmitted to North Bay and displayed on screens
for use by their weapons' controllers." The radar swept the sky
every twelve seconds. Its predecessor had taken twice that. "Very
slow," the major said.

We padded down the passageway to the data centre, a room
illuminated by red warning lights, glowing green screens and
small yellow desk lamps. The old radar console dominated the
space. It was a large, wrap-around arrangement that sat two, built
of heavy gunmetal in the bulbous style of a '55 Chev and festooned with buttons and knobs. It had fallen now into disuse. A
technician sat behind the new console, a single flat screen slightly bigger than a personal computer and with a similar sort of
keyboard. As the cursor arm swept the screen bright squares appeared with tapered tails, like those of meteorites. Radar reflections. "They are returns of some sort," the major said. "They

could just be ground flares. It's when they return sweep after sweep that you know it's a target."

Nearby a sergeant sat at a map covered with plastic and strips of coloured ribbon indicating flight paths and marking the position of every plane over the Arctic. A British Airways jet was being tracked. I thought of the passengers overhead, snoozing or trying to quiet babies or chuckling at a bad movie. In the eye of the system. When the rewiring was complete the technicians were to be replaced by computers. "There will be no more console operators. The equipment itself will channel the information." There was no real reason, the major said, to have humans here.

"The people who run the air battle are Cheyene Mountain, where NORAD headquarters is located, and North Bay, in the underground complex there. They are the people who run the air battles. We just provide them the radar picture for their use."

I thought of an exchange I had had earlier, in another installation. I had been looking over the shoulder of a technician who was peering intently into his scope — "scope dopes" these people were called. His senior officer was standing beside me. A speaker in the console was producing a steady patter of Russian and static. "Radio-free Russia," the officer chuckled. I was wondering what this technician thought he saw when he looked into his scope.

I asked, "Do you imagine the sky out there?"

There was a momentary, awkward silence and then both men laughed. "Why would we?" the officer asked. "It's just empty space waiting for something to return, to tell him there's a heavy metal object reflecting radar energy." The technician said, "That's pretty well it. You don't really think of it in terms of aircraft and sky. You think of it as a blip on the scope. And when it shows up you do your job." He might as well have been a computer.

I left the data centre and went off to interview Captain Chausson, whose job it was to run the air battles. We talked in a room that was very close to the radome and, later, playing back the

tape, I found it had recorded the electrical energy of the sweeping radar dish. Every twelve seconds a staccato electronic wave
broke over his words: sweepitydeep.

"When you sign on that dotted line you are signing the ultimate liability, which is to give your life for your country …
sweepitydeep ….It's just something that you live with, something that you have committed yourself to do … sweepitydeep
….You have entered a community, a military community and
they are paying your salary in return for your services …
sweepitydeep … and if it is a true commitment when you sign
on the dotted line you know that you will carry through with it.
Sweepitydeep."

When I listened to the recording, in my room in the village,
with the sled dogs howling purple and blue outside, it seemed to
me Capt. Chausson and his colleagues were dedicated in both
the traditional sense of the word and the modern. As in dedicated
to his country, dedicated to his way of life; and as in dedicated
facilities and dedicated circuits. They couldn't see the machine.
Because they were the machine. And they were by no means
alone in this. Sovereignty. Security. Sweepitydeep.

A few nights later I went for a walk out of the village under a
perfectly clear and moonless sky. The million lighted windows
of the dead were burning brilliantly. I was on the tundra, between
the village and the radar station. Behind me the cries of kids playing and the thumping of the electricity generator faded into
silence. The station came into the middle distance, alone on the
plain. It was bathed in white light. The geodesic dome gleamed.
What *was* this place? A spaceship? A forbidden palace? The shin-
ing crown of the white man's technological enterprise, charged
by the belief that we could harness the very essence of the
universe and bend it to our will.

*Do you imagine the sky out there?*

(Laughter) *Why would we?*

It depressed me. I turned to go back to the village. Just then, a
slit opened high in the blackness and the ethereal wind of the
northern lights began to blow through. They moved like

luminous sheer curtains billowing in a summer breeze, expanding like the light of dawn until the whole northern sky was alive with a transparent green fire. They would fan across the horizon and then draw into a bright diaphanous column, then telescope and spread suddenly overhead, continually shifting through the colour spectrum — blue, green, red. It was like watching a symphony and I laughed out loud.

The military hates the aurora borealis because it messes things up. This divine light is actually an electrical wind blown down from the sun which charges oxygen atoms, creating x-rays, radio waves, infrared and ultraviolet light. Radars can't tell the northern lights from a squadron of bombers; satellites read them as missile launches and they screw up the guidance systems of weaponry. Knowing that as I watched them dance somehow filled me with optimism. It was as if the sky itself was reaffirming the meaning and power of life by throwing a monkey wrench into the system. The radar station now seemed a dinky, self-important child's toy; a minute plastic conceit. I thought of a man inside, in a darkened room, staring at a dull orb filled with bleeping dots, with an incomprehensible Russian voice chattering in his ear. I wished he could imagine the sky.

# Chapter Four

# Belief

Herodier Kalluk and Gideon Qitsualik, of Resolute Bay and Gjoa Haven respectively, were the best of friends as young men in Pond Inlet, distinguished in the community and bound together by the similarity of their noble noses. "I used to call him 'nose' and he used to call me 'nose,' " they both said. They had also, together, achieved a rare, if temporary and anonymous, sort of fame as literal representatives of Canadian sovereignty. They had had their pictures on money.

For eleven years they were on the back of the Canadian $2 bill, in a frieze called "Eskimos hunting by ice floes." The bill was part of a 1975 issue of pseudo-psychedelic money bordered with wild spiral doodlings intended to prevent counterfeiting. For the first time, the fiction that the note could be swapped for a piece of gold was dropped, replaced with the more tepid assurance that it was legal tender. Heads: Queen Elizabeth is still young and nearly angelic. Tails: Herodier, Gideon and four other men are making ready to hunt whales. They are loading their equipment — harpoons and seal skin floats — into a boat on a desolate beach. With their baggy jackets and long hoods, their traditional bob haircuts, contrasted against a large ice floe just offshore, they look like monks setting out on a journey. Herodier is stepping into the boat. Gideon is blowing up a float. "Unfortunately," noted the Charlton Standard Catalogue of Canadian Paper Money, "no polar bears or seals are shown." More unfortunate still, the picture is a bit of a fake.

"They were preparing to go out for a whale hunt," Gideon said, "although there was no whale at all."

Herodier said, "After they got everything ready, they took off in a hurry. They went behind that ice, the one that's showing. They went behind that ice for a while and came back. They were getting ready for four hours. They just kept doing this, back and forth, for four hours."

They were learning how movies are made. The photograph was taken from a film by Doug Wilkinson, a writer and filmmaker who lived in Pond Inlet in the early 1950s, producing work for the National Film Board of Canada and a book, *Land of the Long Day*. Like most documentary filmmakers Wilkinson shot over a period of months and then reconstructed the material into a coherent narrative. Inuit were used to photography by then, but editing was something new.

Gideon said, "One thing he was so surprised about is that one of the hunters threw a harpoon into the water when there were no whales at all. And, a few years later when he saw that movie, when they were doing that he knows that it's going to be on the movie. He didn't expect to see a whale there. And when the person threw a harpoon it hit a whale. And he still wonders how it happened."

Deceptive editing and the recreation of reality in documentaries for cinematic versimilitude were practically invented in the Arctic. Robert Flaherty, one the pioneers of the genre, coerced the hero of his 1922 *Nanook of the North* to re-enact various routines, at least once putting his life in danger as a result, to obtain the footage that made up the often cloying portrait that defined the Inuit in southern minds for decades afterward. Endless repetitions of this sort of thing have left the Inuit cynical about white representations of them. They expect exaggeration and assume lies. Herodier, for example, criticized Wilkinson's memoir without ever having read it.

The Inuit who had known Wilkinson were surprised and pleased when their image showed up out of the blue on the $2 bill in 1975. It made Gideon feel young again. "He was very pleased to have a picture on the same $2 bill as the Queen. The reason is that he was a child at the same time as the Queen was a child." This was what made the choice of the photo for the nation's money interesting to me also.

The most famous figure in the photo, bending to adjust the kayak, was a hunter named Idlouk. Wilkinson, who had been in the Arctic previously, went to Pond Inlet in 1953 specifically to live a year with Idlouk and his family. "The one Eskimo I have met," he wrote in his introduction, "who has come reasonably close to establishing a balance between the old way of life in his land and that thrust upon him by his contact with the white. Here, in the success of this one man in adapting himself to the changing conditions, perhaps lay the key to the successful development of the Canadian Eskimo as an Arctic citizen. I wanted to find that key."

Wilkinson goes on to describe a man who was shrewd about white ways but firmly rooted in the Inuit reality. For days after Wilkinson told him how many people lived in New York City, Idlouk was kept awake by nightmares. "I awaken thinking about the men and women and children all crammed into such a small place, pushing and shoving, fighting for air to breathe."

Wilkinson closed his book, published in 1955, with an exhortation to Canadians to appreciate the Inuit. For one thing: "As a Canadian citizen the Eskimo helps immeasurably to maintain our sovereignty over this tremendous land mass." By then, Idlouk had already been moved to Resolute Bay for that very purpose. Herodier, who later followed his friend said, "They told him that it was rich here, that they won't need anything, that they got everything here, that he would live an easy life." It didn't work out that way. Like almost everyone else in the village, Idlouk and his wife, Kidlak, who were already almost forty, were overwhelmed by the manipulation of the villagers and the invasion of whites. They began drinking. One night Idlouk, drunk, drove his snowmobile off a cliff and was killed. Speculation about the precise cause and circumstances of the death has continued since.

There is irony, of course, in Idlouk's image being used as a direct symbol of the country's sovereignty almost a decade after he had, in a manner of speaking, lost his life upholding the concept. Irony, too, in that the Inuit in the picture — natural monks, who very rarely used money, setting out to collect their harvest in the sacred lands of the North — had, twenty years later, become anachronisms under the twin pressures of money and government. But the Mint, presumably, had not intended veracity. The image, it seems to me, was not really about the Inuit at all. It was about Canada and Canadians. Its connotation was the same as that of the picture on the $1 bill in the series, a pair of tugs marshalling logs in the Ottawa River beneath the parliament buildings. The message was this: Big Country, Natural Country. Helluva great big, rough and tumble, natural kinda country.

Of an afternoon walk in any Arctic village there were three sounds I could count on: the clattering of hammers, for the winter was coming on, projects had to be completed quickly and, as I may have mentioned, it was an election year; the howling of sled dogs, for they were coming back in some villages where men trying to hunt full-time found them more durable and economical than snowmobiles; the click-clicking of stone being chipped and fashioned into seals by bulky gargoyles squatting on doorsteps. For carving is one of the few ways an unemployed Inuk can make a buck.

Eventually the click-clicking would be lost beneath the sound of a truck pulling up, carrying construction or government workers. Then a man's voice, stumbling, hesitant, sheepish, the way people speak when they don't know the language but are determined to plough ahead with English anyway: "Uh, got any carvings?" A little louder: "Carvings?" He would be given a lumpen seal or a misshapen whale, like a hundred others, which he would bear away to the south and present to someone dear with great ceremony, as if it were an ancient relic.

It is by their carvings more than anything else that most southern Canadians know the Inuit and by which the people of many other countries, particularly in Europe, know Canada. Since the Fifties, when it began to be broadly marketed, Inuit art, especially carving, has steadily increased in popularity. For the Inuit, it has become a vital and relatively huge source of cash. In Baffin Region, arts and crafts make up eleven per cent of the economy and are worth almost $10 million a year. As the industry has grown the cream of it has moved out of the cottage. In larger villages or those with a recognized lineage of talented people, government workshops have been set up, the products of which are marketed throughout North America and Europe. In Lake Harbour, known for its jade-like soapstones, more than a third of the population carves and there are children as young as thirteen who are already said to be brilliant. Accomplished carvers can make $30,000 a year and some as much as $100,000, their work supporting large extended families. Bobbing in the wake of each are dozens of others who chip away on their doorstep to make a little money for gas and cigarettes.

The workshop in Iqaluit was a small factory awash in fluorescent light, a place where small engines might be fixed. The air tasted of dust and smelled vaguely of burnt hair. Country music blared from a ghetto blaster the size of a small car, drowning the intermittent ripping sirens of drills. If you closed your eyes you got the audio track from your worst dentist nightmare. Half a dozen carvers were bent over their work benches fashioning pieces of bone or antler or ivory or stone into birds and earrings and brooches and letter openers. Materials were provided by the government and the carvers worked by the piece. It was a Friday and almost time for lunch, work was winding down and concentration frequently interrupted now by spouses and children appearing at the door.

Pauloosie Ishulutak was polishing a moose antler from which he had fashioned a menagerie of Arctic creatures. He was proud of the tableau and knew it was extraordinary, both reasons for worry. "Sometimes one I like is not so popular. It's hard. There's different people and different things they like." Until recently every Inuk, needing tools, had to be a carver and the people still retained an innate dexterity that helped new carvers to develop their skills at a speed incredible to southerners. Pauloosie was like that. He had come to carving a few years previously by way of various jobs that included driving a taxi and the water truck and working at the jail just outside the town. "Carving is best," he said. It was fun and he could take home $550 a week if he could keep the tourists, who bought most of his work, happy. This was why the moose antler, a departure, made him nervous. It was a little esoteric.

"What I'm making here is what always sold before. Sometimes the people ask for more like this or that. Like, when someone orders a ring, I ask what they want. It's easier like that."

Pauloosie pointed, for example, to an ivory carving in the workshop's store. From a heavy brown, club-like walrus tusk he had drawn out a delicate, bright white totem with an *iglu* at its base and a seal, whale and ptarmigan piled on top. I asked Pauloosie why he carved it as he had. The bird at the top of the totem, he said, had suggested itself. "It's too small for a polar bear so I carve a bird." Of the overall shape, he said, "Mostly I do it that way so it will fit suitcases."

"Suitcases?"

"Yes, people more likely to buy if they can wrap it. It's easier to sell because it's easier to pack."

The exquisite minutia of Pauloosie's marketing sense was not unusual among Inuit artists. It was one of the things that made talking with them utterly different from talking with southern artists. Inuit carvers were not without pride in their work but they had little pretense about it and no romance. Pauloosie said he would not carve if he didn't make money and he seemed to mean it. He did not keep carvings around his house; once they were done he didn't want to look at them. His was a mixture of the oldest and the newest of Inuit attitudes towards their art.

Like Western art before mechanical reproduction, Inuit art was traditionally bound up in ritual, the nature of which changed with their circumstances. The exact and dark miniatures of the Dorset, the howling faces and animal figures with bits of ochre jammed into their throats, appear to archaeologists to have been entirely magical. Dorset shamen, it is thought, spent a good deal of their time wrestling with the forces that must have continually threatened to close in upon their people. The relative wealth of the Thule led to a new art that seems almost decadent in comparison. The critic George Swinton has pointed out that the Thule art was more bulbous, playful and peaceful, more purely decorative and concerned with inducing fertility rather than appeasing antagonized gods.

Traditionally, Inuktitut had no words for art, artists or for the aesthetics of beauty. The shape of Inuit sculpture arose out of the materials used; the final product could not be known until the product was finished. The hunters with whom Edmund Carpenter lived on Southhampton Island in the early Fifties used the small figures they made in various religious ways such as propitiating the spirit of slain animals. The works, he wrote, reflected the Inuit perception of space: they were not meant to be set down and had no favoured angle of viewing, but, rather, had a different appearance from each angle and were thus, in constant flux.

Among the introductions of southerners, Carpenter argued, was linear perspective. From the fifteenth century until the creation of Cubism, linear perspective characterized Western art. "It makes a god of the spectator," wrote critic Robert Hughes, "who becomes the person on whom the world converges, the Unmoved Onlooker." Inuit artists began to learn this way of looking at the world, with its associations of individualism, Carpenter argued, in the Fifties. The Aivilik he knew, particularly the children, were taught the new way of seeing by photographs and by the government teacher who encouraged children to abandon multiple perspective. To draw, as it were, properly.

About that time James Houston happened along. Houston, a young painter, returned from a 1948 trip with carvings from northern Quebec that generated interest in the south and led to the first government-sponsored, widespread promotion of Inuit art. So began what is known as the post-Houston phase of Inuit sculpture.

Inuit had been making carvings to sell whites since the beginning of the nineteenth century. On one of his early voyages, Franklin described sculptures offered for barter by Inuit: "The figures of the animals were not badly executed, but there was no attempt at the delineation of countenances; and most of the figures were without eyes, ears, and fingers, the execution of which would, perhaps, require more delicate instruments than they possess." In the Fifties, when Inuit realized they could make big money from crafts, people began carving relentlessly. An industry was born. Within four years, twenty thousand carvings were exported from the Arctic. Houston wrote, "The supply has not begun to meet the demand."

The demand has not abated since. Nor have the arguments over the nature and value of the art it has produced. Some, like Carpenter, dismiss it as souvenir art while others, like Swinton, see it as a renaissance of Inuit creation. All agree that contemporary Inuit sculpture is completely different than the traditional. Typically, the carvings are large, single-dimensional and consciously fashioned to Western tastes.

According to Swinton, carving has been undergoing a process of secularization since the nineteenth century; but clearly this has intensified in the twentieth. As an opportunity for some economic self-sufficiency, modern carving has brought a new respect to the community and revived some old skills. Ironically, it has become a reaffirmation of Inuit culture. "Today the carvings and prints," the artist and photographer Peter Pitseolak said, "are the great helpers." Nevertheless the art adored by southerners for its primitive naivete is in fact a sophisticated response to a commercial demand.

Craig Hall was a government arts advisor in Iqaluit. He said, "There is still a tremendous amount of romanticism about the North. One of the reasons people buy carvings is for the vicarious, the artifactual value." This is something that even the most talented of Inuit artists are aware of and that the least forget at their peril. "Down south, if an artist gets hungry he can always work at the Seven Eleven. In the North there is more demand to do the business of carving."

Practically, this means appealing to the souvenir market. Inuit carving, as a result, is so easily pegged in the southern mind that a parallel industry has developed producing fake carvings. Every Canadian city has gift shops where glass shelves fairly groan with these things. Some have at least the veneer of authenticity provided by being stamped out of stone. Others are molded plastic and can hardly be bothered to pretend: the pudgy little Eskimos are as cuddly as Cabbage Patch dolls; the muskox have the bodies of baby seals and come-hither eyes. The competition is said to be destroying the market for the real thing. It was a plastic mold, for example, that the nervous Alan Ayak had in his room at the radar site, purchased in the gift shop at the Edmonton airport.

Artists everywhere who try to live from their work are forced to find their place on a continuum of commercial acceptability. The particular misfortune of Inuit artists is that their continuum has been enveloped by the mass image, already a century old, of them as primitives. They appealed to this image and it came back at them.

This was why nobody carved snowmobiles, oil rigs, military bases or television sets. Most Inuit, of course, don't wish to carve these things anyway. Their preferred subject, as their preferred environment, is the land. The point is that, for practical purposes, they couldn't if they wanted to.

Inuit have long known there was a market in playing to southern stereotypes. I think, for example, of Thomas

Anguttitauruq's story of killing his first caribou. As young boys, he and a cousin crept out of camp one summer night under the light of the midnight sun, carrying a bow and arrow his father had made. With this and much resolve, they took what Thomas described as a baby caribou. Their parents were thrilled. Undoubtedly they were all the more so because the boys had used a bow. None of the hunters in the camp would have been able to remember a time when they had not used guns to hunt. The bows they made to sell to traders.

Thomas Anguttitauruq did a little carving, but he did not make much money at it. He genuinely liked carving, as he did making clothes for his daughter and adapting those he bought for himself. But it didn't sell. He liked to put a lot of detail, like fur, into carvings but this is not considered authentic. Not naive. His problem was that his work was too much him. It didn't fit the mold. He said, "I don't carve like Inuit are supposed to."


I stopped, looked: nothing moved. Okay. A few steps more. I was walking up the side of a ridge in a valley on southern Cornwallis Island, not far from the village of Resolute Bay. It was a spectacular day. The sky was an ultramarine dome and there was no wind. Sunlight flooded the valley and it sparkled as if carpeted with crushed diamonds. Yet I walked with trepidation, trying in vain to be soundless. My boots squeaked on top of the snow like wet rubber on a waxed floor. I cursed the swishing admonitions which reverberated across the landscape of my multiple layers of nylon clothing: Swish!! Swish!! Here I Come!! That would bring them on, I thought. I was not much of a runner in the first place. I would be a goner in this get-up. The thing was: there were polar bears about.

This time of the year they hung around the island, waiting for the ice cover to solidify so that they could wander out to sea, hunting. In the village I had been told: "If you see one, just use common sense." Now I realized I had no sense common to this situation and no senses that were very useful in it. Even at its most benign and magnificent, the sheer immensity of the Arctic can be terrifying. It is indifferent to your presence in a way that a forest, say, cannot be. But there was nothing in the image of this valley to warn me. I thought of the Inuit hunter: always afraid, concentrating, wary. I tried to concentrate, to really lock in on the detail of my surroundings. My mind was quickly dazzled by the glittering light, the enormity of the silence. I would bend to look at a rock with a long tapering tail of snow streaming off one side, like an evening shadow, packed so hard by the wind you could cut your finger on its peak. Abstractions. My mind danced off into abstractions. No common sense.

Walking a little further I chanced to look down and I froze. A grinning skull was at my feet. A polar bear's skull. Its teeth were half the length of my fingers and the eye sockets were filled with yellow, pulpy tissue. I looked around. Sunshine, snow, joyous. The village in the distance. For me, to feel afraid in a place such as this was truly surreal. In this, I was a product of my culture.

Small-time fishermen and farmers, peasants, hunters; these were people who still understood the voices of the land and animals. People who knew, in their different ways, both the blessing and terrifying faces of nature. Where I came from, it was only people you had to understand and placate and fear. At its kindest the natural world was a pleasant diversion, a resting place, a park, a pet. At its most fearsome, it was grand spectacle, vicarious thrills, a lightning storm viewed from the balcony, a snowstorm overwhelming the downtown. Big theatre. It *never* frightened me. And I am a nervous person. Understanding this was one way of knowing where all those dozens of thousands of Inuit carvings went. And why.

Inevitably, there was a flip side to the intellectual development of industrial society: the romanticization of animals, people who were considered primitive and everything that falls under the general heading Nature.

The critic John Berger traced the development of this in an essay called *Why Look At Animals?* which was, primarily, about zoos. He wrote, "The zoo to which people go to meet animals, to observe them, to see them, is, in fact, a monument to the impossibility of such encounters." Through the late nineteenth and early twentieth century, animals were gradually pushed out of the lives and consciousness of industrialized peoples. This was partly physical — as trucks and tractors replaced the work of horses and oxen — and partly spiritual — the result of the Cartesian dissection of them which eliminated their mysteries. We do not any longer, as the Inuit do, speak of the Walrus or Caribou to describe the collective spirit of a species. Descartes' legacy is such that we talk about Nature as something completely apart, a notion that would not have occurred to people in the Middle Ages and certainly would not occur to the Inuit.

Institutionalized zoos show the many sides of this process. They were meant to be educational, teaching about animals by isolating and classifying them, and were also symbols of imperial power. Returning explorers were obliged to bring specimens which served as living testaments to a nation's ability to conquer the furthest, darkest corners. Arctic explorers regularly captured muskox and polar bear. Carl Hagenbeck, architect of the modern zoo, toured Inuit and Indians through European zoos and designed a display for the 1904 St. Louis World's Fair which is said to have included a polar bear, a walrus and an Inuit.

Berger's point is that zoos came to represent the marginalization of animals. People go to them trying, as it were, to cross an impossible gap. As this grew, animals became objects of nostalgia. In the nineteenth Century, for the first time, their images flooded into the world of children with the widespread introduction of animal toys. Distinct from the representations children had always had, these were realistic rather than symbolic. They were a replacement.

"The machine," Marshall McLuhan wrote, "turned nature into an art form. For the first time men began to regard Nature as a source of aesthetic and spiritual values. They began to marvel that earlier ages had been so unaware of the world of Nature as Art."

The industrialized mind sees the natural world as uncompli-
cated, free of repression, static, beautiful and innocent. As the
technological world becomes more obviously explosive, these
sentiments only intensify. It seems to me this is some explanation for the immense popularity of Inuit art since the war; over
the last forty years the middle classes have been infused both
with an intense, media-driven desire for fashionability and a
growing, if often unconscious, foreboding. Beyond their intrinsic artistic value, Inuit carvings are innocence as commodity for
the sophisticated mind; Disney for grown-ups. Almost uniquely, they are animal representations acceptable among the fashion-
conscious — and filter down from them — because they are
considered to be unsentimental, unlike the dime-store kitsch that
is much the more common form. And they are also, of course,
political. To have an Inuit carving is, alone, an expression of
solidarity. It was no surprise when the young manager of the
Iqaluit carving workshop said, "This stuff sells particularly well
in West Germany."

"There seems to be one dominating form of modern understanding," Paul Fussell wrote, "that it is essentially ironic." In
*The Great War and Modern Memory*, he argued that World War
I permanently darkened the modern imagination. The generation
that marched off to the slaughter as if to a game "believed in
Progress and Art and in no way doubted the benignity even of
technology. The word *machine* was not yet invariably coupled
with the word *gun*." And they were mowed down like so many
blades of grass by the machines they had put their faith in. The
prevailing sense of irony that resulted has only increased in the
face of the wars, weaponry and environmental disaster since.
Fussell's point, I think, was that this perpetually short-circuits
hope; and makes the hopeful seem stupid. It also, of course, is a
kind of blanket shrug, a permanent justification for the ludicrous.

I think this may be part of the reason for our failure to recognize consciously that our sentiment runs straight counter to our

actions; of why we decorate a dying planet with animal figurines made of toxic plastics. But for the people who try to live in accommodation with their environment, our knowing, ironic smiles are not helpful.

The politician John Amagoalik said, "The Europeans have been having a big love-on with natives for years." He said this with real anger. We were talking about the animal rights movement. For the Inuit, nothing better made the point. During the Eighties, the economically poorest Inuit families, those who tried to survive from trapping and hunting, have seen their incomes steadily drop almost to nothing as a result of the agitation against seal hunting and trapping from the European animal rights movement.

This movement is based in Britain, the imploded empire, Kingdom of Irony. It was the British who invented the notion of pastoral romance at the time of the Industrial Revolution. Two centuries later, the pastoral legacy is a continuing national obsession expressed in a dandyistic love of nature. Nowhere do middle-class suburbanites have such deliberately unkempt gardens, nor are the trips to the countryside so ritualistically rustic nor the television programming so crammed with first class natural histories. The legacy of Industrial Revolution attitudes, however, is one of the most polluted countries in Europe; its cities are blanketed in smog, its countryside replete with leaking nuclear reactors, its shoreline segmented by pipes dumping sewage into the sea. Britain is obvious but not particularly unusual in failing to connect the two.

The most vocal and obvious agitators in the British animal rights movement, as it would happen, are young anarchists who clearly have a genuine fellow-feeling for the trapped and hunted. The movement's sympathizers however, are spread throughout society. Whipping up British support against seal hunting was a cinch. A particularly effective fund and consciousness raiser at one time was a mechanized display that was towed about downtown London which featured a hunter — a Newfoundlander — bashing the brains out of a baby seal. Animal rights activists claim, quite correctly, that it is not aboriginal people who make the bulk of profits from the fur trade. But this is no compensation to Arctic communities that have lost their only source of cash.

Of course, it was the British who initiated the fur trade in the first place, beginning the long economic and social chain reaction within Inuit society. Now the Inuit have found themselves once again undercut by a swing in Western ideological fashion. They have been left infuriated and confused by the destruction of their subsistence economy, which inevitably makes industrial development more necessary. This is as strange to them as our destruction of the natural environment and construction of suicidal weaponry. Inuit have a keen sense of natural irony but no capacity for nihilism. They cannot easily understand a society that wants to have its innocence and eat it too.

Elisapee Davidee said, "Our priority is to be understood. Not just listened to, but understood. Really understood."

Exactly three times in the last two decades the Canadian public has shown a genuine interest in the Arctic; each has been an intense and emotional outpouring. These followed the two American transits of the Northwest Passage and the Mackenzie Valley Pipeline inquiry when Thomas Berger, an admirable man by any standard, became that rarest of Canadian characters, a genuine national folk hero. The significance of this intense sporadic interest, I think, has to do with urban attitudes toward nature. The Arctic sits in the living room of the Canadian psyche like one massive Eskimo seal carving.

Canadians, as a rule, know nothing at all about the Arctic or the people who live there. Few have visited, much less lived, in the North and few are interested in doing so. It is difficult and expensive but, more important, the vast majority of us are urbanites with little interest in getting too far from a city. Because cities, so to speak, are where it's at.

Only in preparing to travel to the Soviet Union have I ever encountered more uninformed opinions than I did before I went
North. People who could recommend restaurants in a half dozen
other countries barely knew the Foxe Basin from the Sea of Tran-
quillity. Several, trying to be helpful, suggested that I not rent a
car in the High Arctic. Driving alone there, they felt, would likely be dangerous. One day I spent a half-hour on the telephone
guiding a ticket agent with the national airline as she ran her
finger from one coordinate to the next on a map trying to locate
Tuktoyuktuk. Throughout, she mumbled, "Chuckee-chuck-
chuck … mmmm … chuckee-chuck-chuck … I dunno why you
wanna go there."

Reports from scientists and bureaucrats with a special interest
are filled with complaints that they receive no public or political
support. "The North," said one, "is not central to our national
psyche. It is not so much a frontier in our consciousness as a
periphery." Franklyn Griffiths has argued that this is a result of
an attitude Canadians inherited with the territory from the
British. The Victorians, he notes, viewed the land as sublime, in-
vested with possibilities of both beauty and horror almost beyond
comprehension. Northward bound, Mary Shelley's ship captain
asks, "What may not be expected in a country of eternal light?"
For Lady Jane Franklin the Arctic was simply "that dark corner
of the earth." For modern Canadians, Griffiths wrote, the land
"brings forth deep seated attitudes of possessiveness on the one
hand and fear and passivity on the other."

It seems to me that the sense of fear no longer has much hold.
The aspect of the national mythology that included the fear and
reverence of the country's great and wild spaces, particularly the
Arctic has atrophied in the contemporary imagination to a
souvenir of its former self. This is partly the result of technology
and, in English Canada, partly a reflection of our shifting attitude
toward ourselves, especially in relation to the United States.

In her 1972 study of Canadian literature, *Survival*, Margaret
Atwood wrote that this was the prevailing theme of Canadian
literature — and, by extension, thought. Mere, grim survival

against overwhelming power, "tales not of those who made it but of those who made it back." She characterized these as falling into different postures of victimization, from the victim who refuses to acknowledge his position to the one who, through progressive steps of awareness, transcends it. Very often she wrote, nature in our stories has been a stand-in for the oppressor — America — while victimized animals have been a double for ourselves.

While the long standing self-torment over identity is by no means ended, it seems to me that English Canadians have come to terms with it by stepping around it. Deep in their resistors, they see themselves as Americans. Only: better.

Despite flare-ups of nationalist sentiment, usually from artists and other malcontents, Canadians' subservience to America hardly merits detailing. The United States dominates Canada's economy, mass culture and foreign policy. The belief instilled in us that we are a quilted, rather than melted, society is increasingly spurious as it becomes apparent that the only common thread in the multicultural tapestry is American culture. As I write, the Canadian government is preparing to formally complete these arrangements by unifying the two nations' economies. Half the country's population is said to be in favor of this, with the other half putting up, at best, a tepid fight. We see the Americans as friends. Just like the Inuit see us.

But Canadians are not quite prepared to swallow America whole either. This is partly because there are all sorts of vile things about American society no one would wish upon themselves and partly because to do so would be to admit a kind of defeat. I think Canadians get around this now by empowering themselves with righteousness, which is also a kind of confidence.

This is the source, for example, of the comic little Canadian conceit that Europeans and most other foreigners like us better. Notwithstanding the fact that the United States' position in the world is such that almost everybody viscerally likes almost anybody better than Americans, it's just not true. Certainly in

Europe, all but the most politicized generally cannot and do not care to distinguish among North Americans.

But we too easily grant ourselves the sleep of the just. In *The Nuclear North*, Carol Giangrande argued that the Canadian desire to perceive ourselves as nice is the reason we refuse to believe that the uranium that flattened Hiroshima and Nagasaki came — as it almost certainly did — from Canada. Why, also, we cherish the myth of being a Peacekeeper Nation and ignore the fact that the only country in the world with more American nuclear weapons installations than Canada is West Germany.

The Arctic, I think, embodies this sense of righteous purity for Canadians. Our contemporary image of the Arctic is a moving one; that is, a tracking shot, from a helicopter flying low and fast, over great white spaces. Now it includes a herd of caribou, perhaps, a thousand tawny specks dispersing before us in a great fan forever to run free. Cut to: the momentary hummocks of Narwhal backs breaking the surface. Cut (perhaps, depends who's paying) to: a mighty oil rig, a clean, non-polluting, well managed, *Canadian* oil rig; standing fast against the ice. The camera spins around it. Dissolve to: a smiling, rosy-cheeked, fur-framed Inuit child. (Music swells) Dissolve to: white. Always white. The Arctic is pure. The Arctic is innocent. The Arctic is clean. That's why people name detergents after it. And the Arctic is ours. It is us.

This is why American challenges to national sovereignty in the Arctic are met with howls of outrage while, from any half-reasonable perspective, much more important areas of sovereignty are blithely abandoned.

In this pretense the Inuit have no small role. As Hugh Brody has pointed out, where Indians were originally stereotyped as savages and, later, as drunks and layabouts, the Inuit have always been cast as cheerful, innocent simpletons. Nanooks. Cuddly pets. One of the ironies of this is that our image of them reflects on us and back at them in yet another closed loop, allowing Canadians the fiction that aboriginal people have had a better deal in this country than, say, in the United States or Australia.

Every country has its mythological territories. America has the rugged west. Britain has the glorious Sea. Canada has the Arctic, the glistening white vessel of our sanctimonious soul. The national halo. The image itself has the ability to conjure innocence, cleanse. Like detergent: *Arctic Power.*

The myth is strong enough that, by association, it can even scrub the filth from nuclear weaponry. When it was bidding for the contract to operate the North Warning System, the company that eventually won, Frontec Logistics Corporation, ran magazine advertisements dominated by a smiling, fur-clad Inuk who stood twice the height of the radar station in the picture. To one side, a polar bear roamed while gulls wheeled overhead. Similarly, in their advertisements to convince the Canadian public that it ought to buy British nuclear submarines, the Trafalgar Consortium ran advertisements in Canadian newspapers. These were dark images, showing the back and conning tower of a submarine, with slabs of Arctic ice sliding off the surfacing beast. The point of the advertisements was to make us think these machines would protect our virginity. Think of us, they said, as atomic chastity belts.


Pretty much single-handed, Bill Zawadiuk hooked Cambridge Bay into the global village. He didn't mean to, but he did. He grinned, now, to tell the way it happened. It was one of those things. An electronic engineer by trade, working for the federal government, he had helped hook up the CBC Northern Service in the village in 1975. After a few years he found he was just sick and tired of that same old CBC stuff. All the more frustrating to know that the satellites were up there and the air was charged with a dozen signals so he decided to build his own dish and pull them in. And then didn't everyone in the village want it?

Before he knew it, Bill Zawadiuk was something of a cable television magnate. Within four years eighty per cent of the homes in the village were receiving nine channels (ten really, but one is slightly illegal, so it doesn't count). Bill spent $100,000 setting it up and now it was just about taking that in annually. No sooner was his empire running smoothly than he decided to move to a more southern locale and sold the service. What was the profit? you might ask. Bill Zawadiuk would only grin.

"What kind of impact has TV had on the community?"

"A real good impact. As you know, there isn't anything up here for other amenities. TV is a good place to keep the kids at home. And this is why it's a good impact."

"What is most popular?"

"The movie channel and PBS."

"PBS?"

"Yes, because of the documentaries and children's programs. The intellectual people in Cambridge watch PBS." (Mrs. Z pipes in here: "Now Biiiilll, I watch it and I'm not an intellectual.")

"Are the Inuit watching PBS?"

"Oh. The *Inuit*. Nah. For the Inuit the most popular things are wrestling and sports. They used to have local Inuit TV but they don't do that anymore. Maybe they ran out of money."

He added: "TV opens a whole new world up here, because we lack what everybody else has down south: the knowledge that the picture presents to the people who watch it. The Inuit and the non-Inuit that are here, that are subscribers."

Television reached the Arctic only in 1967 and didn't get very far then. CBC begin supplying what it called a "frontier package," a four-hour video tape that was carried to Yellowknife daily by airplane and transmitted locally. In 1972 Canada launched its first geostationary satellite, making television and telephone service available in the high Arctic. Appropriately, the satellite and its spinoffs, were given an Inuit name, *Anik*, which Telesat Canada officially translates as meaning *brother*. Actually the precise translation from the Inuktitut means "the older brother of a woman." That is her Big Brother.

Now there is a satellite dish in every village; just on the periphery usually, sitting on top of the little house that encases its brains. Almost always, as if the villagers intended to make a point of the prevailing paradox, eight or a dozen sled dogs would be tethered beneath, howling to run. The dish pointed straight at the horizon, a blank grey metal face staring at two satellites, 40,000 miles away. Anik D1 and Anik D2 spin in lock step with the earth, straight above the equator, transmitting a signal that consists of telephone links, television programming and military communications. It takes one half of one second for these to reach across the continent and into a dish which appears to see nothing but the emptiness of the polar flats.

The television beam carries messages originating in Vancouver (CTV), Edmonton (ITV), Hamilton (CHCH), Toronto (CBC), Montreal (TCTV) and Detroit (ABC, NBC, CBS, PBS, TFN, MTV, HBO), all of which originate, in turn, primarily in Los Angeles. "The beauty of a satellite," Stephen Lowe said, "is that you can get the exact same signal here as they get down south." Stephen Lowe worked for Telesat Canada in Iqaluit, maintaining the electronic links. The military signals, he said, originated at the various Arctic installations and bounced back down to earth somewhere in the United States. Exactly *where* was anybody's guess. "That's the thing with satellites. You don't really know who is receiving the signals or who is sending the signals."

The first day I was in the Arctic, I saw the local news from Hamilton, Ontario (a flipped transport truck was terribly snarling the rush hour), an advertisement for an imitation wedding ring just like Princess Di's (available by mail from Toronto) and *The Young and the Restless*. The last day I was in the Arctic, I saw an afternoon talk show on which a woman named Oprah Winfrey was grilling men who had raped other men. "Did it make you feel really big, really *powerful*?" she was saying to some poor all-but-obliterated soul who stared into his offending lap and clearly wished he had slit his wrists when he had had the chance. In between I saw everything I might have seen living, as I do, in the shadow of the CN Tower.

"We know," George Porter said, "a lot more about the south than people in the south know about the north." George Porter had been to school — "we learned about the whole world" —

and that is what he was talking about. But the comment now applies much more to television. Virtually all Inuit have television and receive, at the very least, ninety-five hours a week of CBC which may include five of Inuit broadcasting. Many have cable also, plugging them non-stop into the Global Village. Even remote and solitary hunting camps are now equipped with VCRs, which are run by generator. As George Porter and I talked in his living room, which is lined with an extraordinary baseball hat collection, the programmes on the television changed over and his wife and daughter spontaneously burst into the infectious little theme song of an American situation comedy about adolescent girls called *The Facts of Life*.

Strictly speaking, what Inuit see on television has little to do with the day to day facts of their lives. Then again, it has everything to do with their lives, because it is their primary representation of how the rest of the world lives and, especially, how things are done in that amorphous region beneath them that they simply call The South where all the crucial decisions in their lives are made. The vast bulk of television images, of course, whether in news, sport or drama come from The South. Middle-class America. What we know of them through seal carvings, they know of us through television.

"It opened everything up," Fr. LeChat said. "This was a very closed world before TV came. They were the Inuit and that was that. I remember once saying that the bishop was going to Rome and a kid asked, 'How is he going.' By boat. 'What? The sea is not frozen?' It was in this part of the country so they thought it was everywhere."

Many people told stories like that. Inuit were not xenophobic but not many got out of the Arctic often and many never had. Their contact with even the southerners who lived among them was — is — limited. In many communities, a social polarity exists between the natives and the newcomers, who are usually just passing through. "Southerners can be pretty cliquey and stick together," Chuck Tolley said. "Sometimes people even develop a kind of siege mentality." Nor do many Inuit even have access to writing from the rest of the world. They have been using the syllabic orthography developed by missionaries since the late nineteenth century but the only outside works southerners have bothered to translate were government manuals and the Bible. Inuit know little of the way whites actually live, but for their outward appearances. Abigail Kaernerk said, "She doesn't have any idea the way white people live. She doesn't have a clue. She can't speak English. She thinks white people pretty well live the same way she does."

With television, Inuit suddenly found themselves overwhelmed by a torrent of impressions of The South and its people. But these, especially at first, were far from totally intelligible.

In the first place, most people do not understand English, particularly the old and those who live in the eastern Arctic where more than sixty per cent of the population, primarily adults, is unilingual. Almost unique in the world, they view television without even the benefit of the incessant commentary that is built into the medium to serve as an easy path through the jungle of disconnected imagery. But the images, of course, are mighty compelling. "My mother," a man said, "is hooked on *All My Children* though she doesn't understand a word of it."

The other translation problem that exists has to do with the language of the medium itself. The essence of television is that it is a bombardment of symbols, a fulsome parade of atomized icons. These are not characters but archetypes, originally vaudevillian, but for decades now taken from television itself, the most self-referential of media. Their purpose is to push emotional buttons.

One of the main themes of every critic of the medium since Marshall McLuhan is that the structure of television is such that it does not attempt to tell a story or to represent life, as such. It's intent is to *be* life. We *feel* television, not from the "reality" of the images — a denotation we can intellectually analyze — but from what they stand for — a connotation that gets you in the gut. Television tries to reach right into viewers and make them feel that the characters on the screen are extensions of themselves. Or, rather, vice versa. To make us, that is, a part of the electronic landscape the way Inuit are a part of the natural one. In *Understanding Media*, McLuhan wrote that medical students who had watched an operation on television had the uncanny sense that they had actually been performing it.

It goes without saying that the job of commercial television is to make the experience pleasant, because its sole purpose is to make us buy things. One of the primary rules within a programme, for example, is what film critics call *closure* and what ordinary people call *happy endings*. Everything gets neatly tied up at the end. Even news gives us a jolly send-off so that the viewer never comes away feeling grim. "Entertainment," critic Neil Postman writes, "is the supra ideology of all discourse on television. No matter what is depicted or from what point of view, the overarching assumption is that it is there for our amusement and pleasure."

Television moves at atomic speed, and for it to work properly viewers must recognize the icons and know the ground rules. Television relies on instant recognition. Casually glancing at a TV in a village hotel one afternoon, I barely acknowledged an auburn summer sunset image of a boy sitting on a wooden porch, with a muskox head beside him, working intently on some tool. I turned back to my writing for a few seconds before snapping to attention. This was a commercial for Bell Telephone and the caribou head was a sheep dog, the furry and cuddly kind manufacturers prefer. I had not been watching television much and had not seen a sheep dog in some time.

Inuit came to television without knowing the rules. Their traditional mode of thinking and story-telling was not linear and their stories certainly did not always have happy endings. Very often they had no endings at all. The water beetle just walks away because he is not good at thinking up answers. Maybe he will come back again. Maybe not. One of the results was that Inuit were not automatically pacified by television or satisfied by its semblance of resolution. Quite the contrary. By many of its constituent parts, they were horrified.

John Amagoalik said: "Overnight the whole world was dropped in our lap. We started seeing all these wars. We used to hear about wars but now we could actually see them; we could see them in our living rooms, we could see the death and suffering it causes. Up until then wars were just stories about war and then television brought them right into our living rooms. Young Inuit started asking: What does this mean for us? We started saying: Okay, we've got to make sure that this military madness doesn't infiltrate into our lives."

The tragic comedy of television in the Western world is that we claim to recognize the grotesqueness of the symbols before us and yet are constantly struck by a sense of verisimilitude. *They look just like us;* only better. *Much* better. We are always challenged to wonder if it is not us — with our infinitely duller and cruder attempts at kinship, at creating and maintaining love, stability and something that passes for security — who are missing the boat. We see ourselves, in short, as lesser versions of the perfection offered on television. Inuit don't recognize themselves at all on television. But they think they recognize us.

Elisapee Davidee, the IBC television producer, had the usual Arctic habit of talking of the Outside World. No such thing, I said. Okay, she said. But: "The southern world is very developed and outside of ours. Our world is living on the land, respecting the land, respecting other people. And the stuff we get from TV is from a very outside world. Because we are not used to seeing people get killed. Up here we kill animals for survival. An expression I have heard is: Don't white people love each other? Don't they care? Are they using humans for target practice?"

McLuhan reported a similar comment twenty-five years ago from a Nigerian who, after seeing an American Western, said he did not realize the West put so little value on life. McLuhan contrasted the reaction to that of American children who, even during gunfights, kept their eyes on the characters' faces. His point was that the kids were not standing back assessing. They were right in there.

The process of being sucked in is a slow one. Our contemporary epistemology, as Postman has shown, began developing more than 100 years ago with the telegraph and the photograph, the prototypical pistol-like media which eventually fused into the imagistic gatling gun of television. We have been here for some time. Not so the Inuit, but they have been given to believe there is no alternative to learning to live with it. Elisapee said, "We can't get away from the world we are living in today." This is, of course, true. And one hears it often in the Arctic. To a certain sort of person, usually Inuit, it means: people have to adapt. This is nothing new. To another sort of person, often white, it means: there's no stopping Progress. And television is the face of Progress. Television teaches television. It is both the landscape and the map.

Above all it is wondrous to look at. In the Arctic, like everywhere else, people cannot get enough. Inuit now giggle away hours before the candy-coloured posturings and buffoonery of the plastic phantoms. Families regularly stay up all night watching television. And fifteen years on, the violence that initially shocked so many has become somewhat more ordinary. People find themselves riveted to the bright snippets of exploding planes, crumbling cities and columns of smoke rising above lands only recently made known to them.

People can habituate to new environments very quickly and aboriginal people, as a rule, much faster than most. A decade ago I happened to spend a day at a hearing before the Canadian Radio-Television and Telecommunications Commission. The commission was in the middle of one of many sets of hearings regarding cable television service. Northern Ontario was being discussed on this particular day. Several earnest public broadcasting advocates gave submissions arguing that the good people of the far north were entitled to the extension of national television so that they might tap into the rich cultural heritage of the country. Ballet, I remember, was mentioned. Eventually a native spokeswoman from one of the communities had her chance to speak. Her comments went something like this: We have been, as you know, getting satellite television for sometime. We steal it. Our people have been able to watch M*A*S*H for years. Now you want to give us ballet. We prefer M*A*S*H.

One critic has noted that American television operates now the way the missionaries did in the nineteenth century, as a herald of the empire. The analogy has particular resonance for the Inuit. Unlike their performance among other aboriginal societies, particularly in South America, where they arrived with armies in tow, the missionaries came gently to the Inuit. They were welcomed with characteristic openness, often entering communities through the shaman. Inuit were always fascinated by the new. When the people grew dependent on other whites, such as fur traders, the missionaries, by then established, had the leverage to begin suppressing the traditional spirituality. The shaman were decried as doing the devil's business and forced, as it were, underground. So it goes.

One evening I went to interview two young Inuit politicians. When I arrived they were watching an old Flash Gordon movie. They had been eager to do this interview — they wanted to promulgate their point of view — but neither could take their eyes off the television. In deference to me, they kept turning the sound down. Then something interesting would happen and one of them would slip over and turn it up a little. Then down. Then up. And so on. It was like interviewing someone who was driving a car.

Afterward, I thought of Thomas Anguttitauruq decades ago, sitting there in his parents' tiny camp on the shores of Garry Lake. He is holding a can of *Klik*. He turns it over and over in his small hands as if it were a cube of crystallized magic. He is simply entranced. He has no way of knowing then what this glowing box means for his future. He cannot. Because he is the answer to the question.


Joe and I were sitting at his kitchen table, drinking tea. The news was spewing out of a far corner. Somewhere, Ronald Reagan was striding past a clutch of reporters who were yelping from behind a barricade. When we looked in, Reagan was striking a familiar pose: hand cupped behind one ear, head cocked, smiling a big, incredulous smile at some silly old question, moving. Joe said, "He must be good, eh? Reagan? He's been there a long time." Cut to: Martin Sheen being arrested in California while blocking the road into a missile plant.

"There's a peace protest, Joe. What do you think about that?"
"Peace protest? What's that?"

Critics of television news and most people who make it agree that it is composed of bits of trivia, out of context, which people either discard altogether or anchor, as they watch, in relation to their personal lives. The only overriding order the news gives us is provided by the proclamations of institutions. These create what Joyce Nelson calls a "structure of reassurance"; the chaos is woven together by pictures of important people doing important things who, we are to assume, have the continuing disaster well in hand. And the very basis of all North American journalism, particularly as presented on television, is opposition; there are always two, and only two, sides facing off with the intensity of pitbulls, no matter how miniscule the issue. This makes for good theatre and is what journalists call objectivity. The sum effect, however, is an impression that the acrimony is relentless but there's no fighting city hall. And, really, no need to.

For Joe, as is common for Inuit, there was a frame of reference for power but not for complaint. When Inuit try to anchor the images of television with their own experience, they must inevitably arrive at the conclusion that the South operates just like the North does. The powerful are always on top of things. Inuit are not culturally disposed to put up much of a fight in the first place. Television only reinforces the logic in this.

This is not the same as saying you have to remain powerless, though. Television promises a straight and certain route to a kind of power: having things. As everyone knows (sort of), its only sustained argument is that money can indeed buy happiness. "Inuit think they are so poor," said Bezal Jesudason, who came from India, where people are. "I tell them that white men look rich, but they are all in debt." But television does not show debt. Nobody is in debt on TV. Sitting in overcrowded, prefabricated bungalows in artificial suburbs surrounded by white officials who, comparatively, *are* rich, it is hardly a wonder that the televised image of the South, where life is one long beer commercial, would lead Inuit to this conclusion. After all, it leads southerners to this conclusion. That's what drives the economy. And as skeptical as Inuit have become over the years, one of the most fundamental tenets of their culture remains honesty and its corollary, the belief that others are basically honest. Needless to say, television is to honesty what fire is to ice.

Thomas Anguttitauruq said, "You know, Inuit believes whatever they are told."

Gideon Qitsualik said, "Everything the Inuit sees makes them want more and more. They are taught to do it nowadays."

There is little question what the main pedagogical force is. Ultimately, what television teaches the Inuit is to see themselves as marginal; no longer at the centre of the earth, but camped on the furthest periphery of the Global Village. It cannot do anything but. They will *never* have the wherewithal to get even a tiny fraction of the baubles dancing before them. All that they will have more and more of is the wanting. This is not a problem specific to the Arctic, though it will always be worse there than in many, many places. But people everywhere have this feeling. It's not that they don't love their own homes or cultures. It's that these are bound to seem wanting under the harsh blue light. All things considered, the Inuit are probably better inoculated against this sort of thing than any people in the world. But they, too, are now starting to interpret their lives through television.

The Gjoa Haven monster comes to mind in this regard. Peter Akkikungak told me about it first. "You know," he said, "we got a monster in this town. Well, just outside of town. In a lake. He's a big hairy thing. His head is the size of a man's body and he has great big eyes." He had not seen it, Peter, but he knew a couple of fellows who had. "These guys aren't lying and they're not stupid." I hadn't suspected they were. I was prepared to entertain any possibility. "I thought maybe we could get some TV cameras up here. If people knew about the monster maybe tourists would come."

In the impossible economic situation a village like Gjoa Haven found itself in, getting the village monster on television was as realistic a plan for revival as any. The next time I saw him he introduced me to the men who knew the monster personally and to several others who could vouch for their credibility. He was certain I had the power to call in gunships full of TV reporters and anxious that I should do so.

Every reporter is used to this kind of harangue and it was all good fun. But it wasn't really very funny. The world is packed with marginal hordes whose problems are irrelevant to their governments, whose claims are easily silenced with a welfare cheque or a rifle butt. For them television is the court of last resort. It has more power and legitimacy than most visible political processes. It is more real than reality. In villages from the Arctic to southern Africa there has erupted a popularity contest amongst the loathed, each vying for the unloveliest or most bizarre wrapping for their problem in the hope of catching the most fickle of eyes. The Inuit situation only called for a tourist-fetching monster. Other people need to riot or blow things up. Television is the closest thing there is to international law. This the Inuit had learned.

As the community fragmented, people were also finding personal meaning in television. They were beginning to see themselves as media archetypes. Consider, to use the anthropologists' device, L. As a child he was raised in a DEW Line Eskimo House, beside the site where his father worked. At six he was sent off to school where he stayed for nine years, returning home during the summers. At school, as was the norm, Inuktitut was forbidden. By the time he was eight, L had forgotten most of his language. "When I would go back home I would try to speak to my mom and my mom wouldn't understand me. And I wouldn't understand my mom. I had to get my dad to translate."

After a few more years in school, he had forgotten most of what he knew about his culture. He felt ashamed of that, he said, but he consoled himself with the knowledge that he was part of Progress. "The world is changing and we're going into the future." Workwise, it could hardly have mattered less. He got a job with the government, working in a village, trying to find jobs for other people.

He said, "Myself, I know I've completely lost my will to go hunting. I've completely lost interest in that. I come to work, I go home, watch TV, go to sleep and come back to work. I don't go out on the land on the weekends because my weekends are pretty tied up. I've just lost that part of the culture. I'm a sports nut. I just watch sports on television and have a few beer. Saturdays and Sundays I just watch sports or visit my friends. That's it. There's quite a few of us in town that aren't going out hunting. We're Yuppies. I guess that's what we're turning into. Yuppies."

When Inuit began to gain local political power the first thing they went after was the school system. More than any other institution they felt it had undermined their culture. They wanted something done so that it didn't turn out another generation of children who could see themselves as Yuppies. No one could argue with this. The school system in the Arctic is haunted the way prison systems are elsewhere; everyone who went through it in the Fifties and Sixties had a personal book of horror stories to relate. The antagonist in these was usually a nun, a huge nun, with a head the size of a man's body. She thought Inuktitut was the devil's voice and she beat it out of kids with a switch as big as a sled runner. Beat them just like they were dogs. Or so the stories went. "They tell us to be nice and I was wondering why they hit us when we disobey. I was told nuns were so gentle."

Education was not compulsory and only a minority of children went to these schools. Some of those who did lost contact with their culture. Others had a fire lit in them and grew into the politicians who worked in the Seventies to force government institutions to begin reflecting Inuit culture. Particularly the schools. They would not stand, they said, for their children being raised in the white man's image. Just about the time that the legitimacy of their argument was being broadly accepted, television came along.

Chuck Tolley, the Baffin educator said, "If you ask the young people in most communities what they want to do they will always tell you that they want to be hunters." Visiting several schools, I found this to be true. Who wants to be a hunter? I would ask, and every boy's hand would go up. Why? "We want to ride around on skidoos all day," came a bright voice at the back of a class of eleven-year-olds in Resolute Bay. I see. What about the girls? The girls were not so sure. If I asked straight out if they saw themselves as hunter's wives, they would not say no. They would just shrug. Dunno. Looking at the old women in the village, their faces lined like tributaries and their hands like leather gloves, was all a girl needed to know how tough was the work of a hunter's wife. And girls, of course, are always more realistic than boys. Usually one of them would venture, in a timid voice, something like, "It's a hard life."

Living where they did, there was no doubt that Inuit children were tougher, physically, than southern children. But to look at them you would never know the difference. Save, perhaps, for their uniformly straight, shiny black hair. No matter how small or how remote the village, the kids all wore the colours of their generation and had every particular of the uniform right. The girls had bright sweat shirts, *Ocean Pacific*. The boys had black T-shirts emblazoned with a *Bon Jovi* or *U2* stencil, a leather jacket if they were lucky and a band for each limb, like tagged geese. Everybody got jeans, of course, and high back runners, to be left open at the top. It might be thirty below outside and storming. But these kids lived in the Global Village, where it's always warm and sunny.

There were pictures of pumpkins and cats on the walls of one of the schools I visited, and in the main hallway there was a stuffed muskox head and three pigeons in a cage. Here, the cultural message of the Seventies had not sunk in. There are no pumpkins or cats in the Arctic, of course. Inuit domesticate only dogs and they make no animals into trophies. At other schools, where the teachers were trying harder, the kids had drawn pictures of whales or cut *ulus* out of coloured paper.

Everywhere educators recognized the need to inject more Inuit culture into the curriculum. But these things don't happen overnight. The basic curriculum and credits are issued by Alberta, the amount of deviation depends on the region. Children going to school in the west might as well have been in a suburb of Calgary. In the east, where the southern influence was less, there is a greater commitment to aboriginal culture. But resources are a problem. Inuktitut is not outlawed any more but it is only taught up to Grade Three, because of a shortage of Inuit who meet the system's standards as teachers and because of the lack of an accepted curriculum. The declared goal is a school system that is bilingual and oriented toward an Inuit viewpoint within the Canadian context. But even the territorial government has had to admit that it does not know exactly what that means. In his 1986 report, the education minister said he recognized that the system had to be more effective and relevant, adding: "Research began to determine the characteristics of 'effective northern schools.'" Certain things were beyond question. Every school, for example, was to be provided with personal computers.

Teachers make it up as they go along. Gone, of course, are the club-wielding nuns and the unarmed young people who replaced them have a much more difficult job. On the one hand they are sensitive to the Inuit culture. On the other, they are white, middle-class professionals who, by temperament and training, are better suited to turning out Yuppies than hunters. Theirs is the same problem that confronts all the sensitive bureaucrats in the North: given the way things are going, the only way Inuit will get power is by being able to work the southern system. And constantly they run up against the contradictions inherent in the position of these kids.

Any of the kids I met, for example, could have been popped into a classroom in suburban Edmonton or Toronto and seemed just another squirming pea in the concrete pod. But if you scratched the T-shirt it was clear that they were firmly rooted in the permafrost of their villages. In smaller villages, the system has not yet been able to provide secondary schooling. As a result, teachers who try to push kids toward high school meet great resistance, because it means they are also pushing them into larger towns, away from their families and their culture. Nevertheless, they push. What else are they supposed to do?

One principal said, "We have five per cent of our kids go to Grade Twelve. But ninety-five per cent of the system's resources go into producing that five per cent. People need life skills; to know how to handle alcohol, take care of their health, set goals. And not just people in the North. If we get one Inuit doctor they say the system is a success. We get that doctor at the expense of all the rest."

Compulsory education in the Northwest Territories was only declared in 1985 and enforcement is still left up to individual communities. Attendance had risen to an all-time high of about eighty per cent. Most parents pushed their kids to go to school but often with little conviction. Peter Akkikungak's son, for example, quit school in grade two. "He said he wasn't learning anything." His teachers confirmed this. "The way they explained it to me was that the classroom was too big, the kids was about fifty in a room, and different levels." We were sitting at the kitchen table of a tiny, three-bedroom house in which seven people lived. Simonie, Peter's wife, was pacing the floor, rocking their teenage daughter's baby. Hulk Hogan was giving someone what for over in the corner. The son in question had just bolted through the house to his room, to immerse himself in *Quiet Riot* or something similar. He felt bad, Peter, that the boy had quit school but children have to make their own decisions. And there were no jobs in the village anyway. So why should he bother? "He doesn't know what else to do better than going out on the land."

What many kids end up with is the least of both worlds. The main job in the short term, the principal said, is to give them positive reinforcement. Everyone agreed with this. In theory. But teachers naturally reinforce their own life style among their charges more than that of the Inuit. And some are zealous about it. Progress was coming, they said. This is the twentieth century. And all that. These kids had to get with it. They considered Inuit ways, given the times, to be crude and children who were interested in them, rather than in school, to be losers. They looked at them, that is, the way many southern teachers look at working-class kids.

"*I* don't care," one teacher said, talking about a pair of boys who were supposed to be in her class but were always skiving off onto the land. She was the sort of teacher who talked about the performance of individual students to strangers and the sort of person who complained, in a scraping voice, that the Arctic was cold. "*I* take the attitude that if they don't want to be here then that's *fine* by me. No skin off my nose. It's *their* future."

This seemed like petty stuff, merely the carping of an unpleasant person. But it was indicative of a much more profound rub fundamental to the system. For middle-class whites, actively supporting a hunting culture is extremely difficult. Because it is inherently political. This was rarely discussed in the North and, I think, had not dawned on many people. It was why conversations about the future were hesitant and often quickly petered out. Inuit culture is egalitarian, individualist, non-materialist and anti-growth in the sense that this is understood in industrial societies. Everything, in short, that southern society is not. Inuit, in their very core, believe in everything that is the opposite of Progress. This is the paradox facing the educational system. But this is being resolved by the Great Educator. Television has no hesitation. Paradox is outlawed in the Global Village.

Abigail Kaernerk said, "Because of the two cultures mixing together, their own way and the white people's way, because of doing the two things — going to school and living the way their parents did — the kids are confused. Because of the two cultures the kids don't listen. It's also TV. They are seeing fights on TV. One of the things that the kids are trying to do is act like the people on TV."

"It hurts me," Elisapee Davidee said, "when a kid here sees people shoot people."

We needn't wonder how often that happens. They see what we see. In the larger villages, there are video arcades that, as in southern cities, rock with the sounds of planets exploding and planes being downed. Even in the tiny village of Hall Beach, where Abigail lived, a less sophisticated version of these thrills was available. After school kids crowded around an old video game in one of the classrooms for their chance to fire at crass, blockish targets labelled "enemy." There were toy guns on sale in the co-ops; not hunting rifles, mind, but Rambo pistols and laser guns with sparkling ionizing chambers and pretend sawed-off shotguns. Western academics have amused themselves for years arguing about the effects these toys and games have on children. Inuit do not bother. It is clear to them.

Of her own parents, Abigail said, "Right up until the time they died, she was getting told how to treat other people. Don't treat them as if they are your enemies. Get along good with them." Her own attempts to impart this message, she said, fell on increasingly deaf ears. Conflict was infecting Inuit lives from many directions but the elders believed that television was becoming one of the biggest problems. A glowing background radiation of acrimony. Today's kids could plainly see that getting along good was not the way the world worked. On television it was cool to be cold. Indeed, on television, it was cool to be everything the Inuit were not: aggressive, acquisitive, fashionable and egoistic. One might argue that all of these traits can come in quite handy in a big city. Quite the opposite on the tundra. What serves a junior stockbroker superlatively is just as likely to get a young hunter killed.

The problem for Inuit parents with television is that they have no way of filtering it. There are many things the kids are seeing that they can not explain. Elisapee Davidee said, "We only get one channel at home. There's lots of garbage people are watching. I discourage my kids from watching too much TV. They see things on TV that I don't understand. They are starting to learn things that I didn't know. I can't force the kids to keep away if they want to learn. I hope they will in their hearts be closer to the land."

This was a common sentiment. But it was not much likely. Of course, a culture cannot be overwhelmed just like that. For me the precociousness of Inuit kids was usually funny because it sat on them like an oversized hat. In Cambridge Bay I overheard a pair of tenish boys being shunned by a few twelvish ones: "You can't come here. This is only for bad boys. We know you are good boys." I was much more taken back by the the strikingly serious, self-effacing, broad mindedness I met in many children. By the sense of *isuma*, the maturity that was so much more developed than that of southern children the same age.

The problem for the Inuit was that the cultural losses of every sort — in knowledge, language, character traits — are increasing progressively. Thirty years ago there was no such thing as a gap between generations. Now the gaps yawned wider between each, not just in attitude and alienation from one another but in the body of the culture that was handed down. To some extent, of course, this has been happening since the nineteenth century. But now it is reaching a kind of critical anti-mass. The children still have an attachment to the land without an understanding of it. This was the point where they fell into danger.

Peter Akikkungak said, "Today everybody is still going out hunting, no problem. They have skidoos and all that. But I'm worried about five to ten years from now. The young are already beginning to lose their tradition of hunting. I'm sure my son knows half of what I know to survive in the winter, to stay out on the land. And ten years from today there will be another half gone. And maybe twenty years time from now there will be nobody who knows how to survive out on the land."

Young people, the elders said, are beginning to take the land lightly, which cannot be gotten away with. There is too much to know about travelling on the land to do it as a hobby. Simeonie Kaernerk said, "Younger people are not asking questions, they don't seem to be curious. He wonders how to teach them to study the weather Inuit way. They don't seem to have the interest he did. If a young person all of a sudden decides to go out hunting and goes out alone, elders are going to worry. He would be happier seeing them knowing how to hunt and see the condition of the weather. They are kind of worried because they don't have as much experience about what kind of weather they are going to run into."

This was a broader matter than knowing specific skills, how to carve a sled runner or mend a *kamiq*. People were losing the language, their map to the land. The deluge of English from the schools and television was swamping Inuktitut. Language grows out of the land and it guides us through it. And it is also an index of perception. The cliche example from Inuktitut is always best. One Inuit orthography lists thirty-five words for snow. The loss of these terms to the Inuit does not just limit their descriptive ability, it changes the way they can use the environment because it alters what they see in it, what distinctions are made.

Jobie Weetaluktuk said, "We are losing the language pretty fast. People my age, twenty-five to thirty, speak to their kids in English. They have found that it has the words that make it easier to talk in English. There are things here that are hard to describe in Inuktitut. If we were on the land it would be the other way around. But Inuktitut is not suited for the community. It is easier to communicate in English, where more things are invented by Europeans. We are losing our language because of the lifestyle we are living."

Perhaps most to the point, the youngest generation is losing interest. The children still say they are keen on hunting, but their ties are fast becoming sentimental. "Too many kids," a twelve-year-old girl told me, "are into wrestling and things like that. They could be going hunting with their fathers but they don't want to." She didn't mean they stay behind in the gymnaseum. She meant they were watching TV.

Her name was Madelaine. I spoke with her, three other girls and a boy one day after school. What did they want to do with themselves? The boy wanted to be a hunter and a pilot of jet fighters. Why? "On the TV it sounds fun." Three of the girls wanted to be stewardesses. But none of them were quite sure they wanted to live in another town. Madelaine wanted to be an Inuktitut teacher; to help preserve the culture. "Our grandparents worry that when they die the culture will be gone. I don't know why I'm so worried but I just don't want us to lose it."

The conversation became a microcosmic explanation for the problem many cultures now face. Madelaine was in uniform and mildly made-up. She wore a motor-racing cap with ATCO, the oil company supplier, emblazoned on it. It was clear that she was in with the in-crowd, if not its leader. Madelaine was glad she didn't have to live the way her parents and grandparents had. "My grandma makes *kamiqs*. It looks so hard. You have to bite it and all that." Madelaine, it was clear, would not put a piece of skin in her mouth if her life depended on it.

"I don't know why I'm so worried. Our mayors and MLAs are working hard, but they are mostly talking about land. They are hardly talking about culture. Since my grandmother told me how hard she worked to raise her kids I think we should work hard to keep our culture alive."

"But none of you look very traditional to me."

"We're shy to wear all those things, Inuit clothes. They brought us up all these things and that's what kids want to wear. Boots, mitts, parkas, I'm shy to wear all those things in public. My grandmother makes *kamiqs* and parkas but I don't wear them. I'd rather wear machine-made jackets like everyone else. We prefer to wear clothes from Montreal. They look so neat. These Inuit clothes, when you wear them other kids will probably tease you about it. Here they are, people with very fancy clothing, you walk beside them with Inuit clothing and you will probably feel left out."

Old Abigail said, "Nowadays the kids don't want to go out with the family when they are going camping or hunting. When you live in a camp or a tent you don't have to have to look for the cleanest area to have your meals. You don't have to worry about getting into something disgusting. The older ones feel they are too old now and they feel more comfortable in a house than in a tent. With younger kids it's easier but the teens don't want to go because of the cleanliness."

Every generation complains about the one that follows and every culture mourns the loss of traditions. And Inuit, like everybody else, have been sucked in by fashion before. There are several reported cases from the nineteenth century of Inuit taking to European clothes and dying of exposure as a result. People kept wearing them, of course, but realized the limits of their use. Over the decades, dozens if not hundreds of specific skills have been forgotten and traditions lost.

People I met — Inuit and white — tended to interpret the attitudes of the children along these lines. They saw it as a continuation of the longstanding accommodation in the Arctic between the traditional and modern, the Western and the aboriginal. Parents spoke hopefully of the need for compromise, for children to learn to live in both cultures, as they had been forced to do. But what was happening, it seemed to me, was infinitely more profound than a further shift in implements. And I think the elders knew it.

The youngest generation of Inuit are undergoing a fundamental shift in their understanding of the world. They are not just losing knowledge about the land, not simply being driven away from hunting for economic reasons — although these are both true. Their culture is becoming dowdy and the land is becoming repellent to them. Dirty. Smelly. The extension of this, of course, is an attitude about their own bodies and about nature itself. It is an attitude they have learned implicitly in their schools and explicitly on television. They are becoming the first generation of Inuit to believe in Progress.

Hunting cultures have been under attack by the Progress ethic since Biblical times. Consider Esau. Esau, the hunter, returns from the fields famished and asks his brother Jacob, the farmer, for some of the lentil soup he has prepared. Jacob, being the sort of person he is, will only give up some soup in exchange for Esau's birthright as first born son of Isaac. Esau does the deal and despises his birthright as a result. Jacob gets ahead because Jacob thinks of the future; Esau, the hunter, motivated by bodily needs, loses out. Biblical imagery, Northrop Frye tells us, generally categorized animals of prey as demonic. Where it detailed the "clean" and "unclean" animals, the former were the ones that could be domesticated.

Feminist scholars argue that the same developments that gave us Progress also provided the theoretical basis of the domination of men over women. The elevation of the knowledge over the known was exploited, the mind came to hate the body. The hatred of the body was synonymous with the hatred of women. Since the eighteenth century this domination has been fueled by the development of technology which seeks not only to control nature, but to recreate it. Only: better. And healthier. And cleaner.

The technological matrix that now envelopes life amounts to man's attempt to supplant women. And this is inextricably tied to economics. "Patriarchal capitalism," Joyce Nelson wrote, "depends on the loss of the body as the basic societal condition." This is because alienation from one's own body creates all kinds of needs and wants, which creates all kinds of markets. All are contained in a kind of metamarket that peddles, basically, immortality. This metamarket is what we call consumerism. And science is now in its employ. As any horror movie can tell you, science is about nothing if not a continuing attempt to eradicate death. And this begins with eradicating shit.

Of course the twelve-year-old Inuit children do not see it this way. All they know is that they would sooner be watching television.

The Global Village did not turn out at all the way it was supposed to. In explaining how electronic technology worked, McLuhan evoked the image of preliterate cultures — like the Inuit —

whose nonlinear, multidimensional way of seeing was apparently replicated by television. Like aboriginal cultures, he said, television was irrevocably bound to the present, eliminating many distinctions, including those of time and space. He also argued that electronic media *could* foster "uniqueness and diversity" on a global scale. The whole idea of the Global Village was that electronic man was returning to a tribal consciousness. McLuhan, of course, saw the down side. But twenty years ago, his vision appealed to many, and to none more than American television corporations, for whose plans it provided a grand moral framework.

The communications system we have ended up with is quite the opposite of that prevailing in the average tribe. It is true that television, like tribal communication, is not linear. Television presents a bombardment of fragments, absurdly juxtaposed. This is also why television critics since McLuhan have argued that it makes rational discourse impossible. Television wants nothing to do with the left side of the brain — the so-called logical side. Many people believe this is something inherent in the technology that has been wildly exaggerated by American television and the many pallid imitations of it, like Canadian television. Nelson speaks of television as a technological cataract. Its social effects, she argues, add up to "having the left hemisphere of one's neo-cortex effectively amputated by TV while the right hemisphere is colonized."

Staring at the fusillade of imagery, the television viewer has little opportunity to discern the important from the trivial, the catastrophic from the idiotic. And because everything happens in the present, there is no access to the past. The viewer is given what Postman calls a "peek-a-boo world" in which nothing matters because nothing lasts for more than four seconds. In *Amusing Ourselves to Death*, he wrote, "We do not refuse to remember; neither do we find it exactly useless to remember. Rather we are being rendered unfit to remember."

This is far from the hunter's way of seeing. His most essential skill is to be able to sort out what matters from the plethora of signals reaching his senses. And his survival depends on interpreting these within a relativist whole, which includes a living past. An Inuk, someone noted, speaks of the whale he is hunting in exactly the same terms as he does of one his father or grandfather hunted.

The world is indeed an interconnected web of nerve endings, like a hunting village, but the difference is that the flow of electronic signals is strictly one way. The United States exports more television programming, some 150,000 hours a year, than everyone else in the world *combined*. The result of this has been the creation of what Brian Fawcett labelled the electronic Imperium. Think of it as trend master control; the Athens of the new world. Postman, for his part, thinks of it as Las Vegas.

It is a place where everybody is happy, everybody is rich, everybody is pretty and getting laid all the time. Except, of course, the bad people, who are getting killed. It is a place everyone wants to be in so badly that they cannot keep sight of the fact that it does not exist. Instead, they are stuck in one of its distant and unloved colonies. It is the destroyer of benign nationalism and the creator of a more radical, violent version. It makes people turn on their own cultures, though more often it makes them simply ignore their own cultures. It makes them also ignore talking to one another, story telling, imagination, friendships. It makes them, in short, into perfect consumers. Because they have nothing else to think about.

This was a part of the problem Inuit children had. And if the people who live in Ottawa or Bonn or Sao Paulo or Moscow did not realize this, there is no reason to believe the Inuit would. The Global Village, it turned out, was just a series of bulls-eyes for *Anik*.

Inuit are no intellectuals, but they knew this would happen. After Igloolik had refused television several times some broadcasting executives were sent to the village to find out what the problem was. This was unheard of. Baffled, they went to see Fr. LeChat, who was the priest at the time. He set them up on the local radio phone-in show so they could hear for themselves. The people gave them an earful. "People said it was foreign stuff. They said the kids would stay up late watching television and that they wouldn't go out and play. They said that when you go to visit people who have television, no one talks. They just watch television. They said they would not have any control."

On certain scales, Inuit have been remarkably successful at using communications technology to reinforce their culture. Thomas Anguttitauruq told me a representative story. Over a number of years when he was moving from community to community and working with the military, he came to speak a jumbled mess of different Inuktitut dialects. When he finally settled in Gjoa Haven, his language was so mixed up that people laughed at him. One day he noticed an advertisement for a small tape recorder in a catalogue and sent away for it.

"I thought I would tape the grown-ups in Gjoa Haven. When that tape recorder arrived I stitched the microphone into the sleeve of my parka and I made a pocket inside so that the tape recorder would be inside and so nobody would see it. So I stitched a few stitches along the wire for that microphone. When I go to the Bay or when I go to the store or when I'm visiting somebody, I would turn the tape recorder on so I could tape them. I would try to get my arm as close to the person as possible so I could tape properly, but without letting them know I was taping. So I would tape them and then when I get back home that night, I would put my headphones on and say those words. At that time my oldest daughter was starting school and she asked me: 'Why are you always talking to yourself? I don't even understand you sometimes.' And I told her I wanted to learn to speak Inuktitut properly. And she said: 'You speak it properly.' But the dialect was so mixed up that I had to learn; so nobody would laugh at me when I was talking. So that's how I learned to speak Inuktitut, Gjoa Haven dialect."

Inevitably, every Inuit village was plugged in to television. "It was genocide," Aimo Nookiguak said. Aimo was manager of the Inuit Broadcasting Corporation in Iqaluit. "It's not too strong a word to use; southern television was a genocide for our culture."

Almost immediately after television arrived, elders began lob-
bying government for access, hoping to put television to their
own use, the way Thomas had done with his tape recorder.

The result was a pilot project that eventually evolved into the
Inuit network. Run from an office in Ottawa, IBC's main production facility is in Iqaluit and has the scale and feel of a local cable
television station. A small one. The network produces five hours
of programming a week, carried by CBC North. Aimo
Nookiguak, for one, saw it as a saviour. "If genocide was still
being practiced IBC wouldn't be here."

The view was widely shared. One often heard it said in the
North that the electronic media would save Inuit culture. There
were academics, in fact, who saw this as a kind of prophetic ful-
fillment. Inuit, they argued, were the perfect McLuhanites. Inuit
had long had community radio, which is still used to great effect
for everything from a bulletin board to bingo broadcasts. In
recent years various sorts of electronic technology had been put
to work in the Arctic to expand the network. Computer programmes were developed in syllabics to teach the language. Tele-conferencing and interactive broadcasting experiments had been
held linking communities from Alaska to Greenland. The IBC
and other Inuit television stations, meanwhile, were recording
the artifacts of Inuit life, broadcasting public events and producing documentaries, talk shows and news. In this, however, there
was a higher aspiration for television and computers. People no
longer see them as simply one big party line.

"These new communications technologies," an academic en-
thusiast bubbled, "... have made it possible to expand the traditional patterns of Inuit village life right across the Arctic, creating
what one might, with a McLuhanesque phrase, call a global igloo
.... The modern communications technologies are ... of fundamental importance to the Inuit in preserving and revitalizing
all aspects of their, and our, Arctic heritage."

Not everybody was so sure of this. "We see ourselves as
recording," Elisapee said. "If we are promoting the culture than
that's good too."

Clearly, IBC was mostly doing the former. For one thing, the ones who needed to have the culture promoted to them, the children, are not watching. More than half of the IBC audience is in the late forties or older, while almost half of the population is under fifteen. The very things that drew the elderly were certain to turn children off. And IBC is nothing if not faithful to its mandate. It prides itself on speaking the Inuit visual language; its programmes are slower paced, languorous even, compared to commercial television. "It's boring," said a southern television producer who had been hired to train IBC staff. They just didn't cut enough. "I keep trying to tell them it's a visual medium. It's lucky they have so much southern television here. They can learn." Creatively, of course, this was exactly their curse. But as much as they tried to avoid it, the young broadcasters could not help but be influenced by southern television. Already IBC had adopted some of its more fatuous habits such as the news anchor. Television teaches television.

Having their own television can not keep the Inuit culture from being marginalized. The potential for tele-conferencing undoubtedly saves native politicians air fare but the paltry five hours a week that IBC staff is hard pressed to generate is no competition for the dominant television. Nor would 500 be. "Any culture," said Elisapee, "will grab what's easiest, especially if it is new." Quite right, as anyone in Canada could confirm. Tokenist national television networks, far from giving people their own voices, function to shut them up.

There are other reasons, more fundamental still, to explain why television cannot keep Inuit culture alive and that also are helpful to understanding the attitudes of the children. These have to do with the nature of the technology.

In the 1930s, critic Walter Benjamin wrote an essay called *The Work of Art in the Age of Mechanical Reproduction*, which, though it predated the medium, was the precursor of much contemporary television criticism. Benjamin argued that the ability to copy a work of art robbed it of its specialness, its aura, its life force. Being able to reproduce an object, by photography say, took it out of the realm of tradition in which it was born. The copying and redistribution of the image in a new context — that is, the erasure of time and space — shattered its connection to tradition. Daguerre, who invented the precursor of the photograph, had a like perception, though an obverse understanding, when he observed that his invention gave nature the power not just to represent itself but to reproduce itself. The image that film and photography reproduce before us is to nature what zombies are to people. They give us the perfect walking dead. In seeking to outwit death, the camera creates an image of death. For the moment captured, of course, is dead a moment later.

"Electronic man," McLuhan said, "is in desperate need of roots. He's lost his body and his private identity. He has an image, but not a body." This is why talk of revitalizing a culture with television is simply ludicrous. The culture of the Inuit — with its elaborate language and skills, its traditions of story telling, its necessary traits of character — exists profoundly in the body. On television it becomes a lifeless image, a ghost of itself. Far from being a halt to the cultural genocide, an operation like IBC becomes a promotion of it because it creates a kind of death mask, a veneer that hides the real loss of culture in the society. It looks just like life. Only: it's not.

Obviously, I would not want to be understood as saying that the Inuit or anyone else should not make moving pictures. Or use computers. I do both. But moving pictures are just moving pictures. They are only a small part of a culture. They cannot replace the corporeal body of a society's knowledge of itself: its environment, the ways its people converse with and entertain each other, the elaborate codes of social behaviour, and ways of relating to other societies. In short, its way of living. When they are allowed to, then begins what Benjamin called "the liquidation of the traditional value of cultural heritage." Which is to say, the murder of memory. The very thing IBC is ostensibly intended to prevent. The very thing that American television actively promotes.

This is something many people realize. Jobie Weetaluktuk, who makes television, and I talked one day about snow. He said, "Something like that is very sophisticated. You have to live with it for it to sink into you. You can have an explanation on tape to preserve the memory. But you need to live with it, to be able to wake up in the day and describe the snow. This is something I've already lost."

It is clear, however, that many people are more inclined to understand this as the limit of the technology, rather than its goal. The emergent class of educated Inuit, from politicians to broadcasters, are engaged in a furious process of trying to hang on to what they have, to keep from being further marginalized, and have been forced to appropriate whatever methods they can, be they drawing borders, creating corporations, or making television.

For decades, Inuit and their sympathizers have been fighting to banish the perjorative image of them as "primitive." It is a good word, *primitive*: "ancient; radical, not derivative, from which another is derived." But the nineteenth century wrecked it; gave it a connotation opposite to its denotation. Made it mean inferior. In the twentieth century, the aboriginal image problem only gets worse and worse. Our society gives them only three possible categories: Pure Eskimo, Perfect Crossover and Fuck-up.

The right-headed thus argue that nobody has any business telling Inuit what technologies they should appropriate and, further, that they will find original uses for them. Both of which, of course, are true. Inuit are not reverent about technology, not bound by our codes. People hold binoculars by one eye-piece and squint to look through the other. They make tea in coffee pots. Sometimes they even use television sets as radios. Nor are they unaware of the inherent powers of machines. Peter Akkikungak's intuition about clocks — "One thing I figured out is that the clock is boss, even the president and the prime minister, they have to serve the clock" — is one that is discussed by few of our philosophers and virtually none of the rest of us.

But this awareness can only last so long. Technological systems are as fundamentally ideological as economic ones. We do not necessarily follow their commands instantly, but sooner or later we come around to doing what they tell us to. The recent history of Inuit society is one long example of this. As is our own. Yet, whether we talk of automobiles or television or computers or genetic tampering, our society refuses to seriously question, consider or debate the social change inherent in new technologies. We are dumb at their arrival, assuming them either essentially benign or inevitable because Progress has told us we have to. So too the Inuit.

Their political attitudes toward this comes through clearly in a comment by the head of an Inuit corporation who, queried about the conflict between capitalism and Inuit collectivist values, responded with the typical anger of the people who feel most bitterly caught between cultures: "The anthropologists and ethnologists from down south who were in the north in the Fifties and Sixties are saying the Inuit are no longer Inuit because they are no longer subservient like they used to be, just listening to the white man. Most of the guys doing all this crying are university professors who want the Inuit to stay the noble savages that they thought they were. I'm sorry, we are not here to live up to anybody's expectations or cultural prejudices."

The comment, I think, underestimates and misplaces the needs of capitalism. We have plastic seal replicas to serve our mythological needs. In real life, Inuit are doing nothing if not striving to live up to our expectations. But they have been given no choice. Rather: their choice has been taken away. Welcome to the Global Village. That's the way it is here.

I had not really thought this through when I was in the Arctic. Now I remember speaking to Elisapee Davidee and her describing, with bitterness, all the cons the Inuit have been through. They were willing to use foreign things — like television — she said, if they could do so to their advantage, but they were tired of being pushed around. The last thing I asked was whether she thought the Inuit could still be conned. "We've come a long way," she said, "I don't know if the cons are gone."

They are not. The promotion of electronic technology, television and its corollary, computers, as a way of keeping the culture alive, is the most elaborate con yet. In being convinced of the need of television for their own cultural protection, Inuit stepped into a con game much more complex than the ruses and lies of the past. And which they clearly play against their better judgement. They have taken up our belief in salvation through technology; a fatal con that Western society originated and that is daily reinforced by the happy puppeteers of the Global Village. To speak of television and other communications technology "revitalizing" — *making alive again* — Inuit culture is to utterly misunderstand both.


I was in Resolute Bay the day greed got slapped on the wrist. Bezal Jesudason said, "I hope you don't have money in the stock market." It had fallen 500 points and the television news that night made it sound as if war had broken out. Black Monday they were calling it. We were all, they were certain, going to really pay for this. As if we had done something wrong. That evening the local news carried a story about the national atomic energy authority beginning to market tiny, village-size nuclear reactors in the Arctic. The market for nuclear reactors, of course, was no longer what it had once been. It was hoped these baby reactors, in distant palaces, would help perk it up. Then a rerun of *Three's Company* came on. It always seemed to be on there, whatever the hour. There was apparently an inexhaustible source. When I went out for a walk that evening, I thought: everything, anymore, is typical. That tells you something.

Outside Bezal's house there was a small, silver monument post, given him by some Japanese polar explorers. It said: May Peace Prevail On Earth. Nearby a dish pointed straight at the horizon. A satellite cruised overhead. There had been polar bears in the village every night that week. I was hoping I would not meet one.

A few weeks later, I found myself walking across Gjoa Haven with a Thomas Anguttitauruq. The village was quiet but for the tinkling of breaking glass underfoot. Thomas was telling me the story of his life as marked out in the deaths of people he loved. There had been several, most recently his brother and his brother's son. The brother had a small company that cleaned out fuel tanks and a contract to do so for the government. His son was working in a tank without proper breathing equipment and fainted. When the father went in to rescue him, he collapsed too. For reasons that were still obscure, it looked like the family was to get no compensation. Thomas told this story in a voice clear and bright as a carillon, with an unspoken sadness but no trace of self-pity. Thomas told me many stories, over a few days, with this voice. Some struck me as outrages, others as poignant. But he never put either of these colorations on them. This is the way Inuit tell stories; the way, at least, they told them to me. *Ayunmut*. "All of our traditions turn toward life."

Very rarely did anyone ask me a question about the south. I concluded from this that they had had their fill of hearing. They appreciated, as they always said, the opportunity to speak. And they knew my business. "What he would like to tell white people," one old man said, "using you as the route ..." But somewhere in this night, Thomas asked me a question. He said, "One thing I've been wondering about and that's Wall Street. I know there's something wrong. But I don't understand what happened. Should I be worried?"

I said no. All things considered, I could hardly see why. I wasn't. Later, I thought that the answer was, of course: yes. I suppose you should. By his account, Thomas didn't know how to build an *iglu* or skin a seal much better than I did. Even if he had, the economics of his community had been gutted. Their only hope was the monster with the big eyes. Or maybe someone would open a mine nearby. Or maybe the oil boom would come and be so loud that people everywhere in the territories would get a little run off. That's what people kept telling them.

Or, the flip side, if the bottom really fell out, then corporations would have another indisputable excuse to keep poisoning the atmosphere. Jobs come first, they would say. It might be just the moment for governments to be prodded into building more weaponry. That always seemed to give the economy a little shot in the arm. Anyway, the people in the village had high expectations now. Higher everyday. Every minute, practically. Life in the village was only going to get more unpleasant if these expectations became even harder to fulfill. And they were impossible now. There would be more despair and fighting. More chances taken. It was obvious.

So I had lied to him. I didn't mean to, but I did. Just wishful thinking on my part. In any case, I'm sure he soon enough figured this out on his own. The television never let up about it.

One can argue that Inuit have been dependent on the whims and fluctuations of southern economies for a good 150 years or so. At the turnYYYYYNN 1700ry, in the MacKenzie Valley, there were trappers who became fabulously wealthy overnight when fur prices shot up and became poor just as quickly when the Depression came and the market disintegrated. This is an old story. But this is a new world. It is not just that Inuit cannot escape the global economy, can't get away from the world they are living in. It is that they are no longer living in the world they are living in. Or if they still are, they soon will not be.

I mean: they know the language of the Global Village. Princess Di, *The Facts of Life*, Hulk Hogan, *Quiet Riot*, Michael Jackson, Rambo guns, Cabbage Patch dolls, whatever. They will all be anachronisms by the time you read this book. Inuit know, too, the sources of power on which life and thought now depend: Wall Street, Los Angeles and the base of a hollowed-out mountain in Colorado. They know to worry about "consumer confidence," cruise missiles, the dollar, AIDS, PCBs, the ozone layer. But they don't really worry, of course, because no one really worries. Television tells them they should not really worry. Yet, as they gain the language of the Global Village, they lose that of their own. They are forgetting how to describe their environment and how to survive in it. And how to talk to the old people. And where they have come from. And where they are.

They are, it seems to me, entering a kind of static, electronic diaspora; becoming wanderers in the technological landscape. Their culture cannot withstand the disintegrating rays of the blue light any more than their economy could the withering blast of the military wind, or their social arrangements the entrenchment of southern laws or their bodies and land the invasion of poisons. They are being uprooted and scattered by the destruction of their knowledge as certainly as if they were driven from their land. They are the inverse of the Jews. And, for just this reason, there will be no fighting their way back, no possibility of return at all.

Talking about the poisoning of the land, Gideon said: "If we try to live alone from the food that we buy from the stores we wouldn't be able to survive." The Arctic produces, for all intents, nothing other than what its people require to live. Inuit have nothing to export to the Global Village. They are offered a world to buy but have nought to sell but a clichéd image. They will be consumers, solo; kept alive by electronic umbilical cords, their villages slowly orbiting the great heart-lung machine like dead satellites.

So this bureaucrat says to me: "There's no question they are being set up for a fall." And an educator, who tries to be optimistic, says: "We have to teach them to deal with leisure time." And now I am flying over Victoria Island. Sitting next to me is an academic who has come to the Arctic to study the social lives of people who live in mining camps ("I wouldn't exactly say they are happy.") We are talking about television. He says, "We don't give them blankets soaked in small pox any more but the effect is the same."

And I think of a small, fanciful irony: say the nuclear winter happens the way the theories predict it will. Say the Arctic, being the sort of place it is, does, as it could, turn out to be the only place that could be considered to have survived the war. Say the

Inuit are the ones left to start over. Only: say they forgot how it is that one lives in this place.


It is not fashionable in the Arctic to doomsay Inuit culture. But, in my experience, the old people had a strong sense that it was ending. There were certain ritual questions I would ask, particularly of the elders. One was what they imagined of the future. This would not have been a sensible question to Inuit thirty years ago. But the elders, more than anyone, understood Progress. Simeonie said, "The Inuit way of life might slowly disappear within fifty years. If we get that far. Every year he senses that we are getting closer to the end of the world."

This was not the ritual post-modern shrug that the world might blow up tomorrow. Simeonie, obviously lacking information, was of the opinion that man could not build a bomb big enough to destroy the world. His belief was based in layers of prophecy that were clearly being fulfilled.

"Some of the things he has heard from his forefathers, his elders, now they are coming true. Like he heard that they are not going to have any very old people living in their community any more, that they will just die away. And in some of the communities now they don't have any very old people living in them anymore. And with the news he's heard: there's earthquakes, there's thousands of lives being taken, there's homes taken. And the land is just disappearing under the feet of the people. So yes, he's heard the whole world's going to end and he believes the world's going to end because of what his elders said before."

Many elders had a similar vision that grew out of shamanism, revelations and common sense. Even before missionaries arrived in the North, it is said that some native shamans, Dene specifically, learning a little of Christianity, made spirit journeys to consult God and Jesus, receiving information on various aspects of the faith, including the promise of Apocalypse. Simeonie said, "That's what makes his belief even stronger now, because it comes from two beliefs, one from shamans and one from Bible.

That's what makes his beliefs much stronger that the world's going to end, it's just going to turn into a ball of fire."

"No one," said Elijah Qammaniq, "can pinpoint the day or the time but signs are showing up." Among these were that children were turning against their parents, races were in conflict and Inuit had become greedy. "Inuit want more money now, more than the white man should have. Even though they don't have knowledge of it from the beginning, they want to grab it from the white person."

There was confusion in the elder's visions, or at least my understanding of them. Sometimes they seemed to speak of the death of the world, sometimes of an apocalypse specific to the Inuit. Perhaps they made no distinction. And calamity seemed inevitable. The world, the elders said, was crawling with signs. It was obvious. Take a look around. "One of the worst signs," Elijah said, "is that the war is expected."

In the nuclear age, apocalypse has become something of a household word, bandied about freely and understood to be synonymous with the sort of scene the Inuit describe: the world consumed in flames. The Bible no longer seems to have much to say about this now that nuclear weapons and other technologies have given us the power it reserved for God. Indeed we shudder to hear the preachers and their political followers whose tongues occasionally slip far enough to muse that nuclear weapons, like the plague of AIDS, are only bringing us what the Bible promised, smugly implying that this was what God had in mind all along.

Northrop Frye has suggested that we ought to read the Bible and more carefully. We would learn a thing or two. In *The Great Code*, he explained that the word apocalypse, from the Greek, has the connotations of unveiling, removing curtains in our minds that hide the truth. The vision contained in the last book of the Bible is indeed one of compound and consuming horrors through which the faithful ride into a new heaven and earth. But we greatly oversimplify, Frye wrote, in believing the apocalypse to be a vision of what will happen. The vision of unimaginable destruction, he argued, is the inner form of things that are happening now. "Man creates what he calls history as a screen to conceal the workings of the apocalypse from himself." This is to say, as I understand it, that the metaphorical fires and plagues are the rendering visible of what we accept as the wages of Progress.

"What is symbolized as the destruction of the order of nature is the destruction of the way of seeing that order that keeps man confined to the world of time and history as we know them. This destruction is what the scripture intended to achieve."

This apocalypse ends with the vision of the restoration of the tree and water of life, the elements of the original creation, and begins a second apocalyptic vision, Frye wrote, ideally, in the readers mind. It is the continuation there of the Bible's visionary aspects; a vision which itself is outside of history, which can come to anyone at any time. The new world that the readers hopefully inhabit is one in which the "the creator-creature, divine-human antithetical tension has ceased to exist, and the sense of the transcendent person and the split of subject and object no longer limit our vision." It is a world beyond the last judgement and thus one no longer mediated by law. It is a world where God is no longer something standing and frowning outside of ourselves, nor we outside of nature. It is a world where God is nature and is us. One where everything is connected and relative; where the hierarchy and the laws that hold it up like struts and beams have collapsed. In this world there is no need for law. Instead there is love. It is an aboriginal world. Or, put differently, the world of quantum science. "The apocalypse is the way the world looks after the ego has disappeared."

What the Inuit see now as the apocalypse is just the opposite. The ego has appeared and been forced to the fore in a society where it was previously absent; even on the economic level the collective ethic has been destroyed. Relativism has been banished and replaced by law. The repressive weight of time and history are crushing the original understanding of nature, in which all time was contained in the present and in which the future was contained in the traditions of the past. Mythology, through which the past was continually recreated in the present, is disappearing.

None of this is new. Visitors to the Arctic have been marking these trends for 100 years. Rasmussen could see the beginnings of them in the Western Arctic. Diamond Jenness never let up about them. Nor did Edmund Carpenter. Farley Mowat made his name predicting the Inuit's demise. More recently, Hugh Brody has been a consistent defender of the people's right to retain their culture against the incursions of the south.

What is new is that the power of the systems enveloping the Inuit have become so great that the fading of their culture is now quite likely irreversible. Barry Lopez thinks of the Inuit as *hibakusha*, the Japanese word for people effected by the atomic blasts. Like the *hibakusha*, it is only decades after the initial blast that the effects of the technological culture are beginning to be understood in full. Only now are the Japanese realizing the extent and depth of radiation poisoning, as only now are the Inuit understanding how basic are the changes the encroaching society has wrought.

Many people who have spoken out on their behalf have done so uninvited and have been considered patronizing by some of the people. They are felt to be expressing a romantic longing for a past that urban capitalist culture has irrevocably rejected, the culture that is now defined by television.

Obviously there is some truth in this. But it is a limited understanding, I think. It seems to me that what shocks us when we look at the impact of our society on the Inuit, the assault of unchecked authority fused with technology, economics and politics, is not just that their traditions are being buried. What is shocking is *how* our society has affected theirs. We do not need to look very closely to understand that all the impacts of our society on the Inuit can he reduced to the destruction of the single binding element in theirs: love.

The apocalypse Inuit are experiencing is the obverse of the Revelation that they believe the Bible has foretold. What they are feeling instead is the fiery disintegration of the love between members of the community, between the old and the young, husbands and wives, parents and children; and, encompassing all, between the people and the land. Inured, as we are, to the fates of other peoples, this is only shocking in so much as it is so palpably indicative of what is happening amongst ourselves. Of what our culture is doing to us.

And so slowly do we come to realize that it is totalitarian. Our culture, for all intents and purposes, is television and our television comes from a single source with a single political message. It makes all previous notions of sovereignty meaningless — whether of countries, communities or individuals — because it overreaches the classical processes of history and beyond all boundaries to directly colonize the mind. It shreds the borders around communities by destroying the bonds within them. Quite the opposite of instilling the tribal consciousness of collective responsibility it destroys consciousness and responsibility altogether. We are left only to follow.

We become oblivious to the system's desires because they seem to be *our* desires. We need only listen to the rhetoric of corporate capitalism to understand this. The way it convinces us that we need its products is not by arguing their intrinsic worth but by associating them with our basic needs: love of family, good health, enough food, a sturdy home, friendship, a feeling of being rooted. The desire, that is, to be secure and weighted within our lives. And the other side of this desire, of course, is fear. Our desire and fear, I think, interact to draw us out of our communities and into this landscape.

And here we drift weightless in this strange static diaspora, like so many space walkers. Individually encapsulated and plugged into a glorious constellation of neon stars, we float in the Sea of Pleasantry. Occasionally we glance nervously over one shoulder at the obsequious faces in the square blue windows of the father ship and they smile and wink their assurances that they know where we are headed and that our line will not be snipped before we get there. But we cannot quite trust them. We remain unconvinced and insecure; afraid. Deep down, on an older level, we can sense the direction for ourselves.

On this road love disintegrates. This, it seems, has become the purpose of Progress: to make love irrelevant. Under such a force a society like that of the Inuit must fade away. But, of course, they will not, as people, really fade away. They will become us. And now we come to a moment when we can begin to understand that the wisdom they have preserved for millennia, daily running their hands along the cord of mortality; their deep understanding that "life is a luminous halo, a semi-transparent envelope surrounding us from beginning to end"; their profound spiritual grasp of what this stuff is that we are which can rise from the hard land and be conscious of itself; that these are the only ways of knowing, the only love, that can save them, or us, now.

But now, to our horror, they come here to sit beside us, taking their place in the Great Audience that grins wide-eyed at the face of the Apocalypse. Phase one.


This house sat on a hill in a village I will not name. It doesn't matter. I happened to stay there by chance and good fortune, when its residents were away, on holiday. The couple who owned it — rented, actually, for something just less than $2,000 a month — were an Inuk woman and her husband, a southerner who worked for the government. She, I was told, had left a traditional marriage in a traditional home. This was not a traditional home.

I knew traditional homes. They were, for me, nice places to be. They were distinguished by having more people than furniture and the fact that no one minded. In the afternoons, the common room in such a home is full of people. The women would crowd onto a couple of old couches shoved up against the walls. There would be women of all ages. The best places, in the corners of course, would go to the old women with tributary faces and hoarse toothless laughs. Their daughters would be there; they would be wearing high leather boots and tight polyester pants and denim shirts, wearing big glasses and bringing everyone tea. Probably their daughters would be there too. They would be skinny and their hair would be razor short on the sides and halfway down their backs, as was the fashion, and they would be the only ones made up. All the women would be talking, fast, at once, and balancing ashtrays and mugs of tea and children on their laps; one sitting in the middle of the couch with no room to move her arms hardly pauses for a breath as she bends to scoop up a baby trying to scale the Olympian heights of her knees and cuddles him and takes a sip of tea.

Off to the side, by himself, would be a boy, sitting in an old kitchen chair. Perhaps he is nineteen. He wears long, straight hair and a black T-shirt cut off at the shoulders to show off tattoos on both thick arms. Half of him is out there, beyond the window, where waves of snow sweep up the road and break over his snowmobile; half is listening to the jokes of the old men at the table and smirking and allowing the baby he rocks in his lap to attempt to disassemble his face. The men, old men, are sitting at the table wearing sweaters and *kamiqs*, though it is at least eighty degrees in here, as if perhaps someone might dash in and immediately require their help outside. A blue cloud obscures their outlines but they can be discerned within, ribbing each other incessantly through pink gums. The oldest son of the house is on the floor, before a piece of cardboard, gnawing his way through a frozen fish. He sends one of the half dozen kids playing tag around him to get me a cup of tea, specifying that the cup should be dirty. He wants to make me feel at home, by not putting on airs.

These people don't think of themselves as traditional, of course. Just plain folks. From the house on the hill, though, I could understand how they would seem that. There were no dirty cups here because there was a dishwasher to sterilize them. It was that sort of kitchen, perfectly appointed with appliances and a wide range of Scandinavian knives. The dining room set was French Provincal and the carpets were quicksand. The police would have been notified right smartly if anyone had put a frozen fish on these floors. This was a house ruled by vacuum; dust had not the chance to float, much less settle. Every cupboard was meticulously lined with paper, including the one that held the garbage can. An Inuk said to me once, "My wife keeps the house *so* clean. Just like a white woman." A child lived here and there was a crib upstairs brimming with toys. These people, some would say, had it made.

There were two kinds of art on the walls. One was American pop: mauve and green prints, for example, of a symmetrical pair of pneumatic women with geometric shapes painted on their faces blowing big kisses at each other. Think: roller skating drive-in waitresses. And there was Inuit art. In the living room, a dog team was being driven across the glass-topped coffee table beside the flat-screen television set. Over the bright and bubbling aquarium, four Inuit were hauling a half walrus each back from a kill. A man walked with a child alone on the tundra.

It was a comfortable home to find myself in, especially after a few weeks of breathing petroleum fumes in hotels. But it was strange also. In the mornings I would listen to pop music from Vancouver and be instructed, given the beautiful day, to be sure to have a stroll in Stanley Park. Heh, heh, heh. In the evenings there was the *CBS Evening News with Dan Rather, Hill Street Blues*, Cosby, et al and my temporary roommate would sit up watching *48 Hours*. "It's silly, but it's funny." I had the oddest feeling all the while that I was in a beach house somewhere on the outskirts of L.A. Or English Bay. Or Cabbagetown. Or nowhere.

Late one night I sat in the living room alone. The flat-screen was spraying the room with red blood and brown girls and voluptuous cans of soda pop. The sound was off; I heard only the aquarium gurgling. The frozen Inuks heaved those bleeding walrus carcasses across the tundra. The dogs on the coffee table snapped and hauled on their harnesses. I was thinking about innocence. "Free from moral wrong, not guilty, harmless," the dictionary said, "guileless, esp. young child, simple person, idiot."

I have been told a story, undoubtedly exaggerated, but some-how believable. A southerner living in the Arctic took an Inuk on vacation to southern California. The first place they went was Disneyland. There they went on one of Disney's famous jungle rides, in which a boat pulls a load of tourists through a plastic bayou. A young, blond unisexual Disney tour guide provided a running commentary. You have to be wary in this swamp, the guide said, anything might leap out. Of course, many things leapt out. Mechanical snakes dropped from trees and paper maché hip-popotamuses reared up out of the water. This tour guide was a sort of perfect American hero: whenever an animal pounced, the guide yanked out a six-shooter and dispatched it, to laughter and amazement. The Inuk, however, found this genuinely frighten-ing. He had never been out of the Arctic nor did he have a television set. He thought it unwise to trifle with the animals this way, to put all these people at risk. He believed the animals to be real.

Later, he was taken to the San Diego Zoo. There he witnessed what everyone witnesses in a zoo: desultory animals slouched in the corners of their cages, barely blinking, avoiding the gaze of the prying onlookers who desperately seek it. The Inuk was not depressed by this. He thought these animals were plastic too. It had never occurred to him that anything a man could do could so break the spirit of an animal. Could make it seem so artificial. I don't really believe an Inuk could be fooled so easily. But this story made a certain sense.

Something blew up on the television. A few days before, on the day the Canadian government signed a deal with the United States to fuse our economies, this news had come across the radio while I was on the telephone trying to gain access to a radar sta-tion. On the other end of the line a man was telling me that I would have to hang in there until Colorado said it was okay. Eight months later, as I was finishing this book, a meeting of the heads of the seven most wealthy nations in the world would be held in Toronto. To protect these seven people, much weaponry would be called back from the various fronts. The streets would be closed down and filled with thousands of soldiers and policemen. Helicopter gunships would sweep low over the city at night, beaming searchlights onto rooftops and into windows. Thousands of television cameras would wait for the proclamations of the privileged septenary. Their images would be beamed in half a second, by way of the equator, into this Arctic beach house, to assure its inhabitants that Progress was proceeding smoothly.

A week after that, another meeting would be held in the same rooms with scientists from dozens of countries. They would gather to confer and agree on the basic proposition that exhausts of the technological society were killing the planet. The flat-screen, however, would have little to say about this. And just before he left Canada, the president of the United States, at an official dinner telecast live, would declare the two nations the best of friends. He would cite particularly their economic union and their pact to rebuild military installations in the Arctic as proof of their love. At the end of his speech he would be given, as a friendly token, an Inuit carving, a jade green impression of a hunter raising his harpoon for the kill. The president would take this and, to great applause, hold it above his head like a trophy.

"Once crime was as solitary as a cry of protest;" Kafka wrote, "now it is as universal as science. Yesterday it was put on trial; today it determines the law."

The Inuks heaved. The dog team hauled. The father and child walked alone on the tundra. All bathed in shimmering blue light. Flicker: guns fire. Flicker: lips glisten. Which of these images was alive and which was dead? What was this place? It was the inside of Thomas' box. Where? Could only be Canada. I could tell by the little halos. And already I knew it would always annoy me to hear Canadians talk of the sovereignty of the Arctic.

There was a porch on the back of this house and, from there, at this time of night you could hear dogs howling, far off. In those months that sound came to seem to me a cry from beneath, from under the asphalt as it were. I know, of course, that this is anthropomorphic. I couldn't help it. It began when I had a roommate in a hotel, an Inuk from Baffin Island, who had been sent several hundred miles away to another village for training. He was working for a company based in the south. His boss was staying in the same hotel and my roommate — call him William — and another young guy were being taught clerical work. This boss was the sort who believed that people who had not been raised speaking English understood it better if it was yelled at them. For hours he would hold court with this pair in the dining room of the hotel, haranguing them at the top of his lungs over and over with details that were unbearably menial. He clearly thought them both imbeciles, which they were not. Afterward, William, who was very quiet, would come back to the room looking utterly exhausted. He didn't like his job much and he hated being away from his family. But what could you do? He would lie on his bed and watch *Three's Company* until he fell asleep. On the table between us there was a big mechanical alarm clock and tethered outside our window were two dog teams. All night long the ticking of the clock reverberated through the room and the dogs screeched and howled as if they were being choked.

The dogs I was listening for now were far, far off, on the other side of a bay. I had to strain to hear them. I could clearly recall the particulars of the place where they were. I had been there the afternoon before. Snow had just fallen then, covering most of the land. But in one place, near the water line, a long, low brown hill had been brushed bare by the wind. In the pink and violet light of the afternoon it seemed to shudder. I never saw a piece of land look more alive. Like the back of a walrus. Like the skin of a brown arm. That was where the dogs were. Over there, near a blinking red light that topped a transmission tower. Their howling was eerie, skipping over the ice, breaking up and soaking into the land, a mournful, warbling cry. But it had power still. It flew through the distance and the darkness as if from another time.

# BIBLIOGRAPHY

Many of the ideas and much of the foregoing information is the result of the work of others. To as great an extent as practicable, I have given credit in the text but there were many useful reports, papers and articles on various subjects which I was unable to include. In the following bibliography I have listed the books and reports which have been particularly helpful to me and which are generally available. To each of these authors I acknowledge my debt.

## Books

Allen, Max (prod.) *The Northern Front* Toronto: Canadian Broadcasting Corporation Transcripts, 1985

Allen, Max (prod.) *Nuclear Peace* Toronto: Canadian Broadcasting Corporation Transcripts, 1982

Arkin, William M. and Richard Fieldhouse *Nuclear Battlefields: Global Links in the Arms Race* Cambridge, Mass.: Ballinger Publishing Company, 1985

Armstrong, Terence, George Rogers and Graham Rowley *The Circumpolar North: A Political and Economic Geography of the Arctic and Sub-Arctic* London: Methuen and Company Limited, 1978

Atwood, Margaret *Survival: A Thematic Guide to Canadian Literature* Toronto: House of Anansi Press Limited, 1972

Berger, John *About Looking* London: Writers and Readers Publishing Cooperative Ltd., 1980

Berger, Thomas R. *Northern Frontier, Northern Homeland* Ottawa: Supply and Services Canada, 1977

Bracken, Paul *The Command and Control of Nuclear Forces* New Haven: Yale Univestiy Press, 1983

Briggs, Jean *Never in Anger: Portrait of an Eskimo Family* Cambridge: Harvard University Press, 1970

Brody, Hugh *Living Arctic: Hunters of the Canadian North* Vancouver: Douglas and McIntyre, 1987

Brody, Hugh *The People's Land: Eskimos and Whites in the Eastern Arctic* Harmondsworth, Middlesex: Penguin, 1975

Burnford, Sheila *One Woman's Arctic* Toronto: McClelland and Stewart Limited, 1978

Cambell, Duncan *The Unsinkable Aircraft Carrier: American Military Power in Britain London:* Paladin Books, 1986

Capra, Fritjof *The Turning Point: Science, Society and the Rising Culture* New York: Simon and Schuster, 1982

Carpenter, Edmund *Eskimo Realities* New York: Holt, Rinehart and Winston, 1973

Cayley, David *History and the New Age* Toronto: Canadian Broadcasting Corporation Transcripts, 1984

Colombo, John Robert (ed.) *Poems of the Inuit* Oberon Press Canada, 1981

Crowe, Keith J. *A History of the Original Peoples of Northern Canada* Kingston: McGill-Queen's University Press, 1974

Dosman, E.J. (ed.) *The Arctic in Question* Toronto: Oxford University Press, 1976

Eayrs, James *In Defense of Canada: Peacemaking and Deterrence* Toronto: University of Toronto Press, 1972

Eayrs, James *In Defense of Canada: Appeasement and Rearmament* Toronto: University of Toronto Press, 1965

Fawcett, Brian *Cambodia: A book for people who find television too slow* Vancouver: Talonbooks, 1986

Foucault, Michel *Power/Knowledge: Selected Interviews and Other Writings, 1972-1977* New York: Pantheon Books, 1980

Franklin, Sir John *Narrative of a Journey to the Shores of the Polar Sea* Edmonton: Hurtig Publishers, 1969.

Freeman, Milton *Inuit Land Use and Occupancy Project* Ottawa: Department of Indian and Northern Affairs, 1976

Frye, Northrop *The Great Code: The Bible and Literature* New York: Harvest Brace Jovanovich, Publishers, 1982

Fussell, Paul *The Great War and Modern Memory* London: Oxford University Press, 1975

Field, Edward *Songs and Stories of the Netsilik Eskimos* Cambridge: Education Development Center Inc. 1968

Gedalof, Robin, (ed.) *Paper Stays Put: A Collection of Inuit Writing* Edmonton: Hurtig Publishers, Ltd.

Gervasi, Tom *The Myth of Soviet Military Supremacy* New York: Harper and Row Publishers, 1986

Ghent, Jocelyn Maynard *Canadian-American Relations and the Nuclear Weapons Controversy, 1958-1963* Urbana, Illinois: University of Illinois (Thesis Paper), 1976

Giangrande, Carole *The Nuclear North: The People, the Regions and the Arms Race* Toronto: House of Anansi Press Limited, 1983

Grant, George *Lament for a Nation: The Defeat of Canadian Nationalism* Toronto: McClelland and Stewart Limited, 1970

Griffiths, Franklyn (ed.) *Politics of the Northwest Passage* Kingston: McGill-Queen's University Press, 1987

Griffiths, Franklyn *A Northern Foreign Policy* Toronto: Canadian Institute of International Affairs, 1979

Hilgartner, Stephen, Richard Bell and Rory O'Connor *Nukespeak: The Selling of Nuclear Technology in America* New York: Penguin Books, 1983

Honderich, John *Arctic Imperative: Is Canada Losing the North?* Toronto: University of Toronto Press, 1987

Holmes, John W. *The Shaping of Peace: Canada and the Search for World Order, 1943-1957* Toronto: University of Toronto Press, 1982

Hughes, Robert *The Shock of the New* London: British Broadcasting Corporation, 1980

Innuksuk, Rhoda and Susan Cowan *We don't live in snow houses anymore: Reflections on Arctic Bay* Edmonton: Hurtig Publishers, 1976

Knelmen, F.H. *Reagan, God and the Bomb* Toronto: McClelland and Stewart, 1985

Lauritzen, Philip *Oil and Amulets: Inuit, a people at the top of the world* Breakwater Books Ltd., 1979

Lifton, Robert Jay and Richard Falk *Indefensible Weapons: The Political and Psychological Case Against Nuclearism* Toronto: Canadian Broadcasting Corporation, 1982

Lopez, Barry *Arctic Dreams: Imagination and Desire in a Northern Landscape* New York: Charles Scribner's Sons, 1986

Lyall, Ernie *An Arctic Man* Edmonton: Hurtig Publishers, 1979

Malaurie, Jean *The Last Kings of Thule* New York: E.P. Dutton Inc., 1982

McCall-Newman, Christina *Grits: An Intimate Portrait of the Liberal Party* Toronto: MacMillan of Canada, 1982

McLean, Scilla (ed.) *How Nuclear Weapons Decisions Are Made* London: The MacMillan Press Ltd., 1986

McLin, Jon B. *Canada's Changing Defense Policy, 1957-1963* Baltimore: The Johns Hopkins Press, 1967

McLintock, Francis *The Voyage of the* Fox *in the Arctic Seas: A Narrative of the Discovery of the fate of Sir John Franklin and His Companions* Edmonton: Hurtig Publishers, 1972

McLuhan, Marshall *Understanding Media: The Extensions of Man* New York: McGraw Hill Book Company, 1964

McGhee, Robert *Canadian Arctic Prehistory* Toronto: Van Nostrand Reinhold Ltd., 1978

McNamara, Robert S. *Blundering into Disaster: Surviving the First Century of the Nuclear Age* New York: Pantheon Books, 1987

Morenus, Richard *DEW Line: The Miracle of America's First Line of Defense* New York: Rand McNally and Co., 1957

Mowat, Farley *People of the Deer* Boston: Little, Brown, 1951

Nairn, Sandy *State of the Art* London: Chatto and Windus Limited, 1987

Nanton, Paul *Arctic Breakthrough: Franklin's Expeditions 1819-1847* Toronto: Clarke, Irwin and Company Ltd., 1981

Neatby, Leslie. H. *In Quest of the Northwest Passage* Toronto: Longmans, Green and Company, 1958

Nelson, J.G., Roger Needham and Linda Norton (eds.) *Arctic Heritage: Proceedings of a Symposium* Ottawa: Association of Canadian Universities for Northern Studies Studies. 1987

Nelson, Joyce *The Perfect Machine: TV in the Nuclear Age* Toronto: Between The Lines, 1987

Pearson, Rt. Hon. Lester B. *Mike: The Memoirs of the Rt. Hon. Lester B. Pearson, Vol. 1, 1897-1948* Toronto: University of Toronto Press, 1972

Pitseolak Peter (with Dorothy Eber) *People from our Side* Edmonton: Hurtig Publishers, 1975

Postman, Neil *Amusing Ourselves to Death* New York: Penguin, 1986

Rea, K.J. *The Political Economy of Northern Development* Ottawa: Science Council of Canada, 1976

Real, Michael R. (ed.) *Mass Mediated Culture* Englewood Cliffs, N.J.: Prentice Hall, Inc., 1977

Regehr, Ernie and Simon Rosenblum (eds.) *Canada and the Nuclear Arms Race* Toronto: James Lorimer and Company, 1983 @SUBBIB = Regehr, Ernie *Arms Canada: The Deadly Business of Military Exports* Toronto: James Lorimer and Company, 1987

Rowe, Dorothy *Living With The Bomb* London: Routledge and Kegan Paul plc, 1985

Royal Society of Canada *Nuclear Winter and Associated Effects: A Canadian Appraisal of the Environmental Impact of Nuclear War* Ottawa: Royal Society of Canada, 1985

Scheer, Robert *With Enough Shovels: Reagan, Bush and Nuclear War* New York: Random House, 1982

Schell, Jonathan *The Fate of the Earth* New York: Alfred A. Knopf, Inc., 1982

Smith, Dan and E.P. Thompson (eds.) *Prospectus For A Habitable Planet* Harmondsworth, Middlesex: Penguin Books, 1987

Sorrels, Charles A. *U.S. Cruise Missiles Programs* McGraw Hill, 1983

Stefansson, Vilhjalmur *The Friendly Arctic: the story of five years in polar regions* New York: The MacMillan Comany, 1921

Stefansson, Vilhjalmur *Not By Bread Alone* New York: The MacMillan Company, 1946

Steltzer, Ulli *Inuit: The North in Transition* Vancouver: Douglas and McIntyre Limited, 1985

Swinton, George *Sculpture of the Eskimo* Boston: New York Graphic Society, 1972

Thompson, E. P. *The Heavy Dancers* London: Merlin Press, 1985

Valentine, Victor F. and Frank G. Vallee *Eskimo, The Canadian Arctic* Toronto: McClelland and Stewart Limited, 1968

Wilkinson, Doug *Land of the Long Day* Toronto: Clarke, Irwin and Company Ltd., 1955

Zaslow, Morris (ed.) *A Century of Canada's Arctic Islands: 1880-1980* Ottawa: The Royal Society of Canada, 1981

## Journals and Reports

Adams, W.P. et al *Canada and Polar Science* Ottawa: Department of Indian Affairs and Northern Development, 1987

Chapman, Peter *Canada and the North American Aerospace Defence Command* Waterloo: Project Ploughshares, 1985

Cox, David *Trends in Continental Defence: A Canadian Perspective* Ottawa: Canadian Institute for International Peace and Security, 1986

Cox, David *Canada and NORAD: 1958-1973: A Cautionary Perspective* Aurora Papers, No. 1. Ottawa: Canadian Centre for Arms Control and Disarmament, 1982

Diepen, Philip Van *The Impact of Mining on the Arctic Biological and Physical Environment* Inuit Tapirisat Renewable Resources Project, Vol. 1. Ottawa: Inuit Tapirisat of Canada. 1975

Demchuk, Andrea *The Risk of Accidental Nuclear War: A Conference Report* Ottawa: Canadian Institute for International Peace and Security, 1986

DeMille, Dianne *Challenges to Deterrence: Doctrines, Technologies and Public Concerns: A Conference Report* Ottawa: Canadian Institute for International Peace and Security, 1985

Department of National Defence *Challenge and Commitment: A Defence Policy for Canada* Ottawa: Department of National Defence, 1987

Hodgson, Gordon (ed.) *Arctic* Vol. 40, No. 4. Calgary: Arctic Institute of North America, 1987

Lindsay, G. R. "Strategic Aspects of the Polar Regions" *Behind the Headlines* Vol. 35:6 Toronto: Canadian Institute of International Affairs, 1977

Mathews, Robert O. and Charles Pentland (eds.) *International Journal* Canadian Institute of International Affairs. Volume XXXIX No.4, Autumn, 1984

Purver, Ronald G. *Arctic Arms Control: Constraints and Opportunities* Ottawa: Canadian Institute for International Peace and Security, 1988

Scace, Robert Chaston *Exploration, Settlement and Land Use Activities in Northern Canada: Historical Review* Inuit Tapirisat Renewable Resources Project, Vol. 1. Ottawa: Inuit Tapirisat of Canada. 1975